The Dream Shattered

Advisor in Criminal Justice to Northeastern University Press
Gil Geis

The Dream Shattered

Vietnamese Gangs
in America

**Patrick
Du Phuoc Long**

with **Laura Ricard**

Northeastern University Press

Boston

Northeastern University Press

Copyright 1996 by Patrick Du Long

Library of Congress Cataloging-in-Publication Data

Du, Phuoc Long.
    The dream shattered : Vietnamese gangs in America / Patrick Du
Phuoc Long with Laura Ricard.
        p. cm.
    Includes bibliographical references and index.
    ISBN 1-55553-232-2 (cl : alk. paper); ISBN 1-55553-314-0 (pb : alk. paper)
    1. Gangs—United States.   2. Juvenile delinquents—United States.
3. Vietnamese Americans.   4. Asian American criminals.   I. Ricard,
Laura.   II. Title.
HV6439.U5D8   1995
364.1′066′0899592073—dc20   95-20446

Designed by Peter Blaiwas

Composed in Baskerville by Coghill Composition, Richmond, Virginia. Printed and bound by Hamilton Printing Co., Rensselaer, New York. The paper is Renew Antique, an acid-free stock.

MANUFACTURED IN THE UNITED STATES OF AMERICA
99 98 97   5 4 3 2

For the bui doi—*the children of dust*

Contents

Chapter 4
Drug Use   128

Chapter 5
Counseling the Alienated   145

Chapter 6
Last Chance Ranches   193

Chapter 7
Xinh Xinh and Tom   209

Preface

In the aftermath of the Vietnam War thousands of refugees from Vietnam, Cambodia, and Laos fled to the United States. They were ill-prepared for life here. They came by way of refugee camps where, sometimes for years, they languished awaiting passage. Many were unaccompanied children, some the offspring of GI fathers who abandoned wives or girlfriends in Vietnam. Few had guidance of any kind; they lacked practical knowledge of what life would be like here, of how, in America, one goes about the task of living day to day. Understanding little or no English, Indochinese people have had to make their way through a frighteningly alien culture. Some have made it.

Tue Nguyen arrived in the United States with thousands of other Vietnamese boat people, and he found the right path. Nine years after he first set foot on American soil, Tue earned a doctorate in nuclear engineering from the Massachusetts Institute of Technology and soon thereafter began a job at IBM on the cutting edge of technological research. Friends describe him as a person "with a lot of willpower."[1]

But for many Indochinese refugees a lot of willpower is not enough. Lacking even the most basic skills for coping with the demands of their new environment, they have found themselves thrust into bad neighborhoods where daily life is deformed by gang warfare and the drug subculture. Many adults totter on the economical edge, and their children, unable to survive in school, attracted by the glitz and false glamour to which they are exposed on television and which gang life seems to promise, turn away from them. These children drop out of school, run away, and turn to drugs and crime. Eventually some are imprisoned, even gunned down on the streets. I wrote this book to shed light on the difficulties that face Indochinese and Amerasian children and to help people who want to help them.

People from Cambodia, Laos, and Vietnam are culturally very different, although they are often referred to collectively as "Indochinese." This book focuses primarily on Vietnamese youths (and chapter 1 provides a brief summary of Vietnamese history) because Vietnamese children constitute the vast majority of the wards whom I counsel. But I counsel Amerasian, Cambodian, and Laotian youths also, and share some of their stories as well.

For nearly seven years I have worked as a counselor to Indochinese children in juvenile correctional and rehabilitation facilities in Santa Clara County, California (the Harold Holden Ranch for Boys and the William James Ranch for Boys). I have spent time on the streets, in the schools, and in the courts with them, logging thousands of hours listening to profoundly troubled young people. Some are the offspring of refugees; others have come to this country on their own and are frightened and terribly alone. Many have come to trust me, and because they trust me they have confided in me. I share their extraordinary stories here.

The Dream Shattered is addressed not to scholars but to general readers, and to the parents and guardians of children who are losing their way. This book does not discuss large-scale, broad-based gang-prevention measures—that will be the subject of a subsequent study.

But it does explain why so many Indochinese youngsters turn to gang life and crime and act the way they do—it illustrates the nature of the difficulties they face on the street and in school and shows why drugs and gang life are so alluring. My objective is to focus attention on a problem that, if ignored, may very well unravel a significant piece of the American social fabric. *The Dream Shattered* will be, I hope, a bridge to understanding.

I gleaned information on the cases of hundreds of children from public records; a lot of material came from the analyses of journalists. But most of what you are about to read I obtained from the wards themselves. (So as not to distract my readers, material in this last category is not footnoted.) Once they see that I am there solely to help them solve their problems and to encourage them to begin new lives, most of these young people are very eager to unburden themselves, and, having come to regard me as a child does a father or a grandfather (I am seventy-five years old), talk to me freely.

They talk about their gun duels, their experiences using drugs and trafficking in them, their criminal activities, their sexual relationships. They talk a lot about their parents, their schools, and their peers. They talk about their hopes, dreams, and fears.

All the details and descriptions that follow are true. Nevertheless, in order to conceal and protect their identities and those of their families, except where the names of young criminals have become a matter of public record, I have fictionalized where necessary. All names have been changed. In a few cases, the individuals I have portrayed are actually composites of several young people, and their words are reconstructions of conversations I have had with several youths. I have altered details and rearranged facts, not only because of the legal constraints that require me to protect the identities of minors, but out of respect for persons in the Indochinese (particularly the Vietnamese) community who cherish their privacy.

I translated the letters and poems of Vietnamese wards and the poems of Nguyen Chi Thien into English. Any error in the text is mine, and if the names I have given to the characters are similar, or even identical, to the names of real people it is coincidental. I have made every effort to capture the moments the children made vivid to me.

PATRICK DU PHUOC LONG

The Dream Shattered

Introduction

Bonset Soun was a toddler in 1975 when the Khmer Rouge, wielding hoes and axes, hacked his father, brother, and two sisters to death and dumped their bodies in a mass grave. They tossed Soun in as well and, because he was unconscious, left him for dead. Miraculously, his mother, Paon Phum, had escaped the fury of the Cambodian communists and was able to save him. Not long afterward Soun again had a brush with death when the Khmer Rouge butchered his sister before his very eyes.

Soun and his mother fled to Thailand on foot. After some time in a refugee camp the United States granted mother and son political refugee status and the two were able to get safely to California.

Then, fifteen years after he was rescued from the killing fields of Cambodia, Bonset Soun himself became a killer. In 1990 he gunned down the Cambodian manager of a video store in San Jose, California, when the shopkeeper refused to hand over money. Found guilty of attempted robbery and first-degree murder, Soun was sentenced in 1992 to life in prison with no possibility of parole. Violence had begotten violence, and Paon Phum lost her only remaining son to the eye of an American dust storm.[1]

A similar fate befell three children of a Vietnamese couple who also escaped the communists in 1975. With four sons and two daughters, Bim Nguyen, an ARVN (Army of the Republic of Vietnam) soldier for twenty years, and his wife, Sao, fled Vietnam aboard a small fishing boat with fifty-one other refugees. Resettled in California, sixteen years after their exodus from Vietnam, the Nguyens were quietly watching television in the small living room of their Sacramento home when an unimaginable drama unfolded before them and thousands of other viewers.[2]

That drama featured their children. The faces of three of their sons and a fourth assailant, a young man named Tran, flashed on the TV screen. The four had stormed into the Good Guys electronics store in South Sacramento, where they had taken forty-one hostages and were terrorizing them.[3]

The Nguyens hastened to the scene. Sao, her cousin, and a Buddhist priest begged to talk to the boys, but police said that the gunmen would not communicate with them. "If they had let me talk to my son, Pham, I could have talked him out of it, to lay down their weapons," the mother said through an interpreter. Eight hours later, a SWAT team shot and killed two of the Nguyen children and seriously wounded the third—but not before the four had killed two store employees and a customer. Police charged the surviving twenty-one-year-old Nguyen brother with fifty-four felony counts ranging from kidnapping and assault to murder as he lay in his hospital bed.[4]

In the aftermath of the murders, Sao Nguyen told reporters how her sons had helped around the house, and neighbors said that nothing in their behavior had suggested they would be capable of such an attack. In fact, that very morning the boys had asked their father for permission to go fishing. A Catholic priest informed reporters that the boys attended Mass every Sunday, and that one of them was an altar boy. "I'd never imagine. Never," Father Nguyen (of no relation to the family) said.[5]

And yet, after the four gunmen allowed two groups of hostages to leave the store (these included five toddlers and their mothers), their behavior toward the remaining hostages was unimaginably cruel. They tied their hostages up with speaker wire and forced them to crawl and kneel. They pointed their weapons at the hostages' heads and swore that they were about to fire. At one point they proposed a "game": they divided the hostages into two groups, then one of the attackers flipped a coin onto the floor, indicating that those hostages on the side toward which the coin rolled would be executed first. "Let's shoot at one of his legs first to show that we mean business," one said, and one of the brothers aimed his gun at a hostage and shot him in the thigh. At nightfall, a seventy-four-year-old man had a diabetic seizure; one of the gunmen shot him in the leg and warned that next time he'd shoot him in the head. A terrified pregnant woman suffered a miscarriage. Wanting to know the time, one of the assailants yanked a wristwatch from a hostage, saying, "We have no intention of ripping off your watch." Then he grabbed a fistful of bills from the register and threw them to him saying, "So we can call it even, keep the change. No problem."[6]

On several occasions the gunmen asked for forty 1000-year-old ginseng roots (a Chinese herb valued for its medicinal properties), four "Robo-Cop" protective suits, bullet-proof vests, one million dollars, a helicopter capable of carrying forty people, a .45 caliber pistol and plane tickets to Thailand to fight the Viet Cong (communist guerilas). "Look there, we are going to be movie stars!" one assailant shouted to another when their pictures appeared on the closed-circuit TV.[7]

Gaining access to the crawl space between the store's roof and ceiling through an adjacent shop, seven SWAT team members stole down both sides of the store just as at least two of the gunmen began to fire on the hostages. But in seconds it was over. "We have four bad guys," a SWAT marksman announced.[8]

Movie stars indeed.

Unlike Bonset Soun and the three Vietnamese gunmen mowed down inside a South Sacramento electronics store, another criminal—let's call him Danny—came to America from Vietnam with several advantages. Arriving in 1975 when Saigon fell to the communists, he was armed with a high school degree, money, some knowledge of English, and, having lived on the border of Saigon's Chinatown, many friends among Chinese businessmen. This last he might have used to great profit. But Danny took the wrong path.

Danny began his life in the United States in Santa Clara County, where he earned a handsome salary as an assembler for an electronics company and a computer component plant. In an effort to fulfill his obligations not only to his wife but to his parents, siblings, and in-laws who remained in Vietnam he worked overtime. He regularly sent them gifts of money and gold.

Danny still managed to save enough to take his first vacation. He decided to look up some old Chinese friends and enjoy a shopping spree. He flew to Hong Kong and was delighted to find his old friends. In one of the most expensive hotels in Kowloon, he discovered that his friends respected him—he was an American citizen now, and was obviously successful. Together they explored the nature of the sophisticated electronics market, discussing items that might readily be sold in Asia: computer parts, microchips, and other high-tech equipment. Danny and his business friends made some commitments and toasted one another.

Back at the electronics plant, Danny took particular interest in the stockrooms where the chips and other computer components were stored. At the same time, he began to visit cafés, nightclubs, and pool halls where he acquainted himself with the Vietnamese and Chinese-Vietnamese adolescents and young adults who hung around these spots. He befriended a few gang leaders. He knew that these people—their contacts and skills—would be useful.

He stole chips in small quantities—tiny and inexpensive chips, at first. He felt his way along and grew confident, delivering and selling the chips himself to buyers in San Francisco and Los Angeles. Gradually he built up his inventory.

Danny now entered a new phase. He cemented his connections and expanded his list of clients. He began to build relationships with employees of other electronics companies in Santa Clara County and continued to pilfer chips worth thousands of dollars from his own employer. Eventually he stopped making the deliveries himself. Teaming up with gang members from other cities in order to avoid identification, he hired juveniles—at two thousand dollars per trip —to transport the chips from the Silicon Valley to Los Angeles. He provided them with shotguns and pistols.

Danny bought himself a brand-new BMW. Not long afterward he bought a big house, equipped himself with a pager, and put a cellular phone in his BMW. His wife quit her job as a restaurant hostess and drove around town in a new Cadillac Seville.

He began to steal more expensive chips, which he sold locally at about one thousand dollars each. He packed the chips in ordinary-looking boxes and shipped them out to Los Angeles, Santa Ana, and San Diego via his teenage gang network. As he established connections with employees of other electronics manufacturers he increased his line of goods, and more and more money came in. His wife began to gamble. He bought her a fifty-thousand-dollar Mercedes Benz. She asked why he no longer brought the stuff home. "*Di dem co ngay gap ma,*" Danny replied (One may run into ghosts if one keeps going out in the darkness of the night).

More cautious now, he stopped stealing from his own company. Besides, he had access to far more of the chips than he could market. He passed around price lists to gang members who hung out in pool halls in the seedier sections of San Jose, and made friends with powerful people in Santa Clara who laundered his money. Now his supply sources were not only in Santa Clara County, but in Stockton and Sacramento.

As his business increased in size and scope, Danny withdrew into the background. Two cronies handled his contacts and transactions, and for security reasons, he relied exclusively on Vietnamese gang members to deliver the goods. All sales were cash-and-carry. He immediately dismissed suspicious delivery boys.

The volume of his business grew to the point that Danny warehoused his inventories. He traveled to Hong Kong nearly every month to expand his market. This brought him the income he needed to invest in land and mutual funds. He added another BMW to the family fleet. His wife began to lose more and more money gambling.

His contacts in Hong Kong asked for more expensive items—disk chips and computer components valued at five hundred dollars or more each. New markets opened up in Singapore, Macao, and Hong Kong. Danny's business was international now. He bought exits from Vietnam for his parents, siblings, and in-laws under the United States Orderly Departure Program.

Growing uneasy, Danny wondered if perhaps it was time to get out of the computer chip business. He decided to diversify. He toyed with the notion of smuggling wristwatches, gold, and automobiles into Vietnam via Cambodia, but changed his mind. Instead, he chose to invest in local businesses and use front men. Increasingly, Danny felt nervous, even paranoid. No longer did he allow the rank and file to see his face. Those he suspected he had executed.

The money came in much faster than he could handle it, so he decided to do a little gambling himself: he and his wife tried their luck in Reno, Lake Tahoe, Las Vegas. One Saturday morning they flew to Las Vegas as part of MGM's "special guests" program; as usual, they planned to return to San Jose on Sunday. They never returned home. Local Big Brothers have told my wards that they have seen them on the streets of Hong Kong. Perhaps Danny and his wife had in mind the ancient wisdom *Di dem co ngay gap ma*—and chose to disappear.

The people in these stories have one thing in common: each was a criminal and became involved with gangs. Bonset Soun was a member of the CWA (Cambodians With Attitude). Unbeknownst to their parents, the three Nguyen brothers belonged to the notorious Oriental Boyz. And Danny's story illustrates the costly connection between white collar crime and gangs.

More than 800,000 Vietnamese live in the United States, and in some states their numbers have doubled in less than a decade. The vast majority of these people are law-abiding citizens and have established themselves in the community. For example, walk down any street in south-central San Jose, a Vietnamese community of approximately thirty thousand people, and you will see comfortable, beautifully landscaped homes, flourishing businesses (Vietnamese-owned bookstores, restaurants, insurance agencies, bakeries, beauty salons, travel agencies), and successful professional establishments (the offices of Vietnamese doctors, dentists, architects, chiropractors, lawyers). You will observe Vietnamese people who are simply going about their business, absorbed by the same concerns that occupy any other group of Americans. Like other ethnic groups, they are proud of their heritage, but they are also eager to contribute to American society. On East Capitol Expressway, a main thoroughfare in San Jose, the Vietnamese community erected three flagpoles to fly the colors of the United States, California, and the Republic of Vietnam. The flags assert the presence of Vietnamese people, show pride in the Republic of Vietnam (the former South Vietnam), and honor the host state and country. In short, the vast majority of Vietnamese are decent, hardworking people.

But the fraction that is not—the fraction that has emerged as a criminal group—has become a serious social problem. In 1981 the FBI began to observe "emerging groups of criminals from outside of the United States," and its study included Asian criminal groups. In its analysis of Vietnamese criminal activity, completed for the Justice Department in March 1993, the FBI observed that the crime rate in the Vietnamese community was "grossly disproportionate" to its size and that "the people in these self-contained communities rated crime . . . as their priority problem."[9]

This is because Vietnamese criminals most often commit crimes against other Vietnamese. The following account from the *San Jose Mercury News* is typical:

> Three armed Vietnamese robbers, one brandishing an Uzi-type weapon, forced their way into an East San Jose house where 18 Vietnamese were holding a family reunion and ransacked the home for two hours, terrorizing the occupants. The young robbers herded the occupants into a downstairs bedroom and tied three men, kicking some of them in the ribs. . . . The suspects are aware that affluent members of Vietnamese communities often keep large amounts

of cash and other valuables in their homes and on their persons instead of in banks.[10]

However, as the attack on the Good Guys electronics store and Danny's activities illustrate, the larger community is hardly immune to the predations of gangs. In California, which is the focus of this book, gang robbery and extortion alone cost private businesses and individuals millions of dollars annually, and rape, assault, and murder take a grisly human toll.

Social scientists are quick to point out that the swelling crime rate and the growing intensity of criminal violence across the country have been accompanied by swelling numbers of gangs. California authorities emphasize that increases in the number and size of gangs and in gang activity have resulted in a dramatic upsurge in violence.

Gangs are a phenomenon of highly industrialized societies. As the pace of industrialization has increased in North and South America, Britain, Europe, Australia, and parts of Asia, gangs have grown commensurately. Today's industrialized societies are increasingly divided into classes of rich and poor, and the children of the poor are often forced to live in ghettos. Forgotten or ignored, in the United States these children live in dilapidated housing projects where they grow accustomed to the sound of gunfire. They attend overcrowded schools, they are raised most often by desperate mothers who have little or no opportunity to improve themselves, and they observe a society in which it appears to them that other people—the people they see on TV and in the movies—are beautiful, comfortable, and rich. The castoffs of the most materially rich society in the history of civilization, these children live their lives without hope and without dignity in an environment where there is almost no regard for human life.

While many of these children become members of street gangs, by no means is the gang phenomenon limited to the children of the poor—upscale families lose children to gangs as well. As one white middle-class mother whose son is a gang leader observed:

Designer gangsters come from beautiful homes with a father working at some place like IBM and the kids are given a $100 bill for the week. This buys the drugs and beer. These kids may take off their red shirts before they get home, but one day it will surface.[11]

Children from all ethnic groups join gangs, but according to federal investigators, Asian American criminal groups are growing faster than any other. Their illegal activities range from drug trafficking, money laundering, bribery, and extortion, to alien smuggling, home invasions, computer-technology theft, credit card counterfeiting, prostitution, gambling, and murder. And Asian American criminals are increasingly skilled in the way they commit crimes. In 1992, after twenty months of surveillance and information gathering by the Bureau of Alcohol, Tobacco and Firearms, the FBI, the Drug Enforcement Agency, the Immigration and Naturalization Service, and the police departments of Santa Ana and Garden Grove, sixty Asian Americans were arrested on charges ranging from drug use and trafficking to homicide. The agencies involved in this operation agreed that the group was extraordinarily sophisticated in its methods.[12]

The sophistication of Asian American gangs is also reflected in the fact that local gangs work hard to develop relationships with Asian American gangs elsewhere. They use these relationships to commit crimes at considerable distances from their home cities. Vietnamese gangs in particular are well organized and have achieved great degrees of mobility in their efforts to exploit new resources. Vietnamese gangs cooperate with one another to plan joint operations that, in some cases, are conducted thousands of miles away. A Santa Clara member of a Vietnamese gang, for example, flew to Boston to direct the robbery of a jewelry store and returned with over two hundred thousand dollars as his share of the loot. More typically, criminal operations are conducted within the state. Law enforcement officials note, however, that with increasing frequency juvenile criminals and their adult leaders are willing to fly to Houston, Dallas, New York, Florida, and even Hawaii to traffic in drugs and exploit vulnerable Vietnamese communities.

The FBI reports that as of spring 1993, Vietnamese criminal activity "can best be described as being in a state of accelerated networking, the precursor to organization." Vietnamese criminal activity is not—at least not yet—"organized crime." But senior research analysts for the New York City Criminal Justice Agency agree that the growth of Asian American gangs on the west coast is a microcosm of what is happening in major cities across the United States and around the world. Gangs are becoming a major problem in Toronto and Vancouver, Canada, and in urban centers in Australia with significant Asian Australian populations.[13]

The sheer ruthlessness and viciousness with which Vietnamese gangsters commit crimes suggest that they have little or no regard for the lives of others or even their own, as the following poem suggests. The poem was probably a group effort of members of the Viet-Ching gang (although one of my wards gave me a handwritten copy of it with his signature on it), who passed it around among the inmates at an institution of the California Youth Authority (also referred to as the C.Y.A. or "YA"), the state's juvenile offender system:

This Country Made Me

Our people set in our own ways
Same old shit day after day.
But our people demands respect
And there's a lot of things our parents expect
Coming to a country that's foreign to us
Looking for people that we can trust
Tired of war, and our gun being loaded
Tired of looking up. A bomb just exploded.
So we come over here for a peaceful life,
Work hard as we can and do what's right
Parents send our kids to school.
Everything is nice, at first.
But one day we come home, running, crying and hurt.
We got beat up, 'cause we're from the Asian race.
So now our kids unite to give them a taste
Of what it is like a real war,
And to get even and even score.

If you wanted to be a gangbanger
Or maybe a dope-slancer,
We will show you how the tough life is:
The real shit, no movies or show biz.
You think you are from the GHETTO and the poor land
If I live like you I consider myself as a rich man.
We don't give a f- - - about death.
We'll still be unloading the gun while breathing our last breaths.
We're the people that's strong and in control
Of our destiny until we're ninety years old.
We have gangbangers from San Jose to L.A.
From San Fran. to New York and all the way back;
Gangs like V-Ching to Dragon, Eagle to Wahching,
Natoma Boyz to O.B. Nip Boys and the rest
Can't be stopped. We're too strong to hold,
No matter the weather hot or cold.
We don't give a f- - -, we just don't care.
Now we give up our own way.
Why is a homeboy dying everyday?
Why do they live like this is hell?
If I have a wish, what will I wish?
That America don't make me like this.
This country made me, can't you see . . . ?

"Many families have lost happiness—their children failed," the father of a Vietnamese minor who was recently committed to a county correctional facility observed sadly. "Some of our children have run away, others have joined gangs and become criminals, causing us heartbreak, suffering, anxiety, weariness, and frustration. Our children hurt us and the Vietnamese community every day. *Why?*"

Pondering the killings at the Good Guys electronics store, T. T. Nhu, a Vietnamese journalist, observed:

If I were to guess what went wrong that day, it could be attributed to a confluence of unhappy events—teenage alienation and unhappiness compounded by the pain and discontent of feeling marginal, impeded by language, cultural, and economic barriers. Demoralized at the thought of facing the law in the form of judge and probation officer [two of the Nguyen boys were facing vandalism and shoplifting charges], the boys decided to "shoot the moon" and go out in a blaze of gunfire. . . . What happened in Sacramento was an American tragedy played out with a new cast of characters who had come to this country, but could not figure out how to get in.[14]

That may very well be why.

Bach Lien

Bach Lien was born on May 14, 1954, one week after Ho Chi Minh's communist forces defeated the French at Dienbienphu. She grew up in a small village a few miles from Da Nang.

Bach Lien remembers the people in their conical hats. She remembers the red tile roof of her home with its big front yard where her parents dried tobacco leaves and winnowed the husks from the rice. In that big front yard they brought in the harvest of corn and potatoes, manioc and rice. In the moonlight she would help them with the rice; in the moonlight it was so very pleasant. She remembers the poetry, the songs of broken love and heartbreak, the clicking of the *sinh tien*, and she remembers her friends, the village children, laughing. Villagers came and went up and down the street talking in low tones and Bach Lien heard a sweet music in their words, a sweet music in the moonlight, and always there was laughter, children's laughter.

She loved the nights. The darkness and the smells, the grassy smell of the paddies—it was a good smell, especially in spring when the rice flowered. She smelled the smell of burning charcoal, of burning betel; she smelled the smell of burning paddy husks and damp soil and manure. Mango and papaya, pineapple, guava, and jackfruit trees: these were citrusy smells, astringent and fine, and they filled the night with unbearable sweetness.

She loved the dark behind the house, so thick you could thrust your hand into it. In the sky burned the Southern Cross, and her father had shown her Polaris, the evening star, and the Scorpion. "Look there," he had said to her one night, and he had pointed out its two claws, its curved tail that ended in a sting, and there was Antares, the giant star, and she could see that it was red, bright red, and her father told her it was very, very far away. Bach Lien loved the cool nights and the starry sky and the sounds of the villagers gathered in her parents' front yard. The pigs grunted. The ducks and chickens bumped against her. The soles of her feet felt cool as she walked in the darkness of the yard. Sometimes in summer they slept outside in hammocks or on beds of bamboo. Babies cried. Dogs barked. Frogs croaked.

But that was in peacetime.

The music went out of her parents' voices. "*Hush!*" her mother ordered her one night. "*Communists!*" Out there, out in the darkness, in the hedgerows, and they were spying on her and her father and others in the village. So her mother said. Communists? It was murky to her, murky as a monsoon rain. What did it mean?

Bach Lien listened to her mother sing, rocking her baby sister:

Ho Chi Minh, the old soldier, is
Determined to sacrifice himself for Vietnam's independence
    and world peace . . .

Bach Lien was mystified. Her parents despised Ho Chi Minh. "Why, Mama, why are you singing so?" Bach Lien asked.

"I sing to fool them, my daughter, I sing because I hate them. I hate the communist scum," and Bach Lien listened to her mother's voice, a voice that was usually as soft as the thread of silkworms:

> Ho Chi Minh, the man who disregards storms and snow, swords, guns and chains,
> Makes himself a suicide pioneer, determined to win every battle.
> Setbacks frustrate him.
> But his soul remains youthful and full of love of mankind.

She spat out the words, and the loathing in her mother's voice chilled Bach Lien, but Mama sang the words forcefully, right out the window and into the hedgerows where communists rocked on their haunches and listened, satisfied. This time they would leave them alone.

Then the Americans came. In Da Nang they built a gigantic air base. Da Nang, Da Nang, her parents took her there every month to market, and Bach Lien loved to utter the name, Da Nang, Da Nang. First, the beach, the beautiful beach, China Beach, and you could smell it, the sea and the beach, before you saw it; it amazed Bach Lien, that ocean smell. Then between the beach and the Da Nang River, the Song Han River. The downtown on the west side of the river; the beach on the other. South of China Beach, the Monkey Mountains—the Americans gave them that name because they were full of monkeys. Then there was that wonderful harbor (no typhoons would hurt them there, no great wind would whirl into Cua Han Bay). The harbor was the gate to the city, Bach Lien's father told her, and the Americans built their air base inside the mountain for security. Da Nang, he added, was part lagoon and part mountain. The mountains came down to the sea and Da Nang rose out of that sea mountain.

Thousands of people came to the American air base, so many, her father said, that Da Nang was almost as big as Saigon now, and Bach Lien knew Saigon only in her imagination. Her father or her mother took her in by bicycle and how strange it was! So many GIs, and her father was able to buy things at the PX that she had never seen before, like round metal cans of food and soft drinks that made her throat tingle. There were convoys of trucks and tanks, and near the base, roll after roll of sharp wire. (Once, on the outskirts of the city, Bach Lien and her father saw a garbage truck full of typewriters. Passersby came and took them and carried them back to their villages.) Many among her people went to work in Da Nang, catering to the American soldiers, and when her father spoke of "American soldiers," he said it fiercely, proudly; American soldiers had come to help them fight the communists.

Night after night her mother sang of Ho Chi Minh, spitting out the words into the hedgerows:

> Even though his hands tremble, his knees weaken, and his voice
>   quavers,
> His steel heart is still fired by his fighting spirit.
> His voice said: move onward and fight.
> And the young rank and file after years of endurance against the
>   elements
> Brightened their eyes, with young arms raising their shining
>   machetes
> Determined to kill and drink the blood of the oppressors. What a
>   pleasure!

Now the Viet Cong (VC) came regularly into Bach Lien's village. They stole the people's chants and songs and took them for themselves: "rice cake never has a bone; the French invaders never loved our people." They had sung that since 1945, her mother said. Now the communists picked up the *sinh tien* and sang it of the Americans, her father said. He was gone a lot now, fighting, her mother said, and she wore a worried look, but she was strong, strong like her own mother had been strong:

Now our husbands and brothers are heading to the battlefield.
Singing the marching song, that resounds
In every direction.
Our flag is floating in the wind
And the entire country is rejoicing.
Brave women, descendants of *Lac Hong* race, hurry
To join the common cause.
As one, all of us young women stand up and fight
For our family cause and national cause.
Let's chase away griefs and sorrows.

Sometimes the Viet Cong would come into her parents' house and her parents had to feed them. Sometimes they came into her village and helped the sick; they helped old Uncle Dung roof his house. "They are masters of propaganda," her father said scornfully. He looked solemn all the time now, but the Americans were here, the Americans, their saviors.

And then one day her father was wounded in the crossfire between the Americans and the VC.

On the last day of January 1968, on the eve of the New Year, the communists launched a big offensive. There was fighting around the airstrip at Da Nang now, heavy fighting, and downtown, by the market, was off limits to GIs. They all fought: the VC, NVA (North Vietnamese Army) regulars, and the Americans. There were artillery and mortars and a lot of fighting at night. Bach Lien lay on the floor of her house with her mother and her sisters and brothers, and the ground shook from the bombs being dropped north of the city. Her village took artillery and mortars, and Bach Lien saw the sky lit up as bright as the noonday sun when giant helicopters dropped white phosphorus flares to expose the VC. The people in her village still wore their straw hats but there was no more laughter, no more tobacco drying in her front yard, and now Bach Lien saw the bodies of her friends torn apart by guns and fire. They lay unburied, in the dirt of the road.

Bach Lien turned fourteen in June 1968.

At night American patrols came through. Her father explained that they were search-and-destroy units, and they would often set the village dogs to barking. Sometimes they walked right past their house, their helicopters landing in their rice and corn fields.

American soldiers poked their noses into their house pretty regularly now. Once, in her yard, a soldier with curly red hair (Bach Lien touched his sun-colored curls and the soldier smiled) showed her his field phone. Bach Lien heard voices on the phone. "How did they get in there?" she asked, pointing to the receiver, and the GI laughed. "They are so big!" Bach Lien said to her mother of the American soldiers, and her mother nodded, "Yes child, they are big." The patrols were in and out of the village almost constantly, and beyond the village, in the paddies and rice fields, there was the *bap bap bap* of AK-47s and M-16s; American marines and VC were killing and killing and killing.

Jets ripped through the sky over her house. Bach Lien did not go out any more to look at Scorpion and the Southern Cross. Her mother told her, "Be strong."

So Bach Lien was strong. She was strong when her mother was injured by "friendlies." An American gunner in an assault helicopter killed the VC gunner at the edge of town, but he got her mother, too, who was hurrying down the road from the well to the house with the red tile roof where her children lay huddled on the floor inside. Bach Lien's mother lost her arm. American doctors treated her at the big military hospital in Da Nang. "Be strong," her mother repeated when Bach Lien's father died of his wounds.

She said that to Bach Lien when in 1973 the last Americans left and Bach Lien married. She married an ARVN soldier. Da Le was away fighting most of the time, but when he came home, Bach Lien felt happy. In 1974 she bore Da Le's first child, a son, Cam Le. In 1975 she bore a second son, Phong Le. In 1975 Da Le was killed by NVA. Seventeen NVA divisions were moving south toward Saigon. "Be strong," her mother told her. The rice fields were in flower. Bach Lien smelled them, and they smelled of sadness, but she would be strong.

She was strong in 1980 when she bought her way out of Vietnam with gold leaves. For five years she had worked for those gold leaves and she and her mother had sold much of what they had. "I will bring you to America, Mama," Bach Lien promised her mother. When the old woman said good-bye to Cam Le and Phong Le, now six and five years old, she wept.

It was in the night when Bach Lien with her two young sons traveled down the coast to Hoi An and boarded the fishing boat that would take her to Malaysia. "That is the light of Saigon," the fishing boat captain said at three o'clock in the morning. Overhead burned the Southern Cross. At dawn they passed some islands. "They are the Con Son Islands," the captain said, and they passed the point, Mui Bai Bung, and the island of Hon Khoai. That was the last she saw of Vietnam. Her young ones slept.

The boat headed for Malaysia. The sea was rough and it rained heavily. Many on board were ill. Cam Le and Phong Le shivered with cold. The boat took on water, but the captain seemed unafraid. Be strong, Bach Lien said to herself. Be strong. She drew her children close to her.

They were a few hours out from Kota Baharu when the pirates came. "*Hai tac* [Pirates]!" the captain hissed. A small Thai fishing boat materialized out of the mist and rain and drew up beside them. There were only three little men, but two had machetes and one had a big gun, the *bap bap bap* kind, and to show that they meant business the one with the gun fired into the people huddled in the Vietnamese fishing boat and one among them screamed. A seven-year-old child went limp. Its mother rose, cursing and screaming, wild with screaming. The pirates shot her, too, and now the two lay dead in the bottom of the boat, mother and child, and the pirates grabbed the child by the ankle and heaved him overboard. Blood pooled on the deck of the boat.

Bach Lien had known fear. She had felt the earth shudder with the dropping of gigantic bombs and had seen people splattered by fire and metal. But always she had been able to flee—for the shelter of her red-roofed house, for the shelter of the jackfruit trees—always there had been somewhere to hide. But not now, not in this boat. She and the others had heard the stories about how the communists would overload a boat in order to get as much gold as possible. Sometimes they would shoot the boat to sink it, just out of meanness. She had heard about the *hai tac* who would molest young girls and even steal them to take inland to sell to Chinese or Thai businessmen, landlords, or rich farmland owners. She heard that on one of the fishing boats a sixteen-year-old girl was raped by different pirates every day of her eight-day flight to

Malaysia. Cam Le whimpered. Bach Lien struck him, fiercely, to silence him. She was terrified. There was no place to hide.

The pirates took their time. They searched everyone and took everything of any value, even the boat battery. Wedding rings were torn from fingers (Bach Lien's wedding ring was long gone, sold for her precious gold leaves). They took brass belt buckles and earrings—they yanked the gold hoops from the ears of one of the women. They reached into the vagina of a thirteen-year-old girl, looking for jewels, then they raped her. And then they were gone, dissolved in the mist. Bach Lien and two other women pushed the body of the dead woman overboard.

With no battery the little fishing boat drifted. It was raining, and the little children cried from cold. They drifted all through the night and into the dawn, until at mid-morning a big mackerel boat out of Malaya drew up alongside and took them on. A few hours later her feet touched the ground in Malaysia. Be strong, her mother told her. Be strong.

Bach Lien, Cam Le, and Phong Le were then sent to a refugee camp in the Philippines where they lived for nearly a year. Finally, the morning came when they boarded the plane for America. When the pilot announced that they had crossed into American airspace, many people on the plane whispered excitedly. An old man in the aisle next to her wept. Bach Lien felt tired.

They landed in San Francisco, California. American officials had encouraged Bach Lien to settle in the Tenderloin district of San Francisco because she had an aunt there. They assured her that many Indochinese lived there, in the western part of the city: refugees from North and South Vietnam, Laos, and Cambodia. She could make a good home there. They promised.

Cam Le and Phong Le rode in the bus from the San Francisco airport with their faces pressed against the glass. Be strong, her mother
had told her, but riding on the bus, with its sickening cigarette smells,
Bach Lien felt a dull weariness that she had never known before—not
in Vietnam, when dead soldiers lay rotting in the paddies; not when Da
Le was killed (he died nobly, for a great cause); not in the fishing boat
when the pirates had tossed the dead child overboard; not in the camps,
when somebody rifled through her belongings one night and stole all
that remained of her money, money sewn so skillfully into the folds of
her *ao dai* that even the pirates had missed it. Cam Le and Phong Le
spoke together in English, spoke words that she, their mother, did not
understand. She looked at her young ones and felt weary, felt an anxiety
that made her gather them close to her. She looked out the window at
the fog.

In her tiny apartment that first night Bach Lien placed the small
woolen blanket they had given her in the camp on the floor in the
cramped kitchen. Rolling it open to examine her few belongings, she
studied the photograph of Da Le and kissed it. Then she picked up the
sandals she had worn on the night she had walked with her sons from
Da Nang down to Hoi An (she had carried Phong Le almost the entire
way), to wait on the beach there for the fishing boat. In the tread of the
soles was dirt. Vietnamese dirt.

Her sandals in her hand, Bach Lien walked quietly into the bedroom to where Cam Le and Phong Le slept heaped together on the
carpet. She would have to clean that carpet, Bach Lien thought; it was
vile. She put her nose to their hair and inhaled their sweetness, their
heartbreaking sweetness. She went to the window to look up at the stars.
Could she see the Southern Cross from here, she wondered? And what

was her Mama doing tonight? But the lights were so bright that they blotted out the stars. A siren screamed. The alien sound made her shiver.

Back in the kitchen, Bach Lien examined the dirt in the sandals again. With her fingernail she scraped it from the treads and put it to her nose, closing her eyes. Then she put it to her tongue. And then she cried.

It had been years. She had not cried for Da Le in years. She picked up the tiny photograph and ran her thumb over it, ran her thumb over the broken glass and the corner that was now chipped (she had purchased the gilt frame in the city's huge downtown, in Macy's. How she had lingered over her choice! This one, this frame, had heft to it). Da Le smiled at her from the photograph. He was in uniform.

She sank to the floor, weeping. If Da Le were here, Cam Le would never have said the harsh words he said to her. "You are *stupid!*" Cam Le had said to her just now, "*Stupid stupid stupid!*" and he had swept the candles, the sweet incense, the fresh fruit and flowers from the altar with his arm, and the precious picture—the picture of his *father!*—it too he sent crashing to the floor. "I go out whenever I please, motherfucker, and you don't tell me not to! I'm sick of your shit!"

Bach Lien got on her knees. She picked up the fruit and the flowers, the incense, and the candles from the floor.

Tinh Duong was the son of a black GI and a Vietnamese mother. Born in the Mekong Delta, he came to America under the Homecoming Program. His mother, however, was unable to assert any real authority over him after Tinh Duong entered the ninth grade. He had done well when they first arrived—he and his mama would spread his lessons out on the living room floor and they would study the English words together—but Tinh Duong was called "Cong" and "Dog-eater" and "Chink" once too many times, and he got mean. He felt meaner when he saw how some of the Americans lived on the other side of town. There were trees there, and flowers, and no graffiti, no garbage in the streets, and once, at night, he saw a mother and father and children eating around a big shiny table together in a gigantic house. He could see it clearly through a great window made of many small, diamond-shaped panes of glass. The table had candles on it. The candles were reflected in the panes of glass. That window made a big impression on Tinh Duong. He had never seen anything so beautiful.

Tinh Duong became the leader of the Thai Bao gang. Despite the fact that he had engineered dozens of home invasions, was running drugs out of the country through his connections with the Wu-Chi, and had masterminded computer heists, he had never been caught. The cops had his name, the FBI knew all about him, but he was untouchable. The younger ones got caught. The younger ones like Cam Le.

Tinh Duong talked gently to Cam Le. They met in a coffee shop, and he talked to Cam Le and Cam Le listened. Like a father Tinh Duong listened to Cam Le ("I am a father to myself," Tinh Duong used to say, and he'd repeat that often to Cam Le: "You don't have a father. Be a father to yourself").

He took Cam Le for a ride in his car. The boy could not take his eyes off Tinh Duong's bomber jacket. Tinh Duong saw this immediately. He took it off and let the boy hold it. "Would you like a jacket like this?"

Cam Le could hardly speak. "A jacket like this?" Cam Le ran his fingers over the leather, touched the fur of the collar. "For a jacket like this, I . . ."

Tinh Duong interrupted him. "You can help me. Help me and I promise you a jacket like this. In fact, you can have this very jacket."

Tinh Duong drove along and let his words sink in. Tinh Duong let the wonder of his words settle over the young boy like a net.

One night Tinh Duong took Cam Le to see the gigantic house with the wonderful window made of many small, diamond-shaped panes of glass where many candles flickered. Only they did not flicker this night. Except for a yellow lamp beside the brick path and a light over the entry-way, the house was dark.

Cam Le and Tinh Duong sat in Tinh Duong's parked car and looked at the great house for a long time. Tinh Duong sighed. Then he started his car, reached into his glove compartment for his MAC 10, and, leaning across Cam Le, aimed it carefully at the window. He squeezed several shots into the window, watched it shatter, and took off down the street.

Bach Lien took Cam Le to school every day now. He hardly spoke to her anymore, except when he wanted to abuse her, and he was good, very good, at abusing her, especially with his tongue. Just last night, when she asked him where he was going (Cam Le was dressed in baggy pants, black leather jacket, and his prized black Hong Kong–made shoes), he responded, "If you keep treating me like this I'll bring home dozens of babies for you to raise to your death! Shut the hell up!"

From her car she watched Cam Le cross the street and follow the sidewalk to the main gate of the school; she watched him enter the build-ing. Satisfied, she pulled away and drove to her job as an assembler at the electronics plant.

Cam Le met My Thu at her locker and gave her a long kiss. To-gether the boy and girl left the building, strolled down the street, and entered the Van Yen coffee shop. Immediately Bo Nham came over, greeted them perfunctorily, and the three of them left the coffee shop and climbed into the older man's van, which was parked down the street. While Bo Nham drove, Cam Le rolled three joints with the grass and the papers in Bo Nham's glove compartment.

Bo Nham headed for the beach. At the beach Bo Nham parked the van in the lot. The three of them climbed into the back of Bo Nham's "Toyota Hilton," as he called it, and "boonged" (smoked) some crack. Cam Le and Bo Nham took turns with My Thu.

Shortly before two o'clock, Bo Nham drove My Thu and Cam Le back to the school. Cam Le went to his last-period class. When the bell rang he met My Thu briefly at her locker, gave her a long kiss, and then left the building. He looked up and down the street and spied his moth-er's car. He waved her over. She pulled up to the curb. Without greeting her, Cam Le climbed into the car. She took him straight home.

Bach Lien had shortened her hours at the electronics plant in order to drop him off at school and pick him up every day. His school coun-selor had suggested that she do so. Cam Le had been cutting a lot of classes.

Tinh Duong drove Cam Le to the airport where they sat together in the Dunkin' Donuts. Tinh Duong bought Cam Le a doughnut, a coffee, and an orange juice. They sat and watched the people a long time. It was just before seven o'clock in the morning.

Then Tinh Duong nodded his head. A slight, middle-aged man walked by. In one hand he was carrying a briefcase, in the other a laptop computer. The man bought a coffee, secured the laptop under his arm, picked the briefcase up and sat down a few tables away from Tinh Duong and Cam Le. He put the computer and the briefcase on the floor beside him. Then he removed the *San Francisco Chronicle* from his briefcase and began reading the front page. Cam Le and Tinh Duong lit cigarettes and smiled at one another. Cam Le smoothed his hair and brushed the crumbs from his neatly ironed shirt. He had dressed for the occasion.

The man finished the front page, checked his watch, and resumed reading the *Chronicle*. When he stood up and gathered his belongings Cam Le and Tinh Duong stubbed out their cigarettes. The man headed for the restroom. Cam Le and Tinh Duong followed.

Nobody was in the bathroom. The moment the man got inside the door Tinh Duong kneed him in the groin. The man groaned and crumpled to the floor. Cam Le grabbed the laptop and the briefcase as Tinh Duong had instructed him. Tinh Duong kicked the man and said, "Make one sound and we waste you," but the man was not able even to whimper.

Cam Le and Tinh Duong left the restroom, walked the corridor to the escalator, rode it down to ground level and strode out to the parking lot to Tinh Duong's van. Tinh Duong pulled out of the parking space and left the lot, collecting five dollars in change from the short-term parking attendant. "This is a thirty-one-hundred-dollar machine we got here," Tinh Duong said, jerking his head toward the back of the van where the laptop sat on the floor. "Why don't you check out the goodies in the briefcase?"

Tinh Duong and Cam Le returned to the Tenderloin district, left the van in a parking garage, and met Bo Nham at the coffee shop. "That's five this week," Bo Nham observed. "And I got a customer for each and every one." Immediately he paid Tinh Duong a thousand dollars. Tinh Duong gave half to Cam Le. Cam Le shoved the wad of bills deep into the pocket of his black leather bomber jacket. The one that Tinh Duong used to wear.

"He is always mad and bellicose. I call Cam Le 'Ready-to-Fight,' " Bach Lien told the counselor at the Ranch. "And now my younger son"—she gestured at Phong Le who sat beside her quietly staring at the floor—"is mimicking him. You know, the clothing, the cigarette burns on the wrist, the hand gestures, and again he has been sent here, this time on a weapons charge."

"I see that Phong Le has been truant."

"Yes. I looked through his books one day and in one of them, there are big Xs on every page, Xs made in such anger that with his strokes, Phong Le tore the pages." Phong Le glanced up at his mother. There was no hatred in his face, no anger.

"I thought Cam Le would turn around after those months in the YA but he uses so many drugs that he was stealing automobiles as soon as he got out and then he was caught in a burglary. I thought his experience would really change him but after only one month he started to go out again, disregarding the advice of the parole officer and saying horrible things to me. He was arrested for attempted auto theft and warned.

I am sure he is a member of the Vietnamese Crips. When he closes our door and steps out on the street I see him put on a baseball cap that says 'CUZZ' on it. A lady at the electronics plant told me that 'CUZZ' means the Crips. She said that the 'VC' are dangerous, very dangerous, and that he probably joined them because of connections made at the YA. The YA changed him, all right." Bach Lien sighed. She listened to the scratching of the counselor's pencil on a notepad. "Had he not been sent to YA he never would have joined the Crips. And he has been such a bad influence on Phong Le." She glanced at the boy again. Phong Le did not look at her. (Phong Le has a round face. He looks angelic. He looks like a son who would be easy to love.)

"Phong Le has a girlfriend," Bach Lien went on. "She moved into my apartment, I mean she actually brought a suitcase to my apartment intending to move in. She was at first the girlfriend of Cam Le. She is older than both of my sons." Bach Lien blushed. "When she came the first time with Cam Le I asked her to go and she refused. Only when I threatened to call the police did she leave. Now that Cam Le is back up to YA, the girlfriend has come and she is sleeping with Phong Le. Right under my nose! Enough is enough!

"I expected Phong Le to be released on his due day, but now he has gotten two more weeks because of fighting, so that has spoiled every-thing. In the next few days my cousin is marrying and relatives will be coming from all over to attend the wedding. But now they will ask, 'Where is Phong Le? Where is Cam Le?' And now Phong Le's release day is extended until after the wedding. What can I tell them? It is all so shameful! I cannot be truthful. I have to kill myself, I don't know what to tell them. Please help me, I will be grateful to you for the rest of my life."

The counselor studied Phong Le. Unlike Cam Le, this boy showed remorse that seemed real—not in front of his mother, but when they were alone, he showed remorse. Once, he cried. He did not want his mother to feel bad. He just wanted to have fun. "Fun fun fun," the counselor recalled Phong Le's saying. "I am crazy for fun." His brother was back in the YA. Cam Le was involved in some big stuff and had gotten himself in some big trouble. Cam Le had orchestrated a home invasion in which the homeowner was seriously wounded. Before that he was transporting stolen computer components up to San Francisco and down to Los Angeles. He carried weapons—AK-47s or sawed-off shotguns. There was little hope for Cam Le.

But the immediate problem: this wedding. The counselor looked at the mother. There was something different about her from the last time. What was it? Her hair. That was it: her hair—she'd cut her hair and dyed it. (The last time she was in to see him she explained that she was seeing a doctor for an irregular heartbeat. She had lost her job at the electronics plant and was worried, worried and anxious all the time. Often she got in her car and drove through the south side, looking into the windows of the coffee shops and pool halls for Cam Le.) This woman had one of the saddest faces he'd ever seen, a sweet, sad face. He'd seen a lot of sad faces in his office.

The counselor excused himself and went to speak with his supervisor. Could Phong Le's IR (extra time a ward must be detained as a result of bad behavior that is written up by authorities in an Incident Report) be reduced? The counselor reported the woman's comment that she might have to kill herself. The Vietnamese people do not joke about killing themselves. "It's a remark we must take seriously," he told the supervisor. The supervisor approved the mother's request.

"Phong Le may go home for the wedding."

"Oh, thank you, thank you," she said. "You have saved me."

"Think twice," Cam Le's counselor at the Ranch had told him. "Ask yourself, 'Is this the right time for a fight?' Tell yourself, 'Postpone it. Look at things later when they're clearer.' You must be *'hien hoa,'* or wise and harmonious, or peaceful and harmonious. Accept defeat and humiliation for the sake of buying time, or avoiding Incident Reports or disciplinary action, only remember, you're not really accepting defeat, you're like the military commander who redeploys or strategically pulls back so you can replan your strategy."

Cam Le liked to listen to talk of military strategy—perhaps it was in his blood. Of course it was in his blood. His father was an ARVN soldier.

Yes, Cam Le thought, redeploy. "Lose the battle so you can win the war," his counselor at the Ranch had said. Lose now in order to win in the long run. At the Ranch he had dismissed his counselor's talk. But here, here at the YA where there were so many crazies, some of the wise words came back to him.

He would do that, Cam Le thought. He would win the war. He would not come back to the YA again. He might even think about *"vuong dao,"* the way of the superior man, of the noble man, of the medieval knight. Yes, he would think about that; those were ideas worth thinking about; those were ideas with martial images marching through them. In the YA there were many who had chosen the way of the mean man. They were *"ba dao"*; theirs was the way of the mean man or the low man. They used tricks, deceit, and betrayal. Cam Le never betrayed anybody. He had done a lot of bad things, but he had never betrayed anybody. Except for his mother. But he would think about her later. There would be time to think about her later. "Do you know the way of the mother bear?" the counselor asked him. He would think about that later, too.

In the bathroom, though, when two of them jumped him, Cam Le fought back. He fought back like a man possessed. But one of them had a screwdriver sharpened to a deadly point. The squat kid drove the screwdriver into Cam Le's rib cage. It pierced his lung and nicked his heart.

Cam Le was conscious when they carried him to the chopper. Blood bubbled from his mouth. "When you deal with a boy who is mean to you in a good way, then you are a superior man," his counselor at the Ranch had admonished him. "Establish your reputation as a superior man." Cam Le heard the *whup whup whup* of the chopper blades. He was scared. Am I dying? he wondered. He felt like crying but he was tired. Very, very tired.

I was opening my morning mail when the supervisor came in and told me that Cam Le had been stabbed, choppered out of the YA, and had died of his wounds just before dawn.

"Does Bach Lien know?" I asked.

"She knows."

I went to my window and looked up into the brown hills. I remembered the first time Cam Le came into my office.

He was perhaps the most angry young man of them all. He would answer none of my questions; he would not even look me in the eye. In group counseling sessions Cam Le would not say a word. He would stare at the wall while the others talked. He made a great show of not listening.

Cam Le had come into the office with a can of Coke. I asked him to put it down and Cam Le did not. He finished the Coke and played with the can, flattening it. Then, looking me in the eyes, he brought it to his mouth and bit through the can.

When he left my office I telephoned Cam Le's mother to report all of this. She was not surprised. "I am ill because of him," she said wearily. She told me her name was Bach Lien. During that first conversation she told me that she wished she had stayed in Vietnam. She told me that life in America had brought her nothing but sorrow and that she missed her old mother. "I don't know how to be strong here," she said. She began talking about the smells of San Francisco ("they are the smells of the dead and dying," she had said), and she told me about a pair of sandals she had worn when she was fleeing Vietnam with her boy children, and that sometimes, in the night, she would pick up these sandals and hold them to her nose and smell Vietnam. "If these sandals could take my feet back to Da Nang I would go. This very moment. But these sandals don't have magic in them, do they? Once I thought they did."

In group counseling the others would talk but not Cam Le. He sat sullenly.

"Do you know the way of the mother bear?" I asked him once. "She allows herself to be torn to pieces for the sake of her cubs. Your mother has wandered all over the forest looking for you. For love of you, she'd allow herself to be torn to pieces." Cam Le did not listen. But Cam Le did say something that day. "I feel the lack of things in my life."

"Things? What things?"

"*Things,* asshole! *Things!*"

I explained to him that because he spoke to me unpleasantly, be-

cause he used a word that was unacceptable, and that he spoke insolently, that his time would be extended. Cam Le shrugged. "Time? Time
is the one thing I have plenty of."

Cam Le fought repeatedly at the Ranch, and for each incident he
was written up and given extended time.

"You have to get out of here," I told him. "If you can't walk out,
then crawl out, because the longer you stay here because you can't control yourself, the longer you'll be confined."

On work crew one day a ward sprayed Cam Le with a hose. Cam Le
picked up a hoe and whanged him over the head with it. He was sent to
Juvenile Hall where the judge decided to send him back to the Ranch. I
counseled Cam Le extensively, but it seemed to be going nowhere.

"Do you remember why MacArthur pulled out of Japan ahead of
time?"

"Because he was so pleased with the Japanese."

"And why was he pleased?"

"Because the Japanese people did everything he asked them to do."

"Yes. The emperor told them—one hundred million people—
'When I tell you to bend you bend, when I tell you to get on your knees
you get on your knees, and when I tell you to stand up you stand up.' "

"No one disobeyed. They had perfect national discipline," Cam Le
said. He had remembered my words.

"And in the end the Americans left early and the Japanese had exactly what they wanted. Do you see the lesson in this?" I asked him.

"Of course. It shows I must behave at the Ranch."

"But you're not behaving."

"No," Cam Le smiled, "I am not. But I have plenty of time."

"Is there a full moon in America?"

—A Vietnamese refugee

Chapter 1
Perspectives

"Where buy dog?" the impossibly frail woman asks the clerk in the American grocery, pronouncing every word slowly and with tremendous effort.

"Aisle four, bottom shelf," the clerk responds. He doesn't bother to look up.

Too embarrassed to ask him to explain, the old woman totters up and down the aisles searching, totally bewildered by the astonishing array of stuff jammed onto the shelves. She did not understand a word he said, and was hoping that he would have shown her. She looks in vain for "dog."

"Where buy dog?" she asks a stockboy, and this time she grasps the boy's sleeve with her spidery hand. He's annoyed. "Aisle four, bottom shelf." He pushes her hand away. The woman gestures and repeats, "Dog, dog." The boy sighs. He walks down the aisle and points to several different varieties of canned dog food. "Dog, lady."

Bewilderment colors the woman's face, but she remembers the cans of pears and chicken from the American PX in Saigon, and figures that this must be okay. She bends down to remove four big cans of dog food from the shelf and staggers with her load to the checkout counter.

Lugging the cans several blocks back to her building, she walks up two flights of stairs to her apartment and sets the dog food on the table in the kitchen. She opens a can using a knife, smells it suspiciously, then tastes the oily-smelling stuff.

But this is not dog! The woman rocks back on her haunches and wails. Wasn't she warned? Hadn't she been told how untrustworthy Americans could be? She wails because she is hungry, and she wails because she is smart—smart enough to know that she is ignorant and that she'll flounder in it, like a too-young water buffalo in a flooded paddy.

We may smile at this pathetic story, as we smile at the thought of a Vietnamese newcomer excitedly telling another, "You can hunt pigeons right in downtown San Jose!" These are isolated incidents and are certainly not typical of the vast majority of Vietnamese, but they suggest that for a small portion of the Vietnamese population ignorance of this country runs very deep.

By the same token, most people outside the Vietnamese community are probably ignorant about the Vietnamese. Who are they? From what sort of past have they come? What kinds of lives are they building for themselves here in the United States—are they adapting successfully? And what about those children we've heard so much about who were born in Vietnam of GI fathers and Vietnamese mothers—the Amerasians—are they making it here?

In order to put Vietnamese criminal activity into perspective, we need to consider these questions.

A Brief History

Vietnamese culture is ancient—it goes back more than 4,000 years—and the Vietnamese have been fighting invaders for centuries. When the Han Dynasty of China conquered Vietnam, it ruled the country for a millennium. In the tenth century the Vietnamese threw off the Imperial Overlord, but for a brief period in the six-

teenth century, the Chinese took over again. The Vietnamese struggled to repel them, and their identity as a people is reflected in the
following lines of poetry, composed in the sixteenth century by
Nguyen Trai, a man who fought the invader:

> We read and learned our warcraft on Mount Lam Son
> The people's welfare was one goal we shared.
> We thrust the flag of justice toward the plains—
> We knew our lord's great mission would succeed,
> All rallied to his virtue far and wide.
> The heathens cowed in terror at his name.
> He waved his sword—like magic he prevailed.
> Wash armour, hang up bows and sing of peace!

The Vietnamese were now free once again to rule themselves.[1]

However, centuries of Chinese domination had influenced them
profoundly: the Vietnamese people embraced Chinese religious and
social values, the Chinese system of government, and even Chinese
agriculture. To this day the impact of a millennium of Chinese domi-
nance is still apparent, and criminal elements—both Viet-Ching and
Vietnamese—carry Chinese "cultural baggage" as well.

In the mid-nineteenth century, the Vietnamese faced an invader
once again—this time, French colonialists. Most Vietnamese detested
the French presence. In the words of a Vietnamese refugee:

> The French were invaders, occupiers who said they came to civilize
> but who only exploited the resources of Vietnam and made the
> country poor and the people bitter. They behaved as if they were
> the masters and we were nothing better than serfs.

Once again the Vietnamese people struggled to free themselves of
an oppressor. A Vietnamese refugee recalled:

> We all supported the resistance war against the French. . . . At that
> time, because they were against the French many supported the
> communists because people thought they were very patriotic. It is
> hard for me to believe now, but when the Japanese occupied [Viet-
> nam] during the Second World War, I too became a nephew [i.e.,

supporter] of Uncle Ho [Ho Chi Minh, the communist leader of the resistance]![2]

After World War II and the defeat of the Japanese, who had conquered all of Indochina, the French reestablished their rule over Vietnam. Resistance to them continued, largely under the Vietnamese communists who, from their power base in the north, capitalized on the fierceness of Vietnamese patriotism.

In the summer of 1954 the Viet Minh (communist rebels who received support from China) defeated the French at Dienbienphu. According to one refugee, most Vietnamese were ecstatic when the French were ousted, but they rapidly grew disillusioned. The Viet Minh defeat of the French paved the way for the partition of the country at the seventeenth parallel, into a rather weak anticommunist government supported by the United States and other western nations in the south, and a communist government in the north.

As soon as the communists installed their government in Hanoi and began to enact their land reform policies, many Vietnamese refused to support them:

> After a Marxist Government was set up in the north and land reforms introduced, many felt that the only thing to do was to go to the area controlled by the French in the south. More than a million northerners made that decision. I was fourteen years old when my parents decided to go. It was very easy because the French arranged transport planes to fly us out of North Vietnam.[3]

The communists took the lives of tens of thousands of landlords and farmers to implement land reform, and between 1954 and 1955 nearly two million Vietnamese living north of the seventeenth parallel fled to the south. The dissident poet Nguyen Chi Thien remembered that time. Until he was released early in 1992 (as a result of the efforts of British Prime Minister John Major), Thien had languished for nearly thirty years in a North Vietnamese prison:

> *Mien Nam oi* (O Southland), from us separated only by a thread,
> Do you see the human conditions here in the North,

With barracks and prisons mushrooming as far as your eyes
  can see?
Hundreds of thousands of husbands, wives, youths,
And thousands of families with tears are flooded.[4]

But meanwhile, in South Vietnam, American-backed regimes grew hopelessly corrupt. Many in the south (in particular, Catholics and the Vietnamese intelligentsia) accorded lukewarm support to the government, but they were not united. In contrast, the communists were. They knew exactly what they wanted and were willing, as their agonizingly protracted war with the United States proved, to fight and die for it.

When the communists entered Saigon in 1975 the independence of Vietnam was secured and its unity achieved, but, as one western writer observed, it was "by means of an ideology, communism, which from the moment of success rejected what many people believed was distinctively Vietnamese": "Our society was completely changed. . . . The most precious thing we lost was our culture and our freedom of thinking. The communists obliged us to throw away our culture that we had acquired; they forbade us to sing the songs we used to sing, to read our favorite books."[5]

The communists perceived themselves to be the inheritors of a literary tradition that emphasized the revolutionary struggle of the Vietnamese people. Consider the following two poems, both of which were written by communist soldiers who fought against South Vietnamese and American troops in South Vietnam:

Winter

Last night it came back, the wind from the eastern sea;
Autumn seems to numb earth and sky,
And the mountains round about are perhaps already cold.
The forest shivers, and the rustling sound echoes away into the
  distance.

In the prison courtyard, some Malabar almond trees;
Leaves and branches sigh under the weight of winter sadness.
With my back to the lonely night, I listen:

The icy wind creeps into the cracks of the cell.

With neither blanket nor mat,
Nakedness of solitude stretched out in the middle of the dungeon,
I hear my voice talking to myself.
Great craving for friends—
I strew my affection to the four winds.

Spring Flowers in the South

In sunny springtime I traveled through the South:
Never will I forget its young soldiers.
They are the tender buds of spring bursting on the trees;
Flowers bloom on their lips, rivers smile in their eyes.
Nineteen, the age when a uniform becomes too tight even before it
    shows signs of wear.
Their step is still unsure, but resolute and keen.
They are unaccustomed to battle—all they know is working in the
    fields;
But they go to their baptism of fire, volunteers to drive out the
    enemy.
They have no sweethearts to write to
Of their hates, angers, griefs, or joys.
In the chilly forest night they share the same blankets,
And squabble laughingly over a brief warm at the campfire.
They dream dreams full of sunshine and roses—the loveliest and
    the most naive of dreams;
They are birds that have never yet crossed the ocean;
They yearn for the open sea;
The horizon seems paltry to them.[6]

In the darkness of his cell, Nguyen Chi Thien had yearnings, too. He felt that there would never be a spring under a communist regime, as the following two poems suggest:

No Spring Out Here

Out here, there is no spring,
But only flung down youths.

Out here, I am experiencing
Only acrid and bitter feelings.

Out here, I have to steal
And hide manioc roots to fill
My flat stomach, before I get ill.

O Spring, although I love Thee
I can't hail Thee, excuse me,
In my unescapable loneliness
Among these remote jungles and forests.
O Spring, since Thou hast come here,
May I share a bit of manioc with Thee
To get "high" with this trustee.
Tomorrow, when I have my day
I will welcome Thee in full honor
To make up for the poor way I am treated.

In My Hilton Cell

After the heat waves, chilly drafts set in.
My flesh grows thinner and thinner,
Then my bones are wrapped with just my skin.
My knuckled legs and feet are swelling
And my skin is erupting.
Mosquitoes and bedbugs drink my blood—their feast.
In the stone-built cell, summer heat
Is like a steam bath—me, sweating and wet.
My daily ration is rice and salt to eat
With stinking mice shit!

In another poem, Nguyen Chi Thien reflects on the harsh treatment the communists inflicted on their enemies:

Killing Fields in the Deep Jungle

In the deep jungles
The Party is hiding thousands of innocent people,
And killing them in hundreds of terrible ways:
Cruelly, barbarously.

Countless numbers of people have died,
Of typhoid, malaria, dysentery;
From eating poisonous centipedes;
For lack of medicine, or wreckless treatment
In a prison system that is one of a kind.
And in these places one finds
Despair and slow death.
Skeletal and sick bodies,
Stricken with tuberculosis and spitting blood,
Were not spared from hard labor.
And complaints, grievances and requests
Only caused more trouble or are useless,
As the clinic is more cruel and wicked
Than the secret police and the security office.[7]

The Vietnamese have a great propensity for poetry. A worker in a refugee camp reported watching a group of refugees who spent their free time writing letters and poetry. One man was seventy-two years old, and he had arrived in Phanat Nikhom, Thailand, after having traveled through the Vam Co delta by boat, "carrying his bag of poems with a stone in the bottom so that he could drop them in the water if he was in danger of being caught." Noting that the old man was laboring over a poem, the worker inquired what it was about. The old man replied that he was writing for his neighbors about the end of communism.[8]

Like the elderly refugee and Nguyen Chi Thien, I too have dreamed of spring in my homeland, but it is a dreamland—a place free of communist rule. In 1967 during the Tet celebrations that occurred amidst the war, I wrote the following poem to express my feelings about the communists. I share these feelings with many Vietnamese who, since that time, have made America their home:

Noi Long: My Heart and Mind

The haunting memory of my Viet Motherland
Makes my heart sink,
The fervent love of Hung Vuong's descendants

Makes my heart ache.
I feel disheartened by those who are not mute
But play deaf,
Sorrowful for those who are not blind,
But persist in following the wrong path.
I empathize with expatriated fellow countrymen
With silver hair, under the burden
Of their age, their lost chance and solitude.
I also feel empathy for the warriors
Practicing their swordsmanship,
And the writers sharpening their pens
To save their countrymen.

The fire of blissful love now is dead,
Tears are no longer shed.
They are only shed for my mother's country,
For my nation's tragic history,
And for my youth's unfulfilled destiny.

When tyranny becomes the champion of love,
Spreading over all the corners of the country,
When the fire of hate becomes the torch of Liberty,
Firming the ideals of our indomitable youths
Fighting for human rights, for clothes that warm, and for food,
When happiness has become truth,
Then I will shed tears of joy for my People.

These poems reflect a fierce anti-communism that characterizes the Vietnamese American community in the United States today. When the American-supported government in Saigon collapsed, for many of us the thought of remaining behind and living under communist rule was unbearable. One refugee communicated the feelings of many other Vietnamese when he said: "It seemed to me that my country which I loved deeply did not belong to me any more, but to the communists, and I was an exile in my own native land. Where then could I find the joy of living?" Thousands left for America. In the words of one chronicler: "When asked why they left the usual reply of Vietnamese was that they were 'looking for freedom.' The phrase covers a wide variety of motives, mainly concerned with self-determination, but the common underlying feature is the wish to preserve a way of life that vanished with communism." Most were so anxious to flee the communist regime that a common expression at the time was "Even the electric poles would leave if they could." One refugee said, "I fear that the reality I am in a wonderful land is a dream and when I wake up in the morning I will be in Vietnam. This is the most fearful thing in my life."[9]

Others found it wrenching to leave friends, loved ones, and country behind, and their sadness, which they carry like an aura about them to this day, makes me think of the Vietnamese saying *"Nam vang di de kho ve"* (It's easy to leave Phnom Penh behind, but it's impossible to return):

> We flew Air France to Bangkok. I couldn't hold my tears looking down saying goodbye and being a thousand miles away. The moment was wonderful but very sad. I was wishing I could have a miracle to have my relatives and friends come along in the air where they can breathe. It was really a hard trip, it made me tired and I couldn't think, smile, or ask for information. . . . The day after I gradually regained my health. In the night I remembered the old house, the loving godson, the friend and the relatives who still live in Vietnam and I wanted to cry. Nothing I could do for them, only my memory of them.[10]

Adaptation to American Culture

There are dramatic differences between Americans and Vietnamese, and some of these differences have made it difficult for refugees to adjust to American culture. Readers should keep in mind that there are always exceptions to any generalizations one might make, but the following differences, compiled by one observer of Vietnamese American culture, have some merit:

• American[s] are generally straightforward and assertive. Encouraged to use the direct approach, they do not avoid confrontation. Conversely, the Vietnamese, indirect and tactful with others, and believing that the most important thing is to please, prefer compromise to confrontation. Humility is one of the touchstones of their culture.

- Buddhism, a principal religion and philosophy in Vietnam, teaches that man is born to suffer continually and that suffering is the result of craving for which the remedy is detachment from all things, including the self. [American] culture teaches that we are born to strive in this, one's short life, so as to make the most and best of it. [American] culture also teaches us to live for the self first of all.

- Confucianism, another basic Vietnamese philosophy, upholds family as a sacred, binding unit. The family is interdependent. They owe allegiance first to the family and think of themselves in terms of their part in the family. This loyalty is carried over into relationships with neighbors in a village. If need be, the entire village will come to aid a member. This loyalty is shown to the extent of ancestor worship and offerings of shrines in their homes on certain days of the year. Americans are self-oriented. They are trained from early childhood to become independent for the time when they leave the parents' home and live on their own.

- In Vietnam, education is a virtue. The people . . . regard it more highly than material wealth. Americans determine social rank by material wealth and value education as the means to achieve monetary success.

- Social relationships between youth of the opposite sex in Vietnam were guarded and the Vietnamese have high moral standards. With little or no dating between boys and girls and no physical contact permitted, there is very little sexual promiscuity, as a rule. Vietnamese parents choose the marriage partners for their children. This is unlike the customs of boy-girl relationships in the American culture. They interact socially and with some restrictions, dating is usually permitted by age sixteen. Sexual promiscuity is much more common.

- Vietnam is a patriarchal, male-dominated culture [in which families sometimes] discounted the birth of a female child (one study reveals that if a family has ten daughters and no sons, they will say they have no children). In America . . . many [women] are educated equal to or better than men, and they hold prestigious positions. In the United States, a woman can be anything she wishes to be.[11]

The differences between the American and Vietnamese cultures are profound. After just one year, researchers studying Vietnamese refugees reported that the newcomers had the most trouble accepting the following features in American life:

- the dispersal of the extended family.
- numerical limits on home occupancy.
- indifference and disrespect toward old people.
- absence of friendly people with whom to socialize in the daytime.
- hectic pace with few breaks in the work day.
- distances that require vehicular transportation rather than including work, family, and social ties in a limited, easily accessible geographic area.
- value on work and achievement rather than interpersonal ties.[12]

Refugees have found it especially difficult to adjust to life here when their children, who are eager to blend into American culture, reject traditional values. Indeed, as a Vietnamese scholar has observed, "For a few youths, the relationship between parents and youths are often filled with uneasiness and conflicts." This unease began even in the refugee camps where, because fathers could do little or nothing to support their families, their authority eroded. Some children stopped listening to them, as the following remarks, communicated to researchers at Camp Pendleton, in California, illustrate:

> My father is too nervous. He always thinks he is right and will not listen to others. In other words, he is too conservative.

> My problem is my father always reprimands me. He does not understand and sympathize with me.

Some disagreements produced actual rifts, with children wanting to separate from their families in the camp. One father confessed, "My son wants to live apart once out of camp. He no longer wants to be in the same group with us."[13]

Some fathers have lost all hope of putting together a truly meaningful career in the United States—or one that is as meaningful as that which they had in Vietnam. For example, Nguyen Kim Huong Giang, a former naval captain, spent more than two decades in the Vietnamese military, but that avenue is closed to him in the United States. He has, as he remarks, "no specialty except leadership."[14]

Andrew Lam was born and raised in Vietnam and has lived in California since he was twelve. He wrote to a cousin in Vietnam:

America is not an easy country to live in. America is violent and fragmented. In certain parts of this country of no core values and dwindling common ground, yellow skin can prove hazardous to your health. . . . [But] I can tell you with confidence that we immigrants from [Vietnam] have given much to American culture and business. We have a gift for hard work and endurance, we have strong family values that the American-born no longer possess. We revitalize areas that have been forsaken by governments and corporations. Families and extended families pool their resources and put a restaurant here, a grocery store there. . . . So, do you still want to come to America, cousin? Don't let my crazy talk scare you. Come. We immigrants are a resilient bunch, after all. We have traveled oceans and survived perilous journeys. There are many immigrant success stories—the lawyers, doctors, engineers. But be prepared to transform, to re-create yourself, to possess great strength.[15]

A story about a Vietnamese refugee awaiting processing on the Cambodian border suggests the cultural chasm between Vietnamese and American minds. It illustrates the deferential posture that figures so prominently in the Vietnamese psychology, their belief that one must always agree with a person of higher status, and that one never brags of one's own achievements in the company of such a person—in other words, it shows how dissimilar Vietnamese and American cultures are:

[The young woman] requested help in writing a letter of application to an embassy. When her final version of the prepared draft was examined it was discovered that she had omitted the sentence that stated that she spoke four languages fluently. She refused to include it because she thought that it was too impolite and boastful. She was shocked that anyone should think she should do so.

Had the woman been an American, undoubtedly she would have demanded to speak to the authority in charge, loudly asserted her *right* to speak to him, and repeatedly stressed her talent for languages, perhaps even exaggerating it a bit.[16]

The first Vietnamese evacuees from Saigon who stepped down from the aircraft on the island of Guam on April 23, 1975, were hardly what one would call a homogenous assemblage of people. One observer remembered:

> [We] saw well dressed people . . . carrying traditional luggage and the usual accoutrements of travel, including tennis rackets and the occasional bag of golf clubs. . . . As the stream of air transports continued, the numbers on the island soon reached the thousands, and the original concept of the refugee became more accurate. Late in April when loads of people picked up off the beaches arrived, they were more miserable than anyone had imagined. [We] learned that the concept of the refugee is an exceedingly broad one, and at least in this particular exodus from Vietnam its characteristics included a wide spectrum of wealth, age, social status, and ethnic background.[17]

Despite initial reports about the heterogeneity of the first refugees from Vietnam, a picture of the nature of the first and second waves of Vietnamese refugees is emerging. The original refugee population (those who came between 1975 and 1977) was relatively young (almost half of the refugees were under eighteen years of age), and because so many men either died, are missing, or are to this day still being detained in communist "reeducation" camps, the majority of first wave refugee families are still headed by women. Most of these refugees are Catholic (a minority are Buddhist), and most are educated, having completed the equivalent of grades 10–12 in Vietnam. About one of four had some university training in the homeland.[18]

The image that many Americans had of the first wave of refugees was of peasants who lived in "hootches" in villages like those depicted in popular movies like *Full Metal Jacket* and *Apocalypse Now,* but the fact is that the majority of adults had white-collar occupations (professional, technical, managerial, clerical, and sales) and one of five held blue-collar jobs. In the second wave (those who came between 1977 and 1985), almost half held white-collar positions and one of five was blue-collar. Most in the first wave owned modern conveniences such as televisions, refrigerators, and motorcycles, and almost half owned automobiles (motorcycles and cars are indicators of status among former South Vietnamese). Clearly, the earliest refugees belonged to an educated elite.[19]

How well have they adapted to life in the United States? Researchers learned that many of the refugees were familiar with American culture and language before they arrived here. Although one of four in the first two waves had no knowledge of English, a large proportion of Vietnamese refugees acquired English language skills rapidly.[20]

Nearly 100 percent of heads of household in the first wave found employment, but for the most part their salaries were not commensurate with their skills and have remained inordinately low. In 1980 nearly half of the first wave and the vast majority in the second wave struggled to get by on yearly incomes of less than fifteen thousand dollars. The first group is improving economically, but the second is not. The latter found themselves in established Vietnamese communities with Vietnamese groceries, newspapers, magazines, restaurants and nightclubs, Saigon-style markets, and so on. In both groups many have been underemployed.[21]

Significant numbers of physicians, pharmacists, and engineers in the first wave reentered their professions in the United States. Some artists and writers also managed to retain their former occupations with the new voices of Vietnamese relating to their displaced compatriots. Lawyers, politicians, and administrators have found it difficult, if not impossible, to apply their skills in equivalent positions.[22]

Researchers discovered that many of the better-educated refugees, while they have adjusted to life in the United States, are not happy here. Medical doctors, pharmacists, businessmen, university teachers, and engineers are forging careers here and are earning respectable incomes, but many cling to the Vietnamese language and culture and miss their homeland deeply. They want their children to learn about Vietnamese culture and speak the language. They remain emotionally attached to Vietnam.[23]

In contrast, refugees of the second wave, which consisted of less educated people who were exposed to communist rule, appear to be more satisfied with life in the United States despite having less income and being less acculturated than those of the first wave. Having enjoyed the advantage of being welcomed into supportive Vietnamese communities, they appear to be attached to their new country.[24]

Vietnamese Criminal Activity

Vietnamese criminal activity (or VCA, as the FBI refers to it) in its present state is not "organized" in the sense that the notorious Cosa Nostra, the Italian criminal group, was organized. It is, as I mentioned in the Introduction, "in a state of accelerated networking." That is, as their criminal groups evolve structurally and organizationally, the Vietnamese are working hard to develop relationships with other Vietnamese criminals across the country (including Hawaii, which has a Vietnamese community) in order to achieve particular criminal objectives.

Nevertheless, Vietnamese criminal activities are a real threat. Although they are not "organized on a national basis with a godfather, underboss, lieutenants, and soldiers with directives flowing down and profits up," the FBI has concluded that "the potential is there": "The rudiments of a hierarchal structure can be seen in those instances where the experienced criminals from the First Wave [of migration from Southeast Asia] . . . begin to orchestrate and direct the activities of the street gangs."[25]

At present, VCA is not a monolithic structure—that is, it is not a unified whole acting as a single, powerful unit. Gang organization is different on the East Coast and West Coast. We are also beginning to see Vietnamese joining ethnically diverse gangs. Another feature of VCA that suggests it is not monolithic is that there are ethnic differences in criminals who are perceived to be Vietnamese, as I will explain shortly. Finally, different kinds of criminal activities are performed by different types of gangs.[26]

The FBI learned that some members of Vietnamese gangs today were criminals in Saigon in the late 1960s and early 1970s:

> They were the backalley, black marketeers who controlled drugs, prostitution, extortions, and other illegal activities at a time when the U.S. dollar was just beginning to establish itself as the Vietnamese future preferred currency of exchange. The black market, under criminal direction, flourished to a point where it was, and perhaps still is, the most stable economic system in the country.[27]

These black marketeers were not ethnic Vietnamese. In fact, the word "Vietnamese" has not always been used correctly in accounts of criminal activity. The FBI has evidence that the above-mentioned black marketeers, the "financiers of the low-class bar area of Saigon," were actually Viet-Ching, or ethnic Chinese who were raised in Vietnam. In the United States, the Viet-Ching who came here during the period immediately following the collapse of Saigon (1975–1977) involved themselves in relatively sophisticated crimes such as extortion, food stamp fraud, and money transfer schemes. Viet-Ching who arrived later (1977–1985) were of a slightly different persuasion. Many of the second wave joined gangs and modeled themselves after long-established Chinese street gangs. According to the FBI, crimes for which ethnic Vietnamese are often blamed have actually been committed by gangs that are largely Viet-Ching.[28]

Many refugees from Vietnam were from the Cholon area of Saigon, which was the city's Chinatown. According to the FBI, the criminal elements from this area pose very real difficulties for law enforcement agencies:

> They easily glide between the [Chinese and Vietnamese] cultures, comfortably camouflaged in either community. They have both Chi-

nese and Vietnamese names and aliases and speak both languages fluently. Often, because of their familiarity with Americans when they were in Vietnam, they have a working knowledge of the English language as well, but will not readily admit this to members of law enforcement.

In other words, when they want to do business with the Vietnamese they say they are Vietnamese; when they want to do business with the Chinese they say they are Chinese.[29]

Both the Viet-Ching and the purely ethnic Vietnamese have joined gangs. But these gangs often welcome Cambodian, Laotian, and Amerasian members into their ranks as well. Thus the "Vietnamese" gangs on American streets today can be purely ethnic or they can be a mixture. This mixture often includes American-born Vietnamese and newly arrived immigrant and refugee criminals.

Some of these gangs are easily identifiable; that is, they bear names such as Action Packed Vietnamese, Born To Kill, and Born To Violence (a female gang). These are active street gangs, and their membership is fairly consistent. Other gangsters come together temporarily for purposes of criminal gain and then break up when they have achieved their objective; their groups are called hasty gangs or phantom gangs. The Viet-Ching gangs generally consist of ethnic Chinese youth, although Vietnamese also join their ranks.

There are no hard-and-fast rules separating members of one type of gang from another: members of one type migrate freely to another, and they learn from one another, sometimes by apprenticing themselves to a particularly admired or powerful gang. Members of the older, more established gang then teach the less experienced youths the ways of crime and the street. For example, newly arrived Vietnamese have worked hard to establish relations with Chinese gangs in order to be tutored by them. The important thing in all this, however, is, "if more and more immigrant youths are unable to find a niche in conventional American society . . . new generations of Southeast Asian gangs will arise . . . and people will die."[30]

The experience of newly emigrated Chinese in the 1960s confirms this. In his study of Chinese gangs in San Francisco, Calvin Toy found that a number of factors fueled the development of Chinese gangs in that period. First, the relaxation of immigration quotas during the Kennedy and Johnson administrations allowed an enormous influx of Chinese immigrant families. Second, San Francisco and its Chinese community failed to integrate the newcomers into the city in any meaningful way—jobs and housing were "severely lacking." Third, newcomers were greeted with racism, violence, and hostility from the general population—the immigrants were abused and even assaulted by other members of the community. These three factors led newly arrived youths to gang up in order to defend themselves. It was clear that "with few choices for survival . . . [criminal activities, especially extortion] were their only viable outlet in fulfilling their dreams in a foreign society." Toy found that "Asian gangs first appeared when Chinese youths were forced into self reliance when faced with a lack of legitimate opportunities combined with hostility and violence from local youths. . . . Gang warfare became a way of life for gang members."[31]

Toy pointed out that years later, after the war ended in Vietnam, there was a tremendous influx of ethnic Chinese from Vietnam into the Tenderloin district of San Francisco. Many were children who became teenagers in the 1980s:

> These refugees often felt as though they were social outcasts amongst Anglo-Americans as well as with the Chinese community. This group of youths were eager to please and sought a sense of belonging. Many in the Chinese community thought of these youths as fearless and "ruthless" individuals. Certain gang leaders realized their attributes and took the opportunity to recruit and train certain Chinese Vietnamese youths for gang activities.

Toy warns that refugee children from Vietnam, Cambodia, and Laos are facing even worse conditions than the Chinese did in the 1960s. Society is not recognizing the needs of these newcomers and another cycle of gang growth and gang violence has begun. History appears to be repeating itself.[32]

The First Wave and Criminal Activity: 1975–77

While American citizens and their dependents were being evacuated from Saigon in April, 1975, hundreds of thousands of Vietnamese were leaving their provincial homes to seek refuge in the cities of the Mekong Delta. . . . The communists advanced [on] Saigon during the last week of April. South Vietnam's President Nguyen Van Thieu resigned and departed with his family to Taipei. Vice President Tran Van Huong became president, but soon transferred his authority to General Duong Van Minh. By April 27, 1975, sixteen divisions of communist troops had surrounded Saigon, and panic spread throughout the city as artillery, mortar [and] rocket barrages on Bien Hoa and Tan Son Nhut air bases intensified. Despite a twenty-four-hour curfew imposed by the government, thousands of Vietnamese sought ways to leave the country, or at least, the capital. "Operation Frequent Wind" was organized by the U.S. Marines to rescue the remaining Americans in Saigon. While frightened Vietnamese converged on the American embassy in quest of air evacuation, other[s] arranged to depart via small boats and virtually any [other] means of transportation at their disposal. At 10:24 a.m. on April 30, 1975, General Duong Van Minh surrendered unconditionally to the communists.[33]

Refugees fled on foot and by boat, in spite of the danger of typhoon and piracy, and came ashore on the coasts of Thailand and Malaysia. They were then flown to American bases in Guam, the Philippines, Wake Island, and Thailand. Next they were transferred to four camps in the United States: Camp Pendleton, California; Fort Chaffee, Arkansas; Eglin Air Force Base, Florida; and Indiantown Gap, Pennsylvania. Eventually they settled permanently.

Two hundred thousand refugees of the "acute" type—that is, "people who are fleeing from great political changes or the movements of armies"—arrived in the United States during the first wave. Nguyen Thanh Liem, the Vietnamese author of the above narration of the collapse of the American-supported Saigon government, added:

Over fifty thousand Vietnamese left the country during the last two days of the war (April 29 and 30). An equal number had been evacuated in advance by American [military] and commercial planes. . . . Most refugees had neither time for planning nor knowledge about where they were going. Many followed the path of least resistance with escape as the sole objective; they sought safety somewhere, anywhere, outside of the area of intense conflict.[34]

Most Americans perceived the refugees to be Vietnamese, but in fact, the exodus consisted of people fleeing from Cambodia and Laos as well, and in addition, there were many Chinese, Hmong, and Mien. These people cannot be lumped together as "Vietnamese." There are considerable differences among them and each has values and customs that are distinct. "To disregard this fact," the FBI warns, is a "fatal flaw" that will "greatly hinder an investigation."[35]

Among the first wave of Vietnamese refugees were people described by the FBI as "high-profile." That is, they were Vietnamese who, because of their association with the American military, feared that the Viet Cong would imprison or execute them. As we have seen, most of these people were highly educated and, having enjoyed close ties with Americans for years, adapted readily to life in the United States (on the surface, anyway). As professionals they were rapidly assimilated into American society and became productive citizens, establishing businesses and paying taxes. Individuals in this first wave were not surprised when the second wave, which included uneducated peasants and a criminal element, created problems.[36]

However, as the FBI reported, the first wave was not free of criminal elements either:

They merely established themselves within their communities and became involved in the more low-profile, sophisticated crimes such as money transfer schemes and welfare fraud. In 1984 for example, 60 Vietnamese pharmacists and doctors fraudulently billed the California Bureau of Medi-Cal for $25 million. The couriers which they [used] for this operation were members of Vietnamese street gangs.[37]

In any case, the refugees of this first wave established close-knit communities across the country, the largest of which were in California (Los Angeles and Orange counties, and the cities of San Jose and San Francisco). Refugees from the second wave, which included the criminal element, headed immediately for these pockets and for Vietnamese communities established in Texas, Louisiana, Florida, and elsewhere.

The Second Wave and Criminal Activity: 1977–1985

There is a world of difference between a refugee and an immigrant. America is a nation of immigrants—people who, of their own accord, departed their native lands to seek a better life here. The immigrant saves whatever money he can to get himself started in the country of his dreams, and plans carefully, even so far as to decide ahead of time the particular community in which he will settle. In contrast, the refugee flees his homeland fearing for his life. Having no time to plan, preoccupied with the loved ones and the land he left behind, he faces the future unsure of anything at all. His flight scars him for life.

Like those in the first wave, the people fleeing Vietnam, Cambodia, and Laos during the second great wave of migration were also refugees. They were totally unprepared for life in America, and the dramatic change was shocking for everyone—young and old alike. The old yearned for home, family, and friends left behind. Lingering over their memories, they struggled desperately to hold on to their customs and traditions. The young were acutely aware of the stress being suffered by their elders, but they also wanted to fit into their new country. Sometimes they rejected the old ways.

Young people who fled Southeast Asia alone—their families either killed or unable to get out—were desperate. First-wave children, the offspring of an educated elite, knew some English or rapidly picked it up at the encouragement of their parents. Most children in the second wave, having come from small coastal villages and the countryside, had little or no English language skills, and this isolated them. Confused and bewildered, many children in this group turned to gangs. Now in their late teens and early twenties, these children are becoming the second generation of gang leaders. The anxiety, hopelessness, and despair of these young people is reflected in the poetry of a California gang named the Natoma Boyz or N-Scar Boyz. Its imagery is haunting:

When we left home it was in the mist of smoke
in quietness without frightened
looking for a house to knock [to rob]
would kill for living [money]
sunk in smoke
never mind a family
day after day look for money
sunk in smoke
and then enter jail
we look out to flee.[38]

The Third Wave and Criminal Activity: 1985–Present

The children I counsel are mostly third-wave refugees—the children of people who have come to the United States since 1985. In Vietnam their families were country folk who lived not in the cities but in the provinces, where they fished, farmed, and kept tiny shops. Uneducated, many are Chinese-Vietnamese and read and write only at an elementary level at best. Very few speak English. Almost none have marketable skills.

In the United States a large proportion of third-wave refugees have ended up on welfare. The children have dim memories of Vietnam, but because they were so young when they left, they are less interested in it than their parents. They did not dream the dreams of refugees. It is the children of third-wave refugees who especially feel the lack of material things in their lives. "I want to wear what the other kids are wearing," they say, meaning baggy pants and Hong Kong–made black shoes. To their parents, who struggle simply to

have enough money for food, their requests are outrageous. If the
child turns to gangs and crime for the money to buy the things he
wants and ends up in a correctional facility, the family loses out on
child care payments. Some desperate parents tide themselves over
by working for cash "under the table."

Others, however, make a fairly good living fishing. Some work
for the Vietnamese owners and operators of fishing boats. Others
work for American fisheries, such as those on the Monterey Penin-
sula, but they have been met with fierce discrimination. In some
cases groups of people picked up and moved from villages such as
Nha Trang, Da Nang, and Phuoc Tuy, and the villagers have pooled
their money to buy small fishing boats here. These people were not
familiar with American life in general, let alone with marine laws.
When they unwittingly violated exacting fisheries rules and regula-
tions (some were using illegal nets, for example), they faced legal
repercussions and found themselves confronted by the bitter hatred
of other fishermen. Some were fined, some had their licenses temporarily suspended, and some were prohibited from fishing in certain
areas. In Florida and Louisiana there was violence: Vietnamese and
American fishermen have shot at each other on the wharves, and
some have died.

The great majority of third-wave children who end up in trouble
have no fathers; most are being raised by single mothers. The father
might have been killed in action during the American war, or he may
be missing in action. He might be languishing in a communist
prison, or he may be alive elsewhere, having sent his wife and children ahead. Some of the children who come are sponsored by relatives. When a child is sponsored, the relatives have no real power,
and the child often disregards their authority. Over and over I have
heard wards complain about their sponsoring relatives. The aunt or
the stepfather is indifferent, even hostile: "she [or he] beats me"; or
"she [or he] talks down to me"; "she [or he] favors her real children";
"she [or he] gives them money but gives me a broom."

These are the children I refer to as the *"bui doi,"* which means
"dust of life" or "children of dust." *"Bui doi"* is a Vietnamese term
that commonly refers to children of Indochinese origin who find

themselves on the streets of American cities. Some of them are Amerasian.

The Amerasian Agony

"Bui doi" originally referred to the illegitimate offspring of American soldiers and Vietnamese women. The parentage of these Amerasian children is stamped on their faces, and as a result they have been outcasts from birth. They are set apart by light hair, freckles, and blue, grey, or green eyes, or if fathered by black GIs by curly hair and different facial features. In Vietnam these children were taunted by peers, humiliated by adults, denied access to schools, and ultimately forced to live by their wits on the streets.[39]

Of all the refugees from Indochina, Amerasians are perhaps most to be pitied. Shunned in Vietnam as half-breeds and as the seed of collaborators, most were exploited or abandoned, coming of age in orphanages or on the streets. As early as 1980 some were permitted to come to the United States, but with the passage in 1987 of the Amerasian Homecoming Act the "children of dust" began to make their way to the land of their fathers in great numbers. In 1984 the State Department's Orderly Departure Program enabled 33,419 Amerasians to leave Vietnam, some with their families. Between 1987 and 1992 the State Department accepted 88,000 Amerasians and family members for immigration and rejected 22,000. Fewer than 1 percent were reunited with their fathers.[40]

They suffered every step of the way. In its "Report on the Amerasian Issue" in August 1989, the Vietnam Veterans of America (VVA) Foundation learned through fact-finding missions to Vietnam and the Philippines that living conditions in the Filipino camps were far from satisfactory. Amerasians were detained for approximately six months to undergo "orientation" programs and to learn English and vocational skills. Despite the good intentions of persons overseeing the Amerasian refugees, the VVA concluded that

> the refugees live[d] in a state of total powerlessness, totally stripped of status, possessions, [living] space, time, and mobility for six

months. . . . Although we saw the crowded living conditions, the inadequate supply of food and water, after listening to the stories of the day to day life told by the [Amerasians] themselves a more desperate picture emerges. The Amerasians that we spoke to described the animosity of the Filipino police. Stories of beatings and rapes were widely known among the refugees, of young women being taken from the camp, later found to be raped or killed. In addition to fears of violence to one's person, the refugees tell [that] the food in the camp was inadequate in amount, inedible in quality, except, as one refugee pointed out, when visitors came to the camp. . . . Quite matter of factly refugees tell of their exploitation in the marketplace by the Filipino tradesm[e]n, resistance to which earned . . . violent suppression by the guards. One young Amerasian told of charging one of the fifteen persons crammed in his billet with the duty of night watchman to ward off theft and physical abuse by the Filipino guards. Another explained that the family was able to secure food only through the actions of his mother, who used the small sum of money [she] brought to the camp to buy supplies in order to sell sandwiches . . . the profits from which fed the family. . . . In response to questions about their instruction in the camp, the refugees expressed their appreciation of the kind Filipino teachers, but also pointed out the barriers . . . [such as] the turning off of electricity in the evenings which prevented studying.

In their own words, the Amerasians reported from the camp:

I try to send you a letter, I have to beg some people I know for stamps.

I have no extra clothes, only one or two that I brought from Vietnam, it almost torn aparts. I thought that when I get here, they will provide some clothes, but nothing. In addition, I don't even get enough food for myself.

Rice are not enough for eating for my family, I don't have any relatives in another country.

There are also many problems in this [camp], it's caused by teenage and youth, so I feel anxious and afraid for my children.[41]

The VVA Foundation concluded that "our desire to provide training and cultural orientation for the [Amerasians] is admirable. Placing them in sub-human conditions in order to provide that experience is deplorable." Clearly, life in the camps was debilitating, forcing Amerasians to make adjustments first to life in the camp and then to life in the United States. These adjustments were compounded by the fact that the Amerasians did not know where in the United States they were going until the very end of their time in the camps. Some observers suggested that the training programs were actually designed to push Amerasians into minimum-wage jobs so that they would be kept off welfare but not compete with middle- and working-class Americans.[42]

The Homecoming Program has been abused. So many persons have exploited it that today Washington is pressuring Hanoi to take back those who have come here fraudulently. So many have settled in California illegally that efforts are being made to deny them access to schools and to state moneys such as welfare assistance.

In two respects, however, the program has been successful. First, thousands of Amerasians have come "home," many with their mothers. Second, as one journalist reported, Americans who visited Saigon after the war were shocked to see gangs of half-American children roaming the streets, begging for food, and pleading with strangers to locate their GI fathers in the United States. Today, because of the Homecoming program, those gangs are gone. But the effort to bring them "home" took too long, and this allowed Vietnamese to use Amerasian children to get out themselves. Unscrupulous and desperate to get out of Vietnam and come to America, Vietnamese have literally bought Amerasian children in order to use them as one-way tickets to America. American officials who have processed the applications by Vietnamese claiming to be Amerasian say that the "*majority* of people approved for entry to the United States faked their American ancestry."[43]

Investigators from the General Accounting Office of the United States (GAO) concur that the program has been abused to an extraordinary degree. According to the law, Amerasians were permitted to bring family members to the United States, but "family," according to a refugee coordinator, "wasn't . . . too carefully defined by our government." In its preliminary report to Congress the GAO indicated that "a serious problem that has emerged for U.S. officials is the large number of fraud cases, particularly those involving so-called 'fake families.' " Newspaper headlines tell it all:

"Resettlement plan riddled with fraud"
"Amerasians pawns in scam to get to U.S."
"U.S. cracks down on phony Amerasians"
"Abuse, disfigurement for a ticket to America"[44]

Resettlement workers estimate that between 20 and 40 percent of their cases—thousands of individuals—came here under false pretenses. One journalist noted that, for Vietnamese who have used Amerasian children to come here, the " 'children of dust' became 'children of gold.' "[45]

Ironically, the children have often been treated badly. According to Catholic Charities in San Jose, they are "used as immigration tick-ets, then beaten, sold into marriage, used as domestic slaves or ditched, penniless, by the families they had helped." The following stories about two young Amerasians, both reported in San Jose's daily newspaper, illustrate how Amerasians have been exploited by other Vietnamese:

Vo Nghia

Vo Nghia was born in the central Vietnamese port city of Nha Trang in 1970. . . . He never knew his GI father. His Vietnamese mother was a secretary to an American firm in Saigon; she abandoned him shortly after he was born. His adopted family beat him and used him as a servant.

Lonely and excluded from school, he tried to swallow pesticide when he was 12 in an attempt to die. When he was 15, a wealthy woman approached his adopted mother, offering to adopt him and take him to the United States. She told Nghia it would be best for everyone.

"I think my mother sold me," he says. "I saw that lady give my mom a lot of money."

Nghia was eager to please. He spent a year preparing for the immigration interview. "That family that bought me, they give me all kinds of good stuff. When it comes to the American interview," he said, "I can say anything they want me to say."

During seven months in a Philippine refugee camp, the woman treated him graciously. She needed him at every turn to sign papers that would get her and her two daughters into the United States. "I think, 'Oh, yes. My life going to be changed,' " Nghia said.

In 1985, they landed in Bakersfield. His new "mother" put him up in an apartment, then moved her family to another home. Disappointed and lonely, Nghia knew no one and spoke no English. But he began to adjust, attending school and working at a fast-food restaurant when, a year later, she convinced him he would be happier out of school. She brought him to San Jose, he said, where she left him with a family and gave him $200 to get started on his new life.

Here, he got help from a program run by Asian Americans for Community Involvement. Today he is still poor, but he moved several months ago to the Tahoe region, where he is working toward a college degree and struggling to send money to the family that reared him in Vietnam.

Tran Giang

Tran Giang's brow is wrinkled with worry as he tells his story. He was born in 1967, he thinks, during the Vietnam War. Three days after his birth, his Vietnamese mother died. He was reared by his grandmother. For a time, his father, an American GI, sent money. Then it stopped. His grandmother lost his father's address.

When Giang was 9, his beloved grandmother died. He lived on the streets, working as a shoeshine boy until the police picked him up and took him to an orphanage where he worked at a sugarcane plantation.

Years passed. He escaped to Ho Chi Minh City, where he lived on the streets. About three years ago, he said, he was sleeping near a church, under a statue of the Virgin Mary, when a woman offered to help him. As it turned out, it was she who needed Giang.

She was trying to replace another Amerasian youth who had

promised to take her to America. "But that guy was so bad, he make lots of trouble for that lady," Giang said through a translator. "That's why she want to replace me for that guy."

The woman had documents with the first youth's photo on them. He didn't look like Giang. "That lady took me to a clinic to have them make my nose look more like that other guy," Giang said.

The nose was a failure. It does not fit his face. But the scheme worked anyway. Once in San Jose, Giang said, the woman kicked him out. He battled depression, living under freeways and in homeless centers until a Vietnamese family took him in.

Giang is embarrassed about his nose. He apologizes, explaining that this is not what he really looks like. He regrets that he helped the woman, but he is a devout Buddhist and he says it would be useless to feel bitterness.

However, he has one request: would the reporter and photographer please make a picture of him here, in the United States, then send it to a certain Buddhist temple in Vietnam so it may be placed on his grandmother's [altar]? It is his greatest wish that she know that he is alive and well in America.[46]

Giang allowed himself to be disfigured in order to be someone's ticket to America. In an effort to make themselves look Amerasian, and thus qualify for the Homecoming Program, other Vietnamese youths have disfigured themselves. They bleach their skin, add freckles, even submit to plastic surgery to pass themselves off as Amerasian. A nose job such as the one Giang endured costs about one hundred dollars in Vietnam and is usually paid for by relatives who have made it to the United States.[47]

Other efforts to look Amerasian are not so radical. For weeks prior to their interviews some candidates stay indoors so their skin is pale. Naturally dark-skinned Cambodian natives and Montagnards (a people indigenous to the highlands of central and southern Vietnam) have attempted to pass as black Amerasians. Officials have reported that during the interview, some "open their eyes as wide as possible . . . so they appear rounder." Others have given their hair permanents so as to look like the offspring of black servicemen:

" 'the test,' officials said, 'is to look at the smallest hairs on the neck to see if they are straight.' " During the series of interviews, conducted in Ho Chi Minh City, "emotions run very high." Applicants are searched for weapons prior to being admitted into the second-floor office where the interviews are held.[48]

By fall 1992 about 80 percent of applicants were being rejected. One interview suggests how American officials were trying to tighten up the screening process as a result of large-scale fraud:

A U.S. official escorted a Vietnamese woman into a barren office where a ranking American looked at the young woman for about two seconds. She stood there, her mouth open in a pose of fear and hope, exposing a missing front tooth.

"No," the official said as he looked down at paperwork. "Go," said the escort, who quickly spun the woman out of the room.

"You cannot look long," the official explained. "You must stay objective. I say no about 10 times a day. And they don't always go so calmly. They throw themselves all over you and sob and weep. They beg. It can keep you awake at night and it often does.[49]

The requirement for papers spawned an entire industry. Many so-called Amerasians backed up their claims of American parentage with phony documents—birth certificates, marriage licenses, or adoption papers. According to a San Jose lawyer who has assisted Southeast Asian refugees and immigrants, "Anywhere in Vietnam you can find people who do the documents—people who work for the government and do it on the side. Or people who have blank forms and fill them out. Or people who just print them up." Sometimes legitimate documents were stolen:

A Vietnamese family "bought" an Amerasian woman and her small child as false relatives more than a year ago and won U.S. approval to immigrate. While awaiting their departure from Vietnam, an official familiar with the case said the family abused the woman and refused to buy the medicine for the child, who died of an illness. Finally, the family stole the Amerasian's documents, substituted someone else for her and left her in Vietnam. The scam came to

light [but] . . . the family went to America with refugee status resettlement benefits because of what . . . [was] described as a "high-
level political decision" not to make an issue of the case. "It was
outrageous," said the official. . . . "It caused a great deal of heart-
burn."[50]

There are actually few legitimate documents. When Saigon fell
to the communists, women who had ties with American servicemen
feared for their lives and destroyed any evidence of their connections, burning their birth and marriage certificates. Today, forgers
are willing to create any document for a fee, so the black market has
thrived. These fees, in addition to the bribes that must be paid by
candidates who are forced to wend their way through a notoriously
corrupt bureaucratic system, have forced many legitimate Amerasians to sell themselves to Vietnamese who are trying to get into
America on their coattails. The going rate is one thousand dollars.

This traffic in human flesh originated in Vietnam with the *"co
lai"* or *"co chay,"* middlemen who made it their business to locate
Amerasians from the southernmost corner of what was once South
Vietnam to the former DMZ (demilitarized zone between the former
North and South Vietnam). They turned Amerasians over to a *"co
ngoi"* (another middleman), who purchased Amerasians and gave
the *co lai* or *co chay* a commission. This *"co ngoi"* referred them to the
"co bao" for another commission. The *"co bao"* sold these Amerasians
to the highest bidders (the prospective fake parents) and with the
assistance of the *"co giay,"* who forged an array of legal documents,
"verified" the Amerasian youths as bona fide members of the fake
families. In each village in Vietnam, the chairman of the people's
committee (formerly the village chief) has the authority to issue birth
certificates and maintains records for each household. These chair-
men help the fake parents meet any other eligibility requirements
they might need in order to migrate with the "homebound" Amerasians to America. The commission for a chief/chairman ranges
from one to two *"lang vang"* (gold leaves valued at $350–400 each).

What did fake families promise their Amerasians in return? In
short, anything: marriage commitments, cash donations to their

mothers or guardians, financial help on arrival, a college education, a car. But these promises were invariably broken. Arriving here under such circumstances, like Giang and Nghia, many legitimate Amerasians were soon abandoned:

- My brother . . . came here under the Amerasian plan. He bought a black Amerasian girl. He has already two cars. As for that black girl, he let her go anywhere she wanted to, we don't need to worry about her. If necessary we just simply kick her out of the house. [Statement made by a Vietnamese woman.]
- In New Jersey, two Amerasian girls were abandoned by husbands who married them to "get the ticket to America."
- In Portland, Oregon, two Amerasians killed their fiancées because they dropped them shortly after having landed on American soil.
- A disabled Amerasian was abandoned by his fiancée immediately after they landed at a Florida airport.
- Young Amerasians who have been abandoned have committed suicide in California, Texas, Hawaii, Alabama, North Carolina, Colorado, and Michigan.[51]

To an extent, the blame for the difficulties Amerasians have faced in the United States must be shared by the voluntary agencies that resettled them here and the Vietnamese community, which has done very little to assist them. This view is shared by the VVA Foundation, which observed that

> the most tragic aspect of the Amerasian legacy is that, after their long-awaited journey to the United States, many Amerasians end[ed] up being resettled into America's urban ghettoes. The opportunities available to those Amerasians who are sent to the ghettoes are as nonexistent in America as they were in Vietnam.[52]

The Foundation sent representatives to visit some of the sites (called "cluster sites") where Amerasians have been settled. They reported that

> although there are some successful resettlement programs run by very dedicated and resourceful volags [voluntary agencies], there

are also . . . programs which are substandard, and resettle Amerasians into some of America's most violent, drug-infested, non-pro-
ductive living environments. The fact that Amerasians are being
placed into these abhorrent conditions [has been] documented.

The Foundation report includes a survey of seventy-eight resettlement areas where Amerasians were living in "high-crime neighborhoods and rodent-infested tenements."[53]

When the facts of their new lives in America began to make
themselves felt, some new arrivals, utterly bewildered and alone,
vented their rage and misery on others. For example, Tuan Den, a
black Amerasian who felt that he was being looked down upon,
stabbed a young American to death following a fight over a girl.
Another Amerasian named Kien wandered shopping malls in search
of his father. When he was arrested several times for drunk driving,
he told police, "What is going to happen to me, I just don't care. I
want the police to get me. . . . I don't know what to do with my own
life anymore."[54]

There are many young people like Tuan Den and Kien. Although groups exist to help them, many of these "children of dust"
will join Vietnamese gangs—in fact, street gangs actively recruit
them. An astonishing 90 percent of the male Amerasians who ended
up in San Francisco are members of gangs. As the VVA observed,
"the Amerasians are truly our own." But when the state no longer
permits an Amerasian child to collect welfare, he or she has nowhere
to turn except to gangs. Some—particularly those who were forced
to turn to crime to survive in Vietnam—quickly become gang leaders, like Anh Ba, who became known as "Big Brother Ba Poppy."[55]

Big Brother Ba Poppy

The Vietnamese young roosters knew him only by his nickname:
Big Brother Ba Poppy. To them he was a hero.

They thought of Poppy that way because he was macho, with a
powerful, masculine allure that they respected and feared. He was

well built, with a neat, black mustache, and there were so many stories about him. Stories about marksmanship that had saved his skin
at least twice in gun battles with Mafia mobs and Los Angeles police.
Poppy was a killer.

Poppy's father was a Hispanic American GI, and unlike so many
Amerasians, Poppy knew his father's name — Marcos Lopez. He inherited his freedom-fighter father's iron-heartedness, and the as-
tute, calculating sharpness of his Vietnamese mother, Mai-Hoa. In
April 1975, when the Vietnamese fled from NVA tanks on the outskirts of Saigon, Mai-Hoa was so frightened for the life of her West-
ern-looking twelve-year-old son that she took him to a naval boat on
the Saigon River in an effort to escape to the United States. Perhaps,
she thought, Poppy might find his father, who had gone home
months before.

Five years later Poppy found himself on the streets of Los
Angeles. His mother died in a car accident, and his aunt, with whom
he had gone to live after his mother's death, died of illness. Poppy
found a home with the Golden Tigers, a Vietnamese American
street gang with a network that included New York City, Louisiana,
Boston, Chicago, and, of course, northern California. The California territory was under the command of Anh Tu Saigon (Brother Tu
Saigon) and his younger brother, Anh Nam Saigon.

One Saturday night in summer 1988, Poppy had a run-in with
Los Angeles police in a Vietnamese night club. He was sentenced to
four years in state prison for assaulting a police officer and attempting to grab his pistol. Instead of "kicking back" (cooling off or retir-
ing) after being released, Poppy gunned down a patron in a bar, and
then, not long afterward, shot and wounded two police officers in
south central Los Angeles from the fifth floor of a hotel. A manhunt
followed, but Poppy escaped.

Poppy never thought about leaving southern California while
things cooled off. It took a gang war with the Mexican mafia, in
which several mafia members were killed or wounded, to convince
him that he should get out while he could. Poppy decided to join
Anh Tu Saigon's "family" in San Francisco. The fit was good, and Tu
Saigon quickly made him his fourth lieutenant. Poppy made a cour-

tesy call to Tu Saigon's godfather, Tam Huu. To Anh Tu he swore, "I'll never let you down. I'll never drop a dime."

Poppy was fearless. Tu and Nam Saigon sent him on missions that others would have found impossible. He escorted stolen cases of computer parts from the Silicon Valley and Sacramento to Los Angeles and Santa Ana, and oversaw shipments of cocaine and heroin from southern California to San Francisco, the South Bay, Alameda County, and Stockton. He had plenty of Hmong and Laotian customers in the working-class neighborhoods.

Tu and Nam were impressed. They gave Poppy even more responsibilities. Now he was to oversee home invasions and out-of-town robberies of commercial establishments. In one operation he masterminded in Texas, Poppy came away with nearly $200,000. Tu and Nam then ordered him to take charge of robberies and burglaries of electronics firms and business extortions in the South Bay. Poppy did this with great skill. Tu made him his right-hand man.

Poppy cemented his relationship with the Viet-Ching, thereby tapping into the resources of Chinese-Vietnamese teen gangs. He used them to expand home invasions of ethnic Chinese, Vietnamese, Cambodians, and Laotians, and to step up extortions of community businesses. The scale of his activities in the South Bay led the news media to report the "rash of robberies and home invasions" between late 1989 and early 1990.

Then Tu Saigon was murdered by a Chinese American gangster. Three other lieutenants and two San Jose gang leaders challenged Poppy's power. Poppy decided to "retire." He married and fathered two children. It was time to tap into the business skills his mother had bred into him. He studied the market and zeroed in on Asian American gang members and other young people. What did they want? Drugs and guns. Fire bombs and grenades. Sex stimulants like Horny Pills and Spanish fly. He could deliver all these things. He opened a "business" in the basement of a small warehouse in southwest San Jose. But he would make himself untouchable.

Poppy hired a young black Amerasian named Lan Den to work on the front lines so that he could melt into the background. Lan Den swore he would never let him down. "I hate American society,"

Lan Den told him once. "And I hate my father most." Like Poppy, Lan Den had been abandoned. They understood each other.

Lan Den turned out to be an excellent choice. He was smart and reliable. He had experimented with all kinds of illegal drugs—cocaine, crack, LSD, methamphetamines, PCP, "ecstasy," even heroin—but he was not addicted to any of them. He knew how to gauge cocaine and fill the vials, how to process crack to make *"trung"* and *"cuc"* (large and small eggballs), and how to mix different kinds of drugs to achieve different effects. Lan Den tried to please.

He knew his customers, from middle school kids who wanted C-2 cartridges to business professionals who wanted a little cocaine. He was always on time and always discreet. He knew how to freebase and how to make 100 percent pure cocaine. He was never careless; it never exploded on him. And he knew how to get high-grade heroin, too, the stuff that his customers found was particularly good when it was inhaled.

Then there was the gun market. High school kids came to him wanting semiautomatic weapons. Lan Den delivered. At two hundred dollars apiece, guns were a lucrative business. And the kids always had the money. As Poppy reported, "Business is getting better and better!"

"I have no faith in anything. I live with the present and for the present."

—Gianh

Chapter 2
Why Indochinese Children Turn to Gangs

In Vietnam, beginning with the French-Vietminh war in the 1940s, the communists used children as spies. The job of the children who belonged to the communist organization *Nhi Dong Cuu Quoc* (National Salvation Children) was to spy on their own families and report their findings to the communist underground. Thus the "enemy" was often under a parent's own roof.

Indochinese refugee parents in the United States have discovered that the enemy wears a different face. It is difficult to fight because it shows itself on so many different fronts. The enemy is in school where their children are failing, becoming truant, and running away. The enemy is on the street where their children are joining gangs in droves. The enemy is the merchant of death who sells children an astonishing array of weapons. And the enemy is, once again, under a parent's own roof: Indochinese children (particularly Vietnamese) are committing heinous crimes, usually against other Indochinese and even against their own families. One horrified Vietnamese mother told me, "He ran away and was living in a safe house with his gang. When he ran out of money from his crimes, he came home, pointed a gun to my head and said, 'Give me all your money or I'll kill you.' "

Some parents—even those with the best of intentions—are unwittingly failing their children. Significant numbers of Vietnamese, Cambodian, and Laotian youths are completely alienated from school, estranged from American culture, and being dragged into a dust storm from which, for some, there will be no escape. Their parents stand by and watch. They do not understand what is happening and they do not know what to do. "It is not like it was in Vietnam," one distraught mother of a runaway lamented. "In America the children run wild." In this chapter, which focuses on the problems of Vietnamese and Amerasian children, we will explore the pressures that push children into gangs.

Shortcomings in the Home Environment

Traditional Vietnamese family values may be summarized in the seven golden Confucian precepts:

Compassion (*Nhan*)
Indebtedness and Gratitude (*Nghia*)
Politeness and Consideration *(Le)*
Learning and Enlightenment (*Tri*)
Trustfulness and Trustworthiness (*Tin*)
Loyalty (to one's country or ruler) (*Trung*)
Filial Piety *(Hieu)*

"*Hieu*," or filial piety, is particularly important: it reflects the Vietnamese belief that a child must care for a parent because the parent has cared for the child. *"Hieu"* contains ideas of sacrifice ("Your father gave his life up for you defending you from the pirates," a distraught mother reminded her runaway daughter), the upholding of family honor, and traditions of ancestor worship.

Many Vietnamese are Christians, and their faith requires that children "honor thy father and thy mother." Buddhism teaches the same lesson, in addition to the belief that one must shun wrongdoing, pride, and attachment to material things (values that differ dramatically from the self-interest and materialism that characterize American culture). Respect for one's elders is a Vietnamese value that has traditionally been "bred in the bone" of children by the immediate and extended family and by the complex networks of kinship that worked themselves out in the context of the village hierarchy. In the "old days," before war and political turmoil unraveled the social fabric of the country, disrespect was practically unheard of. Imagine the horror of a Vietnamese mother who reprimanded her teenage son for his truancy and got as an answer, "Motherfucker, if you keep scolding me I won't come back!" Another mother who implored her delinquent son not to go out late at night told me that he replied, "If you don't let me go out I'll smash the family altar and set your car on fire!"

The differences between Asian and American parenting styles may be summarized as follows:

Asian	American
Children are extensions of parents.	Children are individuals.
Family makes decisions for the child.	Child is given many choices.
Children should remain dependent on the family for most needs.	Early independence is encouraged.
Children should submit to structure.	Children should think about what is right for themselves.
Children should not express anger, frustration, or contempt.	Venting anger and frustration is better than keeping it inside.
Punishment includes shaming, withdrawal of love.	Punishment should be the logical consequence of the misdeed.
Parents provide authority.	Parents provide guidance, support, and explanation.[1]

In Southeast Asia in general and in Vietnam in particular, physical punishment is an important part of child rearing, as the following Vietnamese sayings suggest:

- If you love your children, give them the rod.
  If you don't love them, give them sweets.
  Fish unpreserved in salt will be spoiled;
  Children disobeying their parents are doomed to fail in every way.
- The disciplining of the children should begin at their tender ages; the educating of wives should begin on the first day of marriage.
- If the branches are not bent when they are still tender, they will break when they get stiff.
- Prune the plant when it is still tender,
  Take care of the flowers when they are still on the branches.

The Vietnamese people have a saying that reflects their attitude toward parenting: *"Cha sinh, me duong"* (the father brings the children into life, but the mother rears them). Motherhood is strongly identified with the nation ("Mother Vietnam") and the father's dedication to his family is "as high as Mountain Thai Son." In Vietnam, while their men were away fighting, mothers proved themselves perfectly capable of taking over the discipline of children because the entire extended family and the village were behind them. But in the United States, the Vietnamese mother, especially a single mother, faces enormous obstacles. In our culture, the single mother's authority is not buttressed by an extended family structure or a village. "I feel powerless," one mother confessed. "I cannot do it [raise her son] alone."

American law enforcement agencies recognize the significance of the disintegrating Vietnamese family structure. In its 1993 investigative report on Vietnamese Criminal Activity the FBI outlined the relationship between crime and a traditional family structure that is rapidly becoming unglued in the American environment. It observed:

> The Vietnamese family is a close-knit, tightly controlled unit, that for 2500 years has been dominated by the father. It is a paternal

society. Sole authority and primary responsibility for discipline and harmony in the family reside in the father. Resettlement in America, however, has introduced challenges and problems that threaten to tear this once-close family apart. The Vietnamese youth who was expected to obey without question in his homeland has been exposed to an American community that, historically, has oftentimes questioned authority. This does not sit well with the Vietnamese family. When the Vietnamese youth is exposed to video arcades, overnight parties, and opportunities to experiment with alcohol and other drugs, it becomes increasingly difficult to comply with the father's perception of an ordered family life. What follows far too often is a situation where the youth is punished, to varying degrees of severity, by a father who feels emasculated by a society that guarantees previously-unheard-of rights and freedom to his children. Father and child drift apart and the child becomes part of a new class of disenfranchised Vietnamese youth. Some will remain in the home, others will go so far as to target their own families and other relatives for home invasions as much for revenge as for profit.

What this report fails to make clear is that at least one of four Vietnamese families in the United States today is headed by women.[2]

Fourteen-year-old Helen is a middle school child of Vietnamese parentage, and her father wielded absolute authority over her. Having come from a family where corporal punishment was the only means of discipline, Helen's father beat her when she failed to inform him that she was going to a variety show with her boyfriend. In a letter to her boyfriend she wrote:

> I love my mother, it's just my god damn fucken dad that I hate. The moment I opened the door, he came out with his belt. He tied me to my bed post and started punching, kicking me. He threatened to cut off my hair. . . . He started to mess up bad. He threw anything that was in sight. And then, he burned most of my clothes. Fucken asshole! He even swore to God that if ever I lay my foot out of this house he is gonna shoot me. . . . Right now I'm in much pain. . . . I

might leave tonight. I don't give a shit any more. I hate my life so much. . . . I can't stand my father anymore. . . .

Several days later, in a letter to another boyfriend, Helen recounted her punishment again and added:

I couldn't stand it anymore. I ran away that night. I was halfway down N Street when my father pulled over and dragged me in his car by my hair. When I got home, I got beaten up again. This time, there were marks across my face. . . . What kind of a shitty world is this? Why don't I just shoot myself and get it over with?

Months later Helen wrote to a girlfriend:

My mother is beginning to understand me more now. I don't know about my father. He is still an asshole to me, but he loves me a lot. That's the problem. He loves me too much and it makes me hate him more.

Most adolescents like Helen believe that running away is the only thing they can do, and that it will emancipate them from their families. Helen dreamed of an exciting life-style. "I want to get a big kick out of life," she told me.

Le Thanh Viet is a teacher and educator who works to help Vietnamese families adjust to the culture of their new country. He encourages parents to help their children follow the Confucian "middle path" or "happy medium." He emphasizes that parents should do the same, should strive to understand and accept differences between the two cultures and then work at living in harmony with both—a path that Helen's father would have been well advised to follow. "You can help your child become a strong person by instilling pride in your Vietnamese heritage," reads a pamphlet on drug abuse that was distributed in the Vietnamese community. But becoming American means that parents will have to give up some traditional practices that are backfiring, such as corporal punishment.[3]

"Child abuse" is untranslatable into Vietnamese—the phrase simply does not exist. Many Vietnamese parents are completely ignorant of the fact that in the United States children have "rights"—

the very idea is foreign to them. For example, Bim Nguyen, the father of the three gunmen who killed three hostages at the Good Guys electronics store, was "very strict." A Vietnamese journalist offered this insight into Bim's relationship with his boys:

> As in most Vietnamese families, the children were closely monitored. When the boys began cutting class and were beaten by the father, those close to the family say Bim was warned by the Child Protective Services not to hit his sons.
>
> The father seemed stranded between cultures. Traditionally in Vietnam, a parent always has the authority to discipline a child. The parent's moral authority is supreme in a society where it is forbidden to talk back to your parents, and the parents always have the last word.
>
> Yet in Sacramento, Bim reportedly felt he was losing control, his authority undercut by his own children who could report him if he disciplined them the only way he knew how.

Like their peers, the Nguyen boys probably learned quickly about child abuse from their friends. If they are subjected to discipline that is physically abusive, Vietnamese children beeline for social service agencies or probation departments that bring the parents or guardians to court and charge them with child endangerment, child abuse, or neglect. Many of my wards have warned their parents, "If you beat me, I'll call the police."[4]

Some, like Vicky Phung, have exploited the system for their own purposes. Vicky Phung arrived in California with her parents and two older brothers in 1990. The entire family escaped Vietnam by boat, losing everything, and Vicky's parents, who had been fairly prosperous in Vietnam, had no choice but to accept state assistance. To earn what little extra money they could they both worked long hours at a Chinese supermarket in San Jose. Vicky's brothers got swing-shift jobs as assemblers at a local electronics plant. Vicky was left to fend for herself at home, where she was bored and alone. At school she was lost. In her tenth-grade history class, a remedial course, Vicky could not read a single word. She looked out the window and daydreamed.

Carlos daydreamed, too. A good-looking Hispanic boy, he day-dreamed about going out with Vicky. In history class he whispered to her: "Want to go for a drive with me?" She did.

Every night after his dinner Carlos picked Vicky up. Nobody was ever home when Carlos came around. Nobody knew that they had sex in her bedroom. Nobody knew that they had sex in his car. Nobody knew that sometimes they slept together in Carlos's house. Nobody knew because nobody was home. And even when Vicky's parents or brothers were home, they were sleeping.

One weekend before Vicky's mother went to work, she asked Vicky to help her around the house. Vicky refused—Carlos was waiting outside. Mr. Qui, Vicky's father, ordered her to help her mother. Vicky refused again.

There was a knock at the door. It was Carlos. Vicky's father blocked it. "Open the goddamn door," Vicky said to her father. Mr. Qui, dumbfounded by his daughter's disrespect, gaped at her. Carlos banged on the door. Mr. Qui opened it and shoved him away from the door. Carlos shoved back. "Out of the way old man," Carlos said to him; "don't be a fuckin' asshole." Vicky slipped out past her father. Mr. Qui slumped onto the floor. "What is happening to our daughter?" he asked his wife. "What is happening?" He put his face in his hands.

In school, Vicky reported to her history teacher that her father was abusing her and her brothers were molesting her. "My brothers come to me in the night. They fondle my breasts. My father kicks me and beats me." The teacher took her to a school counselor, and the counselor notified county authorities immediately. They saw that Vicky was installed in the Children's Shelter. Meanwhile, they opened an investigation.

The Child Protection Agency filed charges against Vicky's father and his sons and ordered them to counseling. They sent Vicky to a foster home. A probation officer came to the house to gather up Vicky's belongings. She found a little notebook in a handbag stuffed in a drawer in which Vicky had written boys' names and descriptions of their genitals and sexual habits. She confronted Vicky. "I share information with my friends," the girl said indifferently.

Vicky found herself in a new school near her foster home. Cynthia Ho, another Vietnamese girl, was drawn to her. It was not long before they became good friends and Vicky learned that Cynthia wanted to get out of her father's house. "I hate him," Cynthia said. "I hate him and I hate our dingy house. I want to get out."

Vicky smiled. "I cooked up a story about my father and brothers abusing me. You can, too. Tell the right people that you're being abused and you'll be free."

Vietnamese parents typically are reluctant to share their feelings with their offspring, even though most of the children I have counseled crave their parents' attention. As one boy recalled, "I come home from school and nobody is ever home. I am hungry and no one is there to cook my food. My parents eat out with their friends. I feel lonely. And a lot of times hungry." Another remembered:

> Them [my parents] are never home. Them leave the house for breakfast and then them work the restaurant until ten o'clock at night. Them ate out lunch and dinner and slept at restaurant too because of contacts made and for evening meeting. I have two brother and three sisters. My brother and my sister they run away for fun with other kids. My brother return, but then the other brother run and he no go to school. He a gangbanger [gang member] now.

The fact that some Vietnamese do not speak English very well, or at all, aggravates the problem. Since the children invariably insist on speaking it, the result is that some mothers and fathers are unable to communicate with their own children. Ashamed and embarrassed by this, these children are often rude and disrespectful. In one of my counseling sessions a ward grew so frustrated that, in a rage, he screamed, "Speak English or I'll tell the social worker you're committing welfare fraud!"

Many Vietnamese, particularly those who have come here since 1985, are struggling merely to survive. They subsist on jobs that devour their time and receive government assistance through AFDC

(Assistance to Families with Dependent Children) or other programs. Some work at two or more jobs to pay for a car. A great number take on extra work to help support family or friends who remain
in Vietnam, and some run illegal businesses out of the home. As a
result, these parents do not have time to devote to emotionally needy
children. They cannot help a young child do homework, they cannot
attend PTA meetings, and they do not keep abreast of a child's problems at school. Nor are they alert to the ways in which a child spends
free time.

The results are inevitable. Le Van Co, a young mother, recalled:

> The probation officer called from the Juvenile Hall and advised me
> that my son, Le Dai Giau, was being detained. She asked me to come
> down to answer a couple of questions. When I asked her about
> what, she told me it was about his involvement in a car theft with
> three other minors in San Jose. I asked her, "What are you talking
> about? Giau is a good boy. He never goes out late at night. He always
> does his homework. And after that he watches Kung Fu videos and
> goes to bed. He has the same routine every night. And you're telling
> me that my son steals cars? That's impossible. He can't even drive!"
> She told me, "Your son is small. When police spotted a car that ap-
> peared to be moving by itself, they found a little round-faced boy
> behind the wheel. His name is Giau and he is here with me now."

Giau was sent to a "Ranch," a juvenile rehabilitation and correction
facility, for six months. One week after he was released he ran away
from home again. Obviously Giau did not have "the same routine
every night," but his single mother, who was never home at night,
had no way of knowing this. She worked all night in an assembly
plant and slept during the day.

Many Vietnamese children live with an older sibling, uncle,
grandparent, or guardian, and from what I have observed many relatives and guardians are not raising them successfully. A boy named
Gianh lived with a sister and a brother. The sister told me that she
"tried to be a mother to him," but as Gianh related:

> I have only a sister and a brother. I always felt lonely. Then I had
> . . . opportunities to follow a few friends to their homes. At the

dinner tables were their moms and dads and brothers and sisters. What a happy family life! As for me? I was by myself. When I was hungry, I cooked dinner myself, then ate alone in the kitchen. I felt sorry for myself [and] my life. [Kids like me] feel the same way.

Gianh found a "family" in the gangs. The gangs made a lot of money and spent it recklessly. For Gianh, life with his new friends was exciting. He and his gang brothers spent money on motel rooms, crack, girls. When they ran out of money, they plotted another robbery or burglary, and Gianh took pride in these "accomplishments." They slept in cars and shoplifted from neighborhood supermarkets in order to eat. Like most criminals, they lived from day to day. Gianh told me, "I have no faith in anything. I live with the present and for the present." Gianh was not afraid to die. "You play, you pay," he said. During a burglary Gianh was critically wounded, and because he was the group leader he was sentenced to ten years in the C.Y.A. He wanted to die: "When I was shot, I didn't care for anything anymore; I lost all interest in life. But some Guy up there didn't want me to forget so conveniently about everything I did. He wanted me to live and remember my bloody past." Similarly, the Cambodian refugee Bonset Soun, whose sad story I told in the Introduction, remarked to his attorney, "If my life gonna end, I don't care, you know. Go ahead, end. 'Cause I feel like nothing for me in this world, you know?"[5]

Parents suffer as much as the children. Many Vietnamese parents of rebellious children experience grave emotional problems and become physically ill. Marriages suffer because husbands and wives blame one another for the troubles of their children. Many divorce. Some parents throw up their hands and walk away.

Trung Dang is a boy I counseled when he was admitted to the Ranch for auto theft. He seemed receptive to my counseling, but by the way he dressed when he went home on OT ("Outside Temporarily," or the time an inmate is permitted to visit home), I knew immediately that he was a gang member. I drew his parents' attention to that fact. They listened but seemed not to hear. Both shrugged their shoulders. The father said, "What can we do?"

Because he got involved in a fight when he returned to the Ranch, Trung was restricted for thirty days and was not permitted to go home. When his restriction ended and he expected to go home, his parents were unable to come because each was at work and neither could take time off without losing pay. Several days went by before they were able to come. I asked the three of them to come into my office.

The parents had with them a document from Social Services that indicated how much financial assistance they were losing because of the boy's confinement at the Ranch. They showed it to him, and Trung became furious. "Why didn't you pick me up sooner!" he screamed. The parents patiently explained that they were unable to get away from work and that they were having to work extra hours because of the loss of money. "I don't want you, I don't need you, go home, motherfuckers. Go back to where you came from!" For using obscene language Trung was restricted for another thirty days.

Because this happened in front of me, both parents were humiliated. Trung's father could not even look at me; he stared at the floor. The mother wept. I apologized to both of them. I felt I was to blame because my counseling was not working.

Then Trung escaped. After several weeks he turned himself in at Juvenile Hall (a county-run institution used primarily for the temporary detention of minors alleged to have violated the law). His parents were with him. He finished serving time at the Ranch and was released. But soon after he was released he was back again for auto theft.

I tried to contact his parents, but they had disconnected their phone. I tried to visit them, but they had moved away. These two people, simple country folk, were "peaceful like Buddha." Humble and deeply religious, they were quiet, soft-spoken, sweet people whose son, according to their understanding, had simply gone sour. That he was deeply involved in gangs made so little an impression on them that it was clear to me they simply did not understand. They did not know how to respond to this situation.

For both parents to abandon a child is most unusual. It has been my experience that mothers tend to persevere, sometimes until they literally make themselves sick. One mother told me that she had stomach ulcers because of her constant anxieties about her young son; another developed heart problems. Mothers wander the streets by night, searching for their sons, or drive about aimlessly during the day, checking one café after another in an effort to find their lost children. Exhausted by her efforts to locate a son who had been in and out of detention centers, one mother told me she often thought about killing herself. "I come here to get away from the communists and my children turn against me." She reflected:

> I don't know what I can do for my children anymore. I am thinking lately about what I can do for me. Frankly, I cannot cope. I lost all my jobs because of them. All my time has been spent between the Juvenile Hall, the Court, the Ranch and the YA, or I've been poking my head into one café after another looking for them. One day I went crazy and lost control of my car. I almost got killed. I have wished I were killed to get over with my cursed life. I'm on medication because I worry all the time and can't sleep. I am trying to persuade my husband to move to Texas where maybe I can find a job to cook for a Chinese-Vietnamese restaurant. Our body shop is up for sale. I know many mothers who with children like ours are on medication. Just like me. Sometimes I wonder if we should have never left [Vietnam].

Like this woman, some mothers are so frustrated and bitter that more than one has wished to send her children "back to Vietnam to learn their lessons from the communists." One mother said, "All of us Vietnamese mothers wish to see the U.S. government ship these children, including my son, back to Vietnam. In this country we are totally powerless." One can only guess how many Vietnamese newcomers to the United States have wondered whether they might have been better off staying in their homeland.

Huong Tran may be among them. She arrived in the United States with her twin sons as a boat person in 1983. As they were making their escape, her husband, Tung, was killed by the Viet Cong. A fishing boat caught his corpse in a net along with the bodies of other murdered Vietnamese and brought them ashore. His body was so badly decomposed that Huong Tran was able to identify him only by his belt buckle: before he'd left, Tung and Huong Tran had sold everything they had for a few gold leaves, which Tung melted down and fashioned into a belt buckle that he painted over with a dull, pewtery color. That buckle was everything they had in the world. Huong Tran removed it from her husband's corpse and wore it hidden in a knot of her thick, black hair.

Huong Tran made it to shore in Malaysia and ended up in a refugee camp in Hong Kong. The first night she was there, before the very eyes of her twin sons, Xinh and Xuan, three guards took turns raping her. She became pregnant. In the camp she bore a child, a daughter she named Thu.

She settled in California with Xinh and Xuan and her daughter. It seemed that life was finally granting her a reprieve. She got a job in a Vietnamese restaurant and was struggling to learn English. She was proud that she was able to communicate on the telephone with "real Americans," as she put it. She acquired a boyfriend. He came to her apartment and slept with her. The boys entered the ninth grade. They did not like Huong Tran's boyfriend.

Life began to beat Huong Tran down once again. Xinh and Xuan had had nearly perfect attendance in their middle school, but in senior high they began to cut classes. Both boys hung out with gang members, experimented with drugs and sex, began to shoplift, and committed burglaries for a local gang leader. They watched porno movies compulsively. Huong Tran knew none of this.

One day a school counselor telephoned. Both boys had missed so many classes that they were failing all their subjects. On a bright and sunny Saturday morning that Huong Tran says she will never forget, the police called. Xuan was under arrest for burglary. He was going to be committed to a Ranch. Huong Tran was beside herself with anxiety. *Her son was going to jail!* She was terrified. Her husband had known the inside of Vietnamese jails. "Would American jails be different?" she asked me. At the same time Xinh was taken to Juvenile Hall for truancy.

Then her daughter's teacher called. Seven-year-old Thu had shown her two bruises on the inside of her thigh. The teacher questioned her. According to Thu, Xinh was having sex with her. When Huong Tran visited Xinh at Juvenile Hall and confronted him, he said, "I just imitated my brother. And if I don't do it to her, others will do it anyway." Authorities charged both boys.

When I questioned Huong Tran I discovered that she had known about the molestation. In fact, both boys had tried to molest a babysitter. But Huong Tran did not seek help. "I was too ashamed," she said, and she simply did not know how. When gang members broke into her tiny apartment and robbed her of virtually everything, Huong Tran was too tired to care. She tried to take her own life. "Why? Why?" she cried.

"Because her boyfriend made us work in his restaurant for nothing," Xuan told me. Enraged, he recalled the time his mother took him and Xinh to a department store "and we tore clothing off the hangers and ripped it so she had to pay for it."

Some parents are relieved when their children are imprisoned. One parent said to me, "I wish that Dung's confinement would continue indefinitely." The most embittered parents act as if their children were dead. One Vietnamese mother put a death announcement (or *"Cao Pho Tu Con,"* a formal renunciation of one's child) in the local paper:

> My name is Mrs. Vu Khac Dinh, and I am a widow. My maiden name is Nguyen Thi Suong. I was unfortunate to have given birth to Vu Chi Don. As of the date of this announcement, I wish to let it be known to all that I feel pain to have brought this child into the world. He is a rebellious, ungrateful, bellicose child. I no longer acknowledge him to be my son. It is extremely heartbreaking for me to make this death announcement, but from now on I do not want to see his face, I do not want him to come back to my home, or to call me on the phone. Of all my children, he is the only disrespectful and rude child. It is my hope that you will empathize with my predicament as a mother. It is he who causes me to disown him. What I am doing now is to honor my husband's wish [that he expressed] before he passed away. Before I did not have enough courage to carry out his wish. But now I cannot take it any more. Today,

please be my witness. Mrs. Vu Khac Dinh hereby disowns her son Vu Chi Don, otherwise known as Andy Vu, presently employed at Applied Electronics, Santa Clara.

The words *Cao Pho* are used only in titles of formal death announcements. In using this vocabulary, the mother was asserting that, as far as she was concerned, her son was dead.[6]

Some parents have failed to be good role models. John Do was only ten when he tried marijuana. When he was eleven he began to experiment with amphetamines. After sniffing glue and snorting cocaine, he turned to more dangerous drugs such as PCP and LSD, and when he was thirteen he experimented with heroin. Since the small allowance his parents gave him could not support his habit, John carried drugs and alcohol to school in a backpack and attempted to sell them. What he could not push he used.

When he turned fourteen, John became a member of Asian Pride, which got him into serious trouble. While he was attempting to steal a Mercedes, the police caught him red-handed and arrested him.

After his arrest John claimed that he used drugs to relieve boredom at home and to forget his problems at school. He told me that his father's use of tobacco and alcohol affected him profoundly:

My father admonished me not to smoke or use drugs and alcohol, but I do not remember him without a cigarette between his fingers. His bar was well stocked, he drank heavily, and our medicine chest was filled with tranquilizers and sleeping pills. *Buon gia dinh, toi bo di hoang* (Disappointed in my family, I ran away).

Some parents refuse to acknowledge problems, in part because it is ingrained in Vietnamese culture to feel shame about them. As a result, some do nothing about them. Many, for example, absolutely refuse to get professional help for children who are using drugs. A Cambodian mother in my counseling session admonished her son, "Go to the doctor to get it fixed and don't tell anybody." If a son or daughter serves time at a correctional facility, or participates in a treatment program of one kind or another, parents inform friends and relatives that their child is "visiting family" or "going to out-of-town schools." This kind of attitude, fairly typical of Indochinese, hurts children who desperately need guidance, help, and care.

Sunny Nguy is a Vietnamese teenager committed to a juvenile correctional facility for a third time. In his statement he describes the pressures he feels at home, illustrating some of the family issues examined here:

> The reason I left home is because when I'm at home there is something that does not seem right. When I'm at home I feel worthless to the family. I feel like I'm just there to cause trouble for the family and I can't help my family at doing anything. . . . It seems like I'm not capable to do anything right. Such as school or just being a part of the family.
>
> I usually argue with the family about what I want such as my way of clothing, my hair, or the way I want to be. My family usually doesn't agree with what I do. They tell me what to do and what they want from me. And this makes me don't want to be around.
>
> When I'm by myself or [with] friends I can do what I want and act how I want. Even when I'm locked up . . . I don't have to [be] worried about what my family expect from me. It seems like . . . they were better without me.
>
> Staying home, I have to do what my family wanted and on the other hand when I go out I don't have to do anything I don't want to do. Instead I can do anything I wanted.
>
> The thing I want is that my family not to put so much pressure on me and not expect too much of me. They treat me like a kid. They want me to dress the way they want and even cut my hair the way they wanted. And when I still dress or do what I want . . . everyone says things which I don't like to hear. Such as you look like a punk, or you look stupid. I really don't like to hear these things from them. . . . When watching TV show where there is a guy with shave hair, tattoo, or earring they would tell me that that's the kind of person I am. Sometime I don't say anything and sometime I argue.
>
> I don't know why but home feels more like prison than places like the ranches.

And so I go out and this is how I end up here. . . . What I need is more words of encouragement and not things that would put me down like when my parents compare me to someone else. What I need is comfort and love which my family doesn't show much. When I [am] with my friends they seem to respect me more and care more for me by the attention they give me. They give me respect for the wrongs that I do, but it is better having the wrong kind of respect than having no respect which I've never experienced from . . . my family.

My life is like a gamble. I've earned my respect and love from the street. . . . [I've] never experienced the real love and real life which I've heard [about] and I don't want to risk my friends to search for [it]. . . . I don't know . . . if it's there and would work for me.

Alienation from School

The Vietnamese people have a high regard for education and a great love of books, instilled in them by the teachings of Confucius. In traditional Asian societies men of learning *(Si)* were at the top of the social scale. Next were farmers *(Nong);* skilled workers *(Cong);* and finally, businessmen *(Thuong).* Interestingly, when people ran out of food, the social scale looked a bit different:

First are men of learning
Second are men of farming;
But when the household runs out of foodstuffs,
First are men of farming,
Second are men of learning!

Vietnamese children who end up in serious trouble constitute a small fraction of the Vietnamese population as a whole, and the vast majority of young people are serious students who excel. Some of the children of parents who arrived in the United States with nothing are graduating from high schools and studying at the very best American universities.

Mr. and Mrs. Vuong Dao are the parents of three boys. They arrived in the United States as boat people and in 1978 were resettled in San Jose. Mr. Vuong worked hard and saved scrupulously. With his earnings he could have bought a big house, but he chose to live modestly in a rented house and invest his savings in his three sons. Having had teaching experience in Vietnam, Mr. Vuong provided them with guidance and encouraged their studies. All three sons went to medical school.

Duy Nguyen was born ten days before the fall of Saigon. In the spring of 1993, Duy won a National Honor Society scholarship, an award made to only 250 of 12,000 applicants. Harvard and Stanford offered him full scholarships. In his award-winning essay Duy wrote, "The memories of my past ordeals stir a profound sadness within me. I have practically lost my entire childhood. I never knew the pleasure of Christmas presents, birthday parties, new bikes, Little League." He was aware that his parents struggled to make a new life, and he studied hard to please them, although they never pushed him. "I did it because I know they've given up a lot, and I don't want to waste the sacrifice they've made," Duy said. Like many Vietnamese, he chose to express himself in poetry:

> To leave behind friends and relatives,
> To suffer the pain and grief,
> To witness death and misery,
> To lose loved ones,
> To brave the vast unknown,
> To drift aimlessly at sea,
> To live in run-down hovels,
> To beg,
> To cry,
> To have strength to go on,
> To persevere,
> To fight on,
> To start over,
> To start over,
> To start over,
> Is to be Vietnamese.[7]

The communists imprisoned Binh Nguyen's father because of his association with the South Vietnamese government. Binh's father had been teaching him at home. While his father was in jail, Binh worked in his village collecting cattle dung for fertilizer. By the time he and his family made their way to this country, Binh had had only four years of formal schooling. He knew almost no English and struggled through his first year of school—he spent hours completing his homework. His father got a job as a janitor and encouraged him. Binh recalled, "The more I was afraid, the more I worked. I perceived that I have got to be good in English. That's the first rule of survival." Reflecting on his years of gathering cattle dung, Binh said, "I am proud of that. It forced me to think and strengthened my determination." Now he is at Harvard.[8]

There are many stories like these. A Vietnamese columnist for the *San Jose Mercury News*, T. T. Nhu, reports that "every refugee family I know has one or more children attending college. Although the parents may be washing dishes or doing menial work, they don't mind as long as the children have a chance to do better." She paints an extraordinary image:

> Every night after dinner the table is cleared and homework begins for children in many refugee Asian families. Spared from doing the dishes and other chores which the parents gladly do, older children help younger ones and together they work for several hours. Homework is the dominant family activity on weeknights.

Ms. Nhu reports that research at the University of Michigan has revealed that

> with fierce parental support and determination, the U.S. educational system, in its present state of deterioration, can work, as . . . refugee families have proven. . . . Although the parents often do not speak English and know little about U.S. education, they have a kind of blind faith in the system. . . . Since the children witness[ed] firsthand the hardships the family has experienced, they want to repay the parents in the form of academic success.[9]

Until South Vietnam fell to communist rule, all children attended school. Under communist rule, however, the children of

South Vietnamese government officials and the offspring of American military personnel and government officials were not permitted to go, and children in these circumstances who made their way to the United States had little or no education. Nevertheless, when they arrived here they were plunged into schools with virtually no orientation, no preparation, and often no English. An enormous gap yawned between their skills and the demands of the classroom. Furthermore, children who had had some schooling in Vietnam quickly discovered that the American school setting was entirely different. In Vietnam, they played a passive role in class, listening politely and never questioning or challenging anything the teacher said. In American classrooms the system encourages, even demands, that students question their teachers. The new environment felt so alien and strange that these young people were confused, uncertain, and anxious.

Having come from Southeast Asian refugee camps, where for two to three years they received little if any education at all, most Indochinese children lagged several years behind other students their age. "I'm lost," a Cambodian girl said to me. Her mother is struggling to make her own living and is trying hard to learn English. But many parents like her do not know how to help their children stay in school.

School problems are a major reason children run away from home. A child struggling in the classroom and receiving nothing but criticism at home because of poor academic performance is likely to become truant. Having learned through friends where the coffee shops, skating rinks, and bowling alleys are, he begins to "hang out"—compared to school, these places are fun and exciting. As he misses more and more class time he sinks deeper and deeper into academic trouble. Eventually he gives up hope of accomplishing anything. Running away from his problems, he joins a gang and lives on the street. A Vietnamese juvenile serving at a correctional facility confessed:

> When I first set foot in America . . . I knew nothing about runaway and gang life. Schooling was my only pleasure in Vietnam, and [in

the United States] I knew only school and homework [and] I had no idea of where to go for fun. Then, before long, I made many new friends at school. They knew where to go, such as coffee shops, skating rinks, bowling alleys, and parties. Once I got acquainted with these places I saw the differences between these places and my school. More and more I wanted to go out and felt bored at school. I kept losing interest in my studies and counted every minute for the school day to be over. Eventually I dropped out and before long, I joined a gang. My purpose was to enjoy going from one place to another to have a good time and also to avoid gang fights. These I fear. Confrontations with other gangs [occur] in the coffee shops, with provocative attitudes and verbal abuses. Fistfights happen. Then those who were beaten come back with guns to settle accounts.

To an extent the schools are to blame. More often than not administrators place children with no thought to their English language proficiency. Many children who were high achievers in Vietnam have failed here, and failure in school drives too many of these youngsters into gangs. Embarrassed, humiliated, lacking self-esteem and self-confidence, students on the edge of failure begin cutting classes. Then they become truant and drop out.

Recent arrivals who are deprived of effective guidance and tutorial assistance quickly give up when they are placed according to age and not language ability. They simply do not understand what is being taught in class. Consider the following examples of Vietnamese students who failed as a result of being placed in grade levels beyond their abilities:

Examples of Improper Placement of Refugee Children

Le: Admitted to grade 9; assessed levels:

Reading	grade 1
Vocabulary	grade 2
Math	grade 7

Mai: Admitted to grade 11; assessed levels:

Reading	grade 1
Vocabulary	grade 3
Math	grade 7

Dan: Admitted to grade 11; assessed levels:
       Reading   grade 0
       Vocabulary   grade 0
       Math   grade 6

There are thousands of students like Le, Mai, and Dan who are admitted to classes that so exceed their abilities in English that they are destined to fail. The failure (or unwillingness) on the part of our schools to provide academic assistance in a variety of forms to these young people will drive them out of school and into gangs. As society will pay for this in the long run, it is certainly worth investing in their young lives now. In most schools, however, these kids are left to swim upstream on their own.[10]

Indochinese schoolchildren need more thoughtful attention from school placement officials and should be provided with remedial tutoring services. At home they need quiet places of their own to do homework, to read, and to study. "I have to use a coffee table, the floor, or the family kitchen, and my brothers and sisters are listening to music and watching Kung Fu videos," one of my wards reported. "I can't concentrate on my homework." Studying under these circumstances can be impossible. I have heard youngsters say that they just give up and leave the house.

Parents must do everything they can to encourage the child to study, because failure at school is often the beginning of the road to membership in gangs. The sad fact is, however, that many Vietnamese have been forced to live in undesirable housing. They find themselves in run-down neighborhoods in cramped apartments that are simply not helpful to children who require a quiet space for study.

Thai's experiences illustrate the enormous difficulties faced by refugees struggling to make it in American schools. In summer 1988 Thai's parents put him aboard a fishing boat, expecting that the uncle who was with him would take good care of him. But the uncle was killed, and Thai found himself alone in a refugee camp in Indonesia. His sister had made her way to California, and she sponsored him. When he arrived in the United States Thai knew only the few words of English that he had picked up at the camp. Registering him for school, Thai's sister said he was one year younger than he was. In fact Thai was sixteen and two years older than his peers in grade nine. Thai's sister could not afford tutoring for him, so he rapidly began to fail most of his classes. He grew increasingly frustrated.

He began to cut classes. Then he quit going to school altogether, pretending to set off for classes in the morning so his sister would not question him. When school authorities notified her, she humiliated Thai by comparing him to the successful children of her friends and neighbors. Ultimately Thai ran away, joining other children of the streets. It was not long before he began to use drugs and to find a "home" with the Golden Eagles. Today Thai is a full-fledged member of one of San Jose's most notorious gangs.

Estrangement from American Culture

Question: Do you consider yourself an American?
Answer: No!
Question: Do you consider yourself an Asian?
Answer: No! Everybody treats us like we don't belong here. And nobody seems to understand that we are a mixture. Cambodian, Filipino, Vietnamese.
Question: Are you a member of a gang?
Answer: I am and I'm proud of it [applause].
Question: Why did you join a gang?
Answer: Everybody looks at us as "other." Our parents don't understand us. So where do we feel like we belong? With our friends [loud applause].
Question: There are risks. Didn't you have alternatives?
Answer: Parents don't understand us. The world doesn't understand our parents. Everybody else seems to get attention. Nobody pays attention but our friends. No, there were no alternatives.
Question: Is it easy to join a gang?
Answer: To step in is easy. But to step out, your whole family can be killed.

This interview of a Santa Clara County juvenile reveals two important facts: first, that children need to belong, and second, that teenage Vietnamese gang members feel that society is indifferent to them. That angers them. Uncomfortable at home with parents who are "old-fashioned" and unable to make it in school, children like this gang member hate the law and despise society. Some actually take perverse pride in the fact that they lack the skills and education to live honestly. "I no read and I no write," one ward said to me, "but I can have anything I want—car, jewelry, beautiful girl."[11]

These children are lonely, bitterly disappointed in life, and, as the following poem suggests, longing for attention from their families (the first lines are like a refrain; I hear them over and over):

> Disappointed in my family, I ran away,
> Disappointed in my girlfriend, I joined the gang;
>
> Only now I have realized
> That the vagrants' law is killing me.
> When I leave, nobody sees me off,
> When I come home, I will be carried
> By six or seven pallbearers.
>
> Because of society, I did break-ins.
> Disappointed in my family, I ran away.

Many of these children bear tattoos on their wrists or arms that say *"Han Doi,"* or simply the initials "H.D.", or the word *"Han."* Each means "Resenting Society." Other tattoos that reflect their isolation and pain are *"Doi la So Khong"* (Life Is a Zero); *"Tuoi Tre Thieu Tinh Thuong"* (Youth Lacks Love); or *"Buon vi So Phan"* (I Feel Bad about My Destiny). These marks, often in the form of cigarette burns, are distressingly common on the bodies of the juvenile offenders I counsel.

Whatever the reasons, the juvenile members of gangs are not being integrated into American society. As one horrified Vietnamese observed in the aftermath of the Good Guys electronics store killings, "If the sons of [a respected member of the community] could do such a thing, it shows how far many Southeast Asian refugees are from being accepted into the American mainstream." In a similar vein a Vietnamese grocery store manager noted, "The younger people never saw anything good about Vietnam. . . . Because of the[ir] language problems and other things, they don't see much good here either. . . . The bad ones have many reasons to be bad."[12]

They create a world of their own in the gang. The surrogate family of the gang offers comradeship, understanding, respect, and approval. The world of street gangs is replete with its own rules, vocabularies, dress codes, tattoos, resources, and insignias. Gang names reflect the extent of members' estrangement and their inclination to violence and cruelty. I have identified 231 Indochinese gangs in California, but even a brief list of them suggests how alienated they are from society:

Asian Bad Boys
Asian Kicking Asses
Born To Violence (BTV)
Brotherhood of Crime
Cambodian Boyz Club (CBC, or Cold Blooded Cambodians)
Cheap Boyz
Death on Arrival
Dirty Punkz (Female)
Fuck The World
Innocent Bitch Killers (IBK)
Lao Killer Boyz (LKB)
Lonely Boyz Only
Ninja Clan Assassins
Oriental Killers
Scar Boys
South Side Scissorz
Vietnamese Trouble Makers (VTM)

"Read our message!" these appellations seem to say; "See how hostile we are!" Older Vietnamese people who fled the homeland recall that "in Vietnam I could not afford to buy a chicken, and for any move I made I needed permission from the village chief." For their children, however, "freedom" has come to mean the license to do anything they want in order to get what they want. They join gangs because gang life holds out the promise of material benefits. And yet, so many of these children live without hope or dreams of any kind, for lurking in the background is the ever-present threat of jail and death. As one Vietnamese boy named Dien wrote:

> In this world, no vagrant can elude jail:
> It's no fun to be a vagrant.
> To be so called, you have got to sniff, to inhale . . .
> Tears of pain run down my cheeks
> Make my heart bleak
> And my life a rubbish.

A California high school student observed, "We have been treated like outsiders. We haven't been accepted by the American culture. Gangs allow us to identify with something." The five-dot tattoos burned into their arms with cigarettes say it all: they symbolize *Tien* (money), *Tinh* (sex), *Thuoc* (drugs), *Toi* (crime), and *Tu* (jail).[13]

Amerasians

The extent to which Vietnamese newcomers are estranged from American culture is perhaps best illustrated by the experience of Amerasians. As I explained, Amerasians are Vietnamese born of American GI fathers and Vietnamese mothers. Some GIs married Vietnamese women who bore them children, but only a few actually brought their brides with them to the United States.

According to Vietnamese communist sources (which are not very reliable but generally illustrate the scope of Amerasians' displacement), after the fall of Saigon, over 25 percent of Amerasians were not able to live with their mothers; 76 percent were exiled to the countryside in the New Economic Zones (special resettlement areas set up for families of former South Vietnam civilian and military personnel, and former employees of the United States military and its civilian support); 75 percent of Amerasian children did not finish elementary school; and 77 percent were able to survive only by manual labor. Thousands of young Amerasians were reared as family servants or abandoned. The communists despised them, regarding these mixed bloods as living symbols of America's effort to defeat them, and the children grew up in shame and despair on the streets.[14]

Their stories are poignant, as my daughter, Tiana Thi Thanh Nga, learned when she traveled to the homeland in 1989 to film her award-winning documentary, "From Hollywood to Hanoi." The following is from the screenplay:

> *Scene: Amerasians gather about the filmmaker on a street in Saigon. Tiana speaks with a young man who is clearly of mixed blood. He shows her a photograph of his father, a smiling American GI. The photograph is well worn. It has obviously been cherished.*
>
> *Young man:* This is a picture of my Dad. I never knew my father. Only my mother. Now she's gone. I've applied to go to the States. I have his picture and will find him.
>
> *Tiana:* Do you know your father's name?
>
> *Young man:* Yes. [It sounds like] Ron Tibit.
>
> *Tiana:* Is it on the back?
>
> *Young man:* No.
>
> *Tiana:* How do you spell it?
>
> *Young man:* I don't read or write. I never went to school. How would I know?[15]

Another fellow, a Caucasian-looking boy of perhaps fifteen or sixteen years of age, explains that his mother left Vietnam with his father but that he did not get out. "I was small," he says. "I got left behind during the fall of Saigon." Tiana asks if he is certain his mother is in the United States, and the boy says yes, but that he no longer has her address. He says he "lost it over the years." He can recall his mother's name, but all he can remember of his father's is that it sounds like "Mic Coy, Mic Coy." He says the name thoughtfully, pronouncing each syllable carefully, lovingly.[16]

In Da Nang Tiana encounters a handsome youth of perhaps nineteen or twenty who wears a sad look in his eyes and a dog tag about his neck. She examines the dog tag. It reads, "Ronald L. Robinson, Presbyterian, +" ("+" means positive blood type). The youth explains, "I found it on my mother's dresser. On the altar for my mother. I took it and wore it." But when Tiana asks who his father is, he answers, "I was little when he left. I have no idea."[17]

"America is the land of our fathers," a black Amerasian observes. "But because of the war they came and left us behind like dust." Most Amerasians are motivated to come to the United States because they long to be reunited with their fathers. "America is our parents' home," one youth asserted. "We have to find them so we can go home and have a good life. They mistreat us here."[18]

In the United States many Amerasians have been unable to make themselves at home at all. When they arrived here they lacked supportive families, the most rudimentary education, and marketable skills. Like the young man mentioned above, many are completely illiterate. Dreaming of reunion with their fathers, most have met with bitter disappointment. The find themselves alone. "I want to go to America," a fair-skinned Amerasian woman says in my daughter's film. "They won't discriminate against Amerasians. In Vietnam, the kids beat us and call us names—American halfbreeds with twelve assholes. They hit us and stop us from going to school."[19]

Once they get here, however, many Amerasians are unable to get through a school day because of their lack of education and their inability to speak English. Day and night these young persons can be seen hanging around Asian shopping centers, cafés, and pool halls. Having left their mothers behind, and failing to find their fathers here, they are birds without nests. Few are finding the life they sought. Few are as lucky as Nguyen Thi Xinh who was born on China Beach in Vietnam and was so extraordinarily beautiful that Revlon awarded her $25,000 and declared her "The Most Unforgettable Woman of 1989."[20]

For children who could not fit in in Vietnam and do not seem able to fit in in the United States, gang life is almost inevitable. Linh, a black Amerasian girl, recalled:

> I looked ugly because of my light skin, while my hair and eyes are brown. They pulled my ponytail to the left and the right and burst into laughter. I held back my tears, but I felt like hundreds of needles were plunged into my skin at once.

Linh's GI father returned to the United States after a two-year tour of duty in Vietnam, when Linh's mother, Muoi Lan, was three months' pregnant. Linh was born in 1970 near an American air base. But her stepbrothers and stepsisters refused to have anything to do with her, and the children in her neighborhood taunted her with names like "My Den" (the black American).[21]

Muoi Lan was utterly destitute. A neighbor told her that if she was willing to allow her to pretend that she was Linh's mother, she could take her to the United States. Muoi Lan could not refuse. She dreamed that Linh would find her father and enjoy a good life there. Muoi Lan allowed the neighbor to leave for the United States with her daughter under the auspices of the Homecoming Program. This program gave Linh the right to take her family (in her case it was the family of the neighbor) with her. In exchange, the neighbor paid Muoi Lan two 24-karat gold leaves. Linh did not want to leave her mother, but she reluctantly agreed to go.

In California, instead of helping Linh to locate her father, the neighbor turned her over to a restaurant operator who put her to work as a cook and waitress. Because Linh pestered him to send her to school, eventually he did. But Linh found herself in classrooms where she did not understand a word of what was going on. Classmates mocked or ignored her. She quit school.

A Vietnamese patron of the restaurant told Linh to go to a social service agency where she spoke to a Vietnamese American social worker. She told him that the woman who took her to America was not her real mother. Then she wandered into a church where she kneeled and prayed:

> O Lord! Why [do] I have to endure cruel and unmerited suffering just because of my skin color? And now, why [is] my mind still obsessed and haunted by discrimination and loneliness? The black people stay away from me; the white people do not want to admit that I exist; and [people from] my own country want to make me their servant. O, please, my Lord! Return me to Vietnam so I can live with my mother for the rest of my life. I am not interested in material comfort; I don't need to be well fed or well sheltered. I

only want your love and my mother's love more than anything else in this world. O Lord! Please answer my prayer.

The County Social Services Department provided Linh with assistance so she was able to leave the restaurant. But as if she were an orphan, the agency put her in the care of Vietnamese Catholic nuns who hope they can keep her off the streets. "I long to be reunited with my mother," Linh says.[22]

Peer Pressure

Children want to be liked. They want to feel that their peers approve of them, that they belong, and that they are respected. When peers do poorly in school, experiment with drugs, or become members of gangs, the pressure for a "good" child to behave similarly is great. Drugs are the worst trap, and the pressure to experiment with them is often overwhelming.

Peers are not simply those children with whom youngsters associate at school and at home. Peers are the youths children encounter in the detention quarters of the Juvenile Hall, in the Ranches, and at the training centers of the California Youth Authority. For some inmates, the detention centers are virtual training grounds for criminal activity. The correctional facilities provide them time and opportunity to sharpen their criminal techniques. In correctional facilities, hardened repeat offenders and children like Le Dai Giau (the little round-faced boy who stole a car) are thrown together. The result is that first-time offenders like Le Dai Giau—if they survive the brutality of other inmates—walk out of jail with a more ingrained and sophisticated criminal mentality.

Phu Ly, a high school student, enjoys a good relationship with his mother and father, but he faced enormous pressures from his peers. Eventually he dropped out of school and ran away. He landed in Juvenile Hall many times. Phu Ly explains his situation:

The reason that I'm keep come back to the Juvenile Hall [is] because I'm having a hard time in school every time that I go to school! I see my friends then they would ask me to cut school with them either to go and play pool, or drink café, or else they would ask me to go to the beach.

Well, a lot of people ask me if I have any problem with my parents, because of my record . . . [of] running away from home. But the only real reason that I run away from home is because I like to have some fun with my friends.

I know that my parents love me a lot. But I don't know how to stop doing what I'm doing right now[.] [That is, how to stop] com[ing] back to the Ranch or doing crime. *Bac Long chau muon hoi Bac if chau khong muon di bui nua thi lam sao?* [I want to ask you what I should do if I don't want to run away any more?] And if [I] don't want to rob houses or steal cars and [keep] coming back to the Ranch again, what should I do?

Clearly, Phu Ly longs to "stop doing what [he's] doing." But what are his alternatives? "What should I do?" he asked me.

Other adolescents join gangs for self-defense. One teenager was so fearful of gang members that he carried a gun to school in order to protect himself. The gun went off in class, killing one student and wounding a second. The perceived need to carry a gun for protection is not unusual. One young boy named Huynh, for example, joined the South East Asian Pride gang in northern California not merely to have fun with his peers but for protection:

The reason I joined a gang is just to kick it with my homies, and have fun; and if you need help, they will back you up. Joining a gang is not really fun, because all it does is to get you hurt and killed, and mess you up in school, and [create] family problem[s]. And all you do in a gang is to do crime and [that] get[s] you locked up.

When I join[ed] a gang, I wasn't thinking at all, because I said, "All right, jump me in, I want to be with you guys . . ."

Some adolescents join gangs because they are forced to, and even elementary schoolchildren are being coerced into gang activity. Older adolescents go to elementary schools and bully children into being messengers or drug couriers, and they threaten those who refuse ("do it, or we'll hurt your kid sister").

If young adolescents like Phu Ly and Huynh stay with their gangs, they are destined to grow into young men who will continue to seek respect and approval from peers the only way they know—through criminal activity. The case of Song is a good illustration. Song was a member of the Bloody Boyz. He was a big Amerasian, physically well built and powerful, admired and respected by his peers and other Big Brothers (older gang leaders known as *dai ca* or *dan anh*). Song recalled, "Even in the neighborhood everybody looked up to me. They called me '*Song Ngau*,' which means smart." Song pushed cocaine and crack, and because he manipulated people easily, he rapidly became a gang leader. As a leader Song could have everything he wanted.

But one night Song and a gang brother were riding in the back of a pickup truck when a rival gang member sped by in a car and fired a shot at Song's friend. The gunman missed, but the bullet entered Song's mouth, split his tongue, and exited from the back of his neck, severing his spine. Song is paralyzed from the neck down.

He is unable to speak except in a mumble that only his sister understands. When my wife and I visited him in the hospital, where his mother and father were also at his bedside, Song mumbled to his sister, and she relayed his words to us:

> When I was in the gang I was on top of the world. But nobody loves me now. And nobody will tell of my exploits anymore. I was nothing before the gang. Before the gang I worked washing dishes in a coffeehouse. No way was I going back to that when I could make thousands by running do [drugs] on the street. I was on top of the world.

Song is only seventeen.

Phu Ly, Huynh, and Song spent most of their time in "safe houses," secret shelters known in Vietnamese as *nha bui*. Chronic runaways generally find shelter and comradeship with peers in safe houses. The safe house is a place to eat and sleep and a hideout from family and police. It also provides a place for the *bui doi* (children of dust) to meet their peers for beer busts, drug parties, and sex. After a night of home invasions and burglaries, the safe house is the place to which the children of dust return.

In the safe house, peers cement their relationships and Big Brothers serve as role models to young "roosters" (boys fifteen to seventeen years old). The Big Brother protects the young roosters and is very careful not to show favoritism. Younger gang members learn unwavering allegiance and loyalty to the Big Brother.

I have mentioned that many Vietnamese children do not live with their fathers. Sociological studies suggest that fatherless boys may be prone to hypermasculinity and violence. When former Secretary of Health and Human Services Louis Sullivan observed, "We are raising a generation of young males who measure their manhood by the caliber of their guns and the number of children they father," he was expressing this same view. Sociological studies also indicate that approximately 70 percent of the people in long-term correctional facilities did not live with their fathers while growing up. It is not unreasonable to hypothesize that the loyalty these youths lavish on older members of their gangs is a substitute (albeit a very poor one) for the love, affection, and approval they long to give (and receive from) their fathers.[23]

The Big Brother's greatest skill lies in his ability to create a fanatical loyalty in the younger members who come under his spell (the next chapter examines this phenomenon more closely). As he initiates his young charges into the world of crime, the Big Brother orders them to deny any knowledge of him in the event that the group is caught engaged in criminal activity. He instructs a child to say that he only just met the Big Brother, that he knows him only by a first name or nickname, and that he has no idea where he lives. If a group of gang members is arrested, a "little brother" will come forward, accept all responsibilities (thereby making apprehension of the older criminal difficult), and be punished. "I won't step back in facing any danger when it comes to help[ing] my friends," one of my wards said to me proudly. In other words, the child is taught to sacrifice himself—for it is likely that he will be sent to a correctional facility—for the good of the group.

Invariably the child is willing to do so. Inspired by the camaraderie and brotherhood he sees repeatedly in Kung Fu movies, which are immensely popular in the Vietnamese community, he is delighted to live among his peers under the watchful eye of the Big Brother. Among them he feels that he belongs, and he is able to show his sense of belonging by wearing his gang's colors and style of clothing or by burning a particular tattoo into his wrist.

One such boy, Billy, spent a long time in a Malaysian refugee camp before he settled in northern California with his Chinese-Vietnamese parents. During a brief period in Oakland he was frequently arrested and spent a lot of time in various counseling and rehabilitation programs. A chronic truant, he divided his time between the public parks and coffee shops of Chinatown.

At the age of seventeen Billy was proud of his "achievements": ten home invasions, expertise in car theft, and robbery. He was the first young refugee to be admitted into the ranks of the notorious Wah Ching gang after he scored a big victory over five rival gangsters in a Vietnamese café. "I was given whatever I needed," he said, "with no questions asked. Whenever I got loot I handed it over to my *dai lao* [Big Brother] and he gave me money." Billy carried out his first successful home invasion when he was only eleven. The gang relied on Billy to shut the mouths of victims with duct tape, to tie them up with stereo or telephone wire, and to threaten the head of the household with a gun. The Big Brother usually assigned this last job to Billy because Billy was always "in control of the situation." Billy looked for approval from his Big Brother, and he got it. This was satisfying.

Billy was never able to find satisfaction and a sense of belonging elsewhere: not in his family, which he felt failed to love him; not in his school, which failed to teach him; not in his church or temple, which seemed irrelevant to him; not in his community, where his neighborhood was run-down and uninspiring and there was little evidence that people cared. Billy's neighborhood was characterized by hate crimes, racial harassment, and violence; a notable lack of any kind of recreational facilities or activities; residents who used and sold drugs; the failure to provide adolescents with summer jobs; juveniles who coerced children to join gangs; the lack of positive role models, especially male role models; the lack of institutions that provided meaningful alternatives to gang life. In other words, Billy never saw any alternatives.

Children whose lives are proscribed by conditions such as these will find identity and respect only among their peers. "Junior" gangsters boast of their loyalty to their peers in an old Vietnamese saying:

Tram nam bia da thi mon,
Ngan nam tinh ban van con tro tro.
[In a hundred years the tombstones will wear out;
but in a thousand years, friendships will not be obliterated.]

Among their peers children like Billy feel "free." That freedom—plus the lure of seemingly endless money to buy expensive jewelry, the latest French and Hong Kong clothing designs, and mood-enhancing drugs—makes gang life irresistible.

Two years ago a young Vietnamese boy named Tho Tran wrote these lines:

Muoi sau tuoi toi vao bang dang
Giat giay chuyen de tang nguoi yeu.
[At sixteen I joined the gangs.
I snatched necklaces to give to my sweetheart.]

Tho Tran did exactly that. With his gang brothers he invaded a home to snatch valuables for his sweetheart, tying his victim up and threatening her. But luck was not with Tho Tran: a friend of the victim recognized her jewelry in a downtown jewelry store. She informed the victim, who notified the police. Plainclothes officers accompanied the victim to the jewelry store. As they were talking to the shopkeeper, a Vietnamese boy entered the shop with his Vietnamese girlfriend. "It's them!" the victim screamed, and he was arrested.

Gang members have what one might call a philosophy—they're fatalistic. If there is a problem, a gang member does not go home at night to solve it with the help of his family. He solves it with guns (after all, an Uzi or even an AK-47 can be bought on the street for only $150). "How does it feel to be writing poems from Juvenile Hall?" I asked Tho Tran. He shrugged. "It's all a roll of the dice," he replied. "Besides, I want a reputation as *ngau* [bold, smart, and belligerent]."

"Tell me where your mother keeps her jewelry box."
—A Vietnamese Big Brother

Chapter 3
Learning the Trade

Of thousands of South Vietnamese soldiers who returned home when the American war in Vietnam ended, those who had no place to live, nowhere to go, and nothing to do organized gangs of young criminals in order to survive. They enticed them with money, drugs, and young girls. Between 1975 and 1977, the period during which the first wave of refugees arrived in the United States, a number of these former soldiers also came. In this country they continued to exploit children in order to survive, using the same lure of money, drugs, and young girls. Over time, these former soldiers passed their skills on to other Vietnamese who became gang leaders or Big Brothers themselves.

Some former soldiers—and other men who found themselves unable to survive unless they engaged in illegal activities—began their criminal lives in Southeast Asian refugee camps. Located in Malaysia, Indonesia, Thailand, and Hong Kong, the camps were operated jointly by the International Red Cross and the United Nations High Commissioner for Refugees. They were a temporary haven for people fleeing Cambodia, Laos, and Vietnam on foot ("foot people" walked into Thailand) or by boat ("boat people" came ashore on the beaches of Malaysia and Indonesia).

The camps provided refugees with food and rudimentary shelter, and volunteers also taught them some English. But the demands on official personnel were overwhelming and staffing was woefully inadequate. As a result, the camps offered little to do, and supervision was minimal. Nobody had an opportunity to do much that was meaningful or productive. As I observed in chapter 1, this was particularly hard on the men whose traditional authority as the virtual "rulers" of their families eroded in the camps. "I watch my children grow up behind barbed wire," one man said. "We be here two years. And what can I do? What do I do? Nothing."[1]

In virtually all the camps theft and violence were common, and many refugees felt compelled to take turns staying awake on guard throughout the night. The majority of the refugees were young men between the ages of eighteen and thirty. Having nothing to do and no legitimate way to support their families (who were either in the camp or left behind in the homeland) or to develop relationships with potential mates, they felt guilty, angry, and frustrated. Sometimes they exploded in acts of violence that got them up to twenty-eight days of solitary confinement.[2]

In the open camps (where refugees were free to come and go as they pleased), easy access to drugs and crime on the outside (most notably in Hong Kong) fueled criminal activity. Officials in Hong Kong assert that of all the crime committed in the city, at least one tenth of it originated in the open camps. Police raids were common:

> On one such occasion at 2 A.M., amidst sirens and searchlights, all the men were ordered out and spread-eagled on the ground. Forty were eventually taken back to the station and held for several hours after which one man was charged.

Many Vietnamese men sought work in Hong Kong, and while some were successful, as one observer pointed out, they also were subjected to "all the other social problems of drug trafficking, gang activity, and gambling rackets."[3]

Many of the refugees in the camps were unaccompanied chil-

dren who came to the United States under the sponsorship of relatives (and fake relatives); some came under the auspices of various
government programs designed to help them. Many of them turned
to gangs and crime in the camps because they had no family to look
out for them. Instead, they attached themselves to older criminals
who gave them sympathy and knew exactly how to exploit them.

Within the Vietnamese American community today, young Vietnamese juvenile criminals continue to be exploited by older gang
leaders (although gang intelligence to which I have access suggests
that former ARVN soldiers are mostly "retired" from the gang
scene). These Big Brothers know how to use children. Teenagers are
useful to Big Brothers as "insiders." They can, for example, provide
a Big Brother with all the information he needs in order to rob businesses and to invade private residences to steal cash and valuables.
Big Brothers also use teens to transport deadly weapons, and they
pay them handsomely.

Illegal weapons—guns of every imaginable type with their serial
numbers removed, and even weapons such as fragmentation grenades—are being smuggled into this country, and there is evidence
to suggest that some of these may be coming from communist Vietnam, Laos, and Cambodia. When the weapons arrive, Big Brothers
market them through "wannabes" (children who "want to be" full-
fledged gang members and are generally ten to fifteen years old).

Several years ago my wards gave me some extraordinary intelligence. They warned me that two rival Vietnamese gangs from the
Monterey and Oakland areas were planning a shootout at the San
Jose fairgrounds, where celebrations for the Tet New Year were
about to begin. I informed the organizers of the festival, and they in
turn notified the police, who beefed up security.

The two gangs (about thirty juveniles) showed up and confronted each other at an outdoor café. Someone hurled a chair at a
rival, and the incident escalated rapidly into a brawl in which gang
members used knives and guns and inflicted some serious injuries.
The gang members tried to flee as the police began to arrive. With
the help of dogs, the police captured nearly everyone, but one youth

climbed a chain link fence and threw (or dropped) a grenade, simply to get rid of it. How was he able to acquire such a deadly weapon?

When American soldiers left Vietnam, they left behind a staggering amount of weaponry—M-16s, grenades, mines, and so on. These were stockpiled for the use of the South Vietnamese army. During the Vietnam War I worked in Washington, D.C., with a group of other Vietnamese translating technical material on the maintenance of war materiel used by the Army of the Republic of Vietnam. These documents suggested that the American government intended to turn the war over to the Vietnamese (which in fact it did, through Nixon's Vietnamization program). After the communists took over South Vietnam they inherited this vast military stockpile, which included even jet fighter planes. Unable to obtain the simplest replacement parts, the communists sold a lot of this military hardware to the Chinese as scrap metal. The communists kept a lot of the guns (M-16s) and grenades to use, but apparently some are falling into the hands of Asian arms traffickers and are being smuggled into the United States.

Some of these weapons have surfaced in California. Vietnamese and Chinese-Vietnamese gun dealers sell them to Big Brothers, who in turn put them in the hands of young roosters and wannabes. In casual conversations and during counseling sessions, a number of my Indochinese wards have told me that some of the guns they have purchased come from Vietnam, Laos, and Cambodia. This reflects the high degree of corruption in the communist military (stealing government property, in this case weaponry, to sell for personal gain). It is not unlikely that, given the nature of other black-market activities between the United States and Asian countries, there is a "gun connection" linking Vietnam, Hong Kong, and the United States. It is clear that Asian American (particularly Vietnamese) gang members are the "delivery boys." And Big Brothers are running the show.

Adolescents are often frustrated by parents who refuse to dole out pocket money, and Big Brothers play on that frustration. They ask naive adolescents for inside information about their families and relatives and in exchange promise them money or gifts. For instance, the adult will say, "Tell me where your mother keeps her jewelry box or where your father hides his cash, and I'll give you fifty bucks and a gold necklace." To some children, the promise of money or a piece of glamorous jewelry is irresistible. The young adult criminal works hard to cultivate relationships with teenagers; often this is all a juvenile needs to begin a life of crime. He has learned from the Big Brother that it pays.

Kids who want to belong to their Big Brother's gang serve what we might call an apprenticeship. The adults tutor younger children in how to be streetwise. They also teach them how to steal car stereos and cars, commit home invasions, and extort money from businesses. They obtain guns for them and instruct them in their use. Meanwhile, they also supply them with mood-elevating drugs that make them feel good and powerful. They even feed, clothe, and shelter them (and so indeed act like older brothers). Over time the relationship between the adult Big Brother and the adolescent deepens. When the child passes on accurate crime tips and Big Brother cashes in, he is quickly rewarded with loot or cash, and sometimes with drugs. Eager for more, the child becomes increasingly willing to provide the adult with whatever information he requests and to cooperate with him in other ways. For example, a child will deliberately leave a front door, garage, or bathroom window unlocked. He will inform Big Brother about the times when his parents are not home, or tip him off about the dates of family reunions, weddings, gambling events, and so on—times when the Big Brother is most likely to cash in on family valuables, caches of savings, or business receipts.

Tien Dang, Bien Le, and Dam Phung are members of EST (East Side Troublemakers). They are all Vietnamese youths in their early teens (thirteen to fifteen) who have dropped out of San Jose's middle schools. As wannabes and young roosters, they have "proven themselves" by fighting with members of other gangs, mostly Hispanics and other ethnics who hurled racial epithets at their "homies" (gang brothers). Their Big Brothers introduced them to alcohol and drugs—marijuana, Kool cigarettes laced with the "white stuff" (cocaine), and wine coolers. These new habits created a new need for money. Big Brothers also introduced them to ways to get it. Under their guidance, Tien Dang, Bien Le, and Dam Phung learned how to break into cars, homes, businesses, and warehouses.

In spring 1992 all three boys were arrested. The police raided a motel room, where they discovered stolen car stereo systems, video-cassette recorders, cameras, jewelry, a cellular phone, Nintendo cartridges, and several hundred dollars in cash. In the trunk of a stolen car officers discovered a .22 caliber pistol and a MAC 10 (a semi-automatic handgun). In the glove compartment were two homemade crack pipes, three butane lighters, and a plastic bag containing powdered cocaine; beneath the seat in a first-aid box were capsules of some kind of hallucinogen and a small bottle of PCP. On the floor of the back seat were two six-packs of empty beer bottles. Police also found crack processed with baking soda into large balls *("trung")* and small balls *("cuc")*. Two of the teenagers possessed Kool cigarettes stuffed with marijuana and "Turbo," or crack rolled in cigarette fashion. Police concluded that the teenagers stole the property in order to support their drug habits.

Tien Dang, Bien Le, and Dam Phung spent several months in the Ranch, where I counseled them. All are chronic runaways; all had been sleeping for weeks on mattresses thrown on the floor of the motel room, which was paid for by their Big Brothers. They tell their stories here.

Tien Dang

One Monday morning we were sitting with our girlfriends at Café Thong Reo on Santar Road, when Big Brother Dung Hoang walked in. Immediately he walked over to our table and sat down with us. He asked us if we could use two thousand dollars. At first I thought he was kidding, but I wanted to show him I was *ngau* [gutsy], so I told him to tell us more. We all pulled our chairs closer and our girlfriends listened too. He told us that if we got him a van for a pickup he needed to make in Santa Ana that we'd make *hai xap* [two thousand dollars] just like *that*—he snapped his fingers. Then he put a twenty-dollar bill on the table and told us to use it for gas and

pho [beef noodle soup]. He told us that he had whatever tools we
needed and that Candy and Christina [the two older girls present]
could be the lookouts. He told us that he had the money on him and
that if we got him the van it would be all ours. In cash.

Bien Le

That night we drove off in a car belonging to Candy's father. Candy
simply helped herself to it. On a side street in South San Jose Dam
spotted a van. Not a new van, but certainly one that would do the
job. The team jumped into action. In a matter of seconds Tien was
at the wheel of the stolen van, nonchalantly driving through the
city. Tien looks old. No *canh* [cops] would suspect him. Behind him
Candy drove the family car. We had plenty of time before we had to
have the van in Dung's hands. Tien drove for Hellyer Park Creek—
the "Cricket Motel," as the Americans call the steep dry creek that is
perfect for having sex—but Thuy [Bien's girlfriend] gave me thirty
dollars in bills and quarters that she'd stolen from her parents'
lunch truck receipts. So Tien turned the car around and we left the
creek. We checked into a cheap motel in town.

The next day we went to Café Lang Dzu on Tally Road in East
San Jose and Dung paid us the two thousand dollars. Toan Pham
[another Big Brother] came over and sat with us. He said he knew
about the van and the two thousand dollars and he asked us if we
wanted to grab more.

He told us he knew of a *Xi* [Mexican] who sells car stereos at the
big Flea Market in North Valley. He told us he knew the inside of his
house because about six months earlier a friend of his had helped
paint it. Toan told us the guy kept a lot of cash in his house because
most of his stereos and car speakers and stuff came from the grey
market. Toan said the Mexican treats himself pretty good. He drives
a brand new, gorgeous Cadillac—a gold Seville. Toan also said that
the *Xi* and his wife are partners to a couple of money-laundering
joints in the Bay Area.

I told him that between us we had only a couple of small butcher
knives. I told him that we needed guns. He said he'd loan me a .45
semi-automatic that was in his car.

Toan gave us instructions and he took all three of us in his car. A good distance from the *Xi*'s house Toan pulled the car over. The car was still running while he told us what to do. He told Tien to climb through the kitchen window first; then me and then Dam. Tien and me were to use the butcher knives to threaten the *Xi* and his wife. Dam was to hold the semi-automatic and use it if they resisted. Toan told us he'd wait in the car for us.

Dam Phung

The man and wife woke up when they heard noise in the kitchen, but before they could get up, Tien put a butcher knife to the man's throat. Bien told the wife to get down on her knees on the floor. I stood between the two bedrooms with the .45 ready to fire. We all wore white masks. The wife asked if we wanted money. Tien said, "Yes, yes, we want money." But Bien said, "No! Not just money!" The woman started to scream. Bien told her to shut up, but she wouldn't stop screaming. I had electrical tape in my pocket that I should've used, but the woman continued to scream. We all ran downstairs. The husband must have dialed 911.

I got into Toan's car and Toan took off, but Bien and Tien ran and hid in a cornfield. A mile or so on East Capitol Expressway police pulled Toan over for speeding. Bien and Tien were sniffed out by police dogs in the cornfield. They got sent to the Ranch. Toan got a ticket and was told to slow down.

The following descriptions of criminal activity come from public records. Each was committed using information that Vietnamese children passed to Big Brothers about their own families:

• After a wedding banquet, the parents of the bride drove the newly-weds to the airport for a honeymoon trip. Seconds after they left the house for the airport, gang members entered the house through a door left deliberately open by their son. They cleaned out the house of his mother's jewelry, cash wedding gifts, and thousands of dollars in savings from the family's catering business in a carefully hidden wooden box.

• In an early hour of the morning, five masked bandits stormed into the home of nine Vietnamese. The bandits forced two teenaged members of the household to the floor at gunpoint. They nicked one man in the back with a butcher knife, kicked and hit three men repeatedly, and put a pillow over the head of another, firing a round into the pillow case close to his head. They escaped with an undetermined amount of hidden cash and electronic equipment. The victims indicated that the cash was being saved to bring other relatives from Vietnam to the U.S. and that only family members knew its whereabouts.

- At ten o'clock at night, young Vietnamese adults showed up outside the home of the Vietnamese owner of a beauty shop and knocked at the door. The victim's ten-year-old son opened the door. Brandishing a revolver and pistol, they bound both mother and son with telephone cord and ransacked the house, stealing cash and the mother's car. Young roosters asserted that the ten-year-old had planned this with his big brothers.

- On a hot July night a group of five hooded robbers invaded a South San Jose home. They pistol-whipped the older son, sexually assaulted the twenty-year-old daughter, and ransacked the house, terrorizing the family for more than three hours. Having gained entrance through a bedroom window, they stole a lot of jewelry and the family car. The family operated a jewelry business out of their home. Friends of the family blamed their youngest daughter, who was a chronic runaway and lived on the streets, for the break-in.

- Four young robbers rang the bell of a West San Jose home and a child opened the door. Pushing their way inside, they forced the occupants upstairs, tied them up, covered them with blankets, and fired one bullet into the bedroom floor to keep the victims quiet. They fled with money and jewelry they found easily in hidden locations throughout the house. The oldest son had been incarcerated in Juvenile Hall several times and authorities believed he revealed the location of the cash and jewelry to the intruders.[4]

According to the FBI, this kind of criminal activity is not at all unusual among recently arrived Vietnamese refugees:

Not prepared to function in, nor even to immediately understand a new culture, the refugee experiences "culture shock." With Viet-

namese, culture shock is not experienced on an individual level, but
as a family unit, resulting in friction between the generations. The
stress felt within the family, combined with the pressure from the
outside to learn a new language, a new culture, a new profession,
and family roles affects the psychological well-being of the refugee,
especially the younger family members. It is not unusual to see the
involvement of some adolescent family members, in a rebellious
spirit, in setting up their own relatives as targets for home invasions.[5]

Vietnamese children find it hard to say no to the easy life that
older and more experienced men promise. They are determined to
claim their share of the material luxuries they see all around them
and crave what one of my wards called "the easy life." "Goodies" and
"an exciting life" are far more alluring than parental admonish-
ments to "study and work hard to achieve success." So children drop
out of school and join gangs, committing themselves to their peers
and their Big Brothers "unto death." As the above incidents suggest,
children are willing to see a parent robbed, beaten, and even raped
in order to get what they want. The following poem was written by
a young Vietnamese gang member:

Power

Money is power,
The strength of the spring,
The laughter of youth,
The health in the Juvee [Juvenile Hall].
Far away from the homeland,
I think of my mom.
But when close to her,
I think of her purse.

Indeed, some Vietnamese children are apparently willing to do just
about anything to her in order to obtain mother's purse. They want
it so that they can buy material things, motel rooms, and girls, to
achieve a sense of belonging to a peer group, or to gain the attention
of a Big Brother whom they admire. Through their association with

criminal elements these adolescents learn criminal skills and, perhaps more significant, develop a criminal mentality.

This mentality is encouraged by the Vietnamese themselves, because they often choose not to report crimes or they succumb to threats and intimidation. A nineteen-year-old former gang member explained that Asian gangsters target Asian homes because they know there is less chance of getting caught. "With white people, there's a 90 percent chance that they'll call the cops. Asians are safer, they don't usually call the cops because they are scared to get involved, or because they are afraid they'll be attacked again."[6]

The following story illustrates many Asians' fear of involvement. At ten o'clock on a hot summer night in Little Saigon, Orange County, the Tu Hai Restaurant was packed with Vietnamese customers. Suddenly, gunshots shattered the glass. Patrons screamed in terror; people dove under tables and scattered in every direction. They heard the sharp report of answering gunshots as two restaurant employees fired back into the street.

Was it a drive-by shooting? Was it gang related? The preliminary to an extortion attempt? Nobody could come up with a satisfactory answer. The police investigated, but when they attempted to question the thirty-two patrons who witnessed the entire episode, each and every one of them asserted that during the shooting, he or she was in the restroom![7]

Both boys and girls are sucked into the vortex of gang life. Girls are victimized sexually. (Boys are too, but not as often.) A Big Brother hangs around a school, looking for female prey. When a particular girl is to his liking, he approaches her.

Her slippery descent into gang life often begins with a single puff on a marijuana cigarette or with "joyriding"—that is, a drive with Big Brother in his fancy car "just for fun." Having been in the United States for perhaps only a few months, the young girl is naive, and Big Brother's offer is irresistible. It is an exciting opportunity to "see the sights."

Fourteen-year-old Jacqueline Hoang was in the United States less than one year when she was picked up by nineteen-year-old Big

Brother Chinh as she was walking home from Sylvan Middle School with two friends. Chinh, a handsome fellow who prides himself on being a "fast worker" with girls, is a member of the Oriental Boyz, and has come by a lot of money through the sale of drugs, stolen cars, and valuables obtained through assaults and home invasions. He usually carries hundreds of dollars in cash with him. In and out of correctional facilities, he is a seasoned veteran. Jacqueline spoke of her encounter with him:

> A beautiful car came beside us and drove along as we walked. Two men were in the front seat of the car. The handsome one, Chinh, was in the passenger seat and playing cassettes. He asked us if we wanted to go on a little tour, maybe a drive to the beach. I wasn't so sure, but Cathy Dzung whispered to me that he was certainly good looking and what a fancy car he had. I told him for an hour because we had homework. Chinh jumped out of his car to let Jane Dao and Cathy Dzung into the back seat. I sat beside him in the front in the middle. We drove to the beach where Chinh bought us ice cream, sodas, and sunglasses. He had a lot of money on him, a lot of paper money that he kept in his pocket. They kept us out for two hours. My mother was worried and reprimanded me sharply. I told my mother that I stayed after school to get help from a teacher. She told me not to do so again unless I told her first.

Unbeknownst to her parents, Jackie snuck out with Chinh again and again. He pursued her with Vietnamese dinners out, movies, and drives to the ocean in his fancy car. Like many Vietnamese immigrant girls her age, Jackie had many fantasies. She had been in America for only a short while, but she knew what she wanted: fancy sundresses, expensive shoes, a watch, and a gold necklace. Chinh was a veteran. He promised Jackie that she would have all those things and more.

One night Chinh urged her to try marijuana. Jackie refused at first, but the allure of his maturity and the money that seemed to flow without limit overwhelmed her.

At school Jackie became truant. Eventually she dropped out and ran away to live with Chinh at a safe house, where she began to smoke crack. Soon the "white stuff" was all she thought about. Chinh supplied her, but only in exchange for sex. Eventually he tired of her. When he did, Jackie, like so many *bui doi* her age, was left to her own devices. Unwilling to return home, she joined The Lazy Ones, a female gang. Now she lives on the streets or in safe houses and steals to survive. When she is caught she spends time at the Ranch:

> At the Northridge Mall, we stationed ourselves on a bench in the middle of the promenade. Linh and Bich pointed out the fashion store to me and told me that in that store the clothes aren't tagged, so you have to study the security people. They told me to see how they walk up and down the aisles. Linh said to walk into the store separately and to make sure you know exactly where the security people are. She said to decide what it is I wanted and then just take it. Bich said don't hurry out after you take it. That I should take a good leisurely look around; maybe even ask a salesperson to show me something in order not to arouse suspicion. She said if you think you've been seen, drop the thing.
>
> I had never stolen anything from a store before and so I was nervous. Linh went in first and told us to meet at the car when we were ready. She said that if anybody was *bi chup* [caught], that we were on our own.
>
> I entered the store. I spotted a lizard-skin purse I liked. I glanced all around to be sure security was elsewhere and then I slipped the purse into the inside pocket of my baggy jacket. As Bich suggested, I walked casually down the same aisle. I stopped at the scarves and tried a few on, folding them neatly and putting them back. A salesperson approached me and asked if she could help me. I said I was just looking. Then I left. I could feel the purse against my heart.

Recently Jackie was arrested for selling crack to an undercover agent.

Indochinese Big Brothers who deal in drugs exploit the fact that if a minor like Jackie is caught selling drugs her punishment will be light. Thus, their very youth makes children attractive to a dealer: he can sell his wares through them with little risk to himself. A "homegirl" serves time at a correctional facility for only three to five months, and after her release gang members and drug dealers welcome her back into their ranks. These children, who are frequently addicted to cocaine themselves, also have to cover their Big Brother's "expenses," or what it costs him to pay for their food and shelter. So the children (who are sometimes only ten and eleven years old) go back to "work" immediately. If they are caught, they find themselves back in a correctional facility. Such children are likely to find themselves moving through life in an endless cycle of exploitation, arrest, incarceration, and release.

Big Brothers exploit minors in a variety of ways, and of course the children are learning the tricks of the trade while they are being exploited. Older gang members use minors to act as lookouts for police or passersby while the gang is conducting a criminal operation, such as a home invasion or a drug sale. In this role, a young child can earn one hundred dollars or more per day. In addition, Big Brother will often reward a "little brother" with expensive new shoes, a black leather jacket, a fancy wristwatch, or marijuana. Such gifts are enormously satisfying to wannabes. These children crave the jewelry and the clothes they see on TV, but many of their parents are on welfare, or earn just enough money to make ends meet; they certainly cannot afford Rolex watches and designer leather jackets. Perhaps more important, these gifts are satisfying because they represent acceptance and approval—things that are often sorely lacking at home.

When a child has proved himself a capable lookout, Big Brother will then entrust him to transport or deliver drugs. As a drug runner a child can earn more than three hundred dollars per day. If he is caught, the child always says he's working alone.

With these experiences the children eventually become dealers, and in California cities they can clear more than three thousand dollars daily. Because of the astonishing sums they make on the streets, they arm themselves for self-defense, not with mere pistols but with semi-automatics and sawed-off shotguns.

Willy Hong is Chinese-Vietnamese. When he was fourteen, Willy sold marijuana and cocaine, turning over a percentage of his profits to his Big Brother. A born entrepreneur, he outsold other dealers by offering his clients free samples and by running promotional "two-for-one" sales of crack on weekends. The secret of his success was, as he put it, "to serve the customer good." At one point Willy made almost $150,000 a year. He sported designer clothing and jewelry, and owned two Toyota Supras for which he paid cash. Fortunately, Willy's story has a happy ending. When he was caught, my counseling enabled him to put his life back together; he went on to finish high school and get an associate degree at a community college. But the stories of other children just like Willy usually do not have happy endings.

The majority of crack dealers and crack runners are juveniles like Willy. Some are locked into crack houses by older dealers to cook, weigh, package, and sell it. They live from day to day in a sordid underworld among people who carry Uzi submachine guns, .357 magnums, and MAC 10s, people with no respect for life. Children like Willy are tortured by rival gang members or exploited by child pornographers; often they die in the street with bullets in their backs.

These children are fanatically devoted to other "homeboys" and their Big Brothers. Feeling unwanted and unloved at home, they turn to their peers and leaders in the gang for loyalty and respect. To be "down for" (or loyal to) their Big Brothers and homeboys is the principle that governs their lives. They take fierce pride in their abilities to invade a home and terrorize their victims because it earns them the respect of fellow gang members. This pride in their accomplishments is too often denied them at home or in school.

Big Brother My Lai

In Saigon a gang of children worked for me and my experiences there served me well. I bought my house on the proceeds of stolen goods I sold on the grey market. Because my father was American, I was barred from schools in Vietnam. I joined street gangs there when I was seven. I came here with a phony family under the U.S. Homecoming Program for Amerasians, but my "mother" put me out of the house not long after we got here. She said I was unmanageable.

I have a lot of children who work for me here, girls and boys. I take care of them and they take care of me. These children are my spies. They tell me exactly what I need to know about their families and relatives and neighbors and friends. They tell me where the loot is. The cash and the valuables. They tell me when people will be on vacation or out of town for a night. Is there a house where people are gambling? I want to know about it. Is somebody getting married? Celebrating an anniversary? At those kinds of parties everybody shows up loaded with money and jewelry—genuine diamond rings, not the phony stuff—and presents. That's the kind of stuff I need to know. They tell me something as simple as when their mother leaves the back door unlocked.

I tell them about the Monday Draw. Lots of people did it in Vietnam and now they do it here. Say a bunch of people want to get together to start a business—say they want to buy a fishing boat. Five or ten people get together and put up a thousand dollars a month each into their own "bank." It doesn't take long for money to accumulate, and before you know it, the group has ten thousand dollars to bankroll a new business. People got to have capital, you know? My wannabes tell me when banking day is.

In Vietnam nobody had guns. Back in Vietnam I heard that practically everybody in this country keeps guns in the house. The kids ask me, how do you know if anybody's inside? They are my eyes and ears. They have to thoroughly investigate. They watch for *canh* [cops] and if suddenly the wrong people show up, like the homeowner who forgot something. I teach them how to use the filed-down car key, screwdrivers, wire cutters, jumper wire, jacks. Break-in stuff, you know. I show them how to do the jobs themselves so they know how to bust the little telephone box with a hammer before they break into a house. They know how to cut the wires so the phone can't be used. They know why Japanese cars are easier to break into than American and French cars, which are the hardest. They know how to silence car alarms and remove stereos and speakers. They know that stereos come out of Celicas and Supras in a snap but that Toyota Camrys are pretty hard to crack. They know how to pry open car trunks to look for loot and how to use a slide hammer to extract ignition locks. It always amazes me how many people keep jewelry, even cash, in the trunks of their cars! They do so because they don't trust banks or the people they're sharing rooms with. Or they hoard cash they've gotten illegally—say through gambling—that they don't want to pay taxes on, or they hoard it because if the welfare people find out that they have money they lose the welfare. The best car opener is the Datsun 280 ZX key. Just file it down and it will unlock just about anything—American, French, Japanese—you name it. Little brothers always carry around a screwdriver to punch the ignition key hole. A simple screwdriver can do the job. Insert it at the top of the window, force the window down until you can use your hands to jam it down, and pull the lock up.

Take home invasions. You've got to plan very carefully. You make cold calls first. You knock on the door and pretend to ask for somebody; somebody that you know doesn't live there. If nobody comes to the door, you know it's safe to break in. That's a cold call. Before you break into a place you drive by it a lot to figure out the comings and goings of the people who live there, and you check for cars in the driveway. You also make sure that nobody's at home on either side of the target house—you ring the doorbells and knock. When you're sure, as sure as you can be, that is, that nobody's home in the target house, you knock on a back door. If nobody answers, you pry it open, or jack the sliding door or windows, or the garage. In case the garage has an electric door, you use a jack to crack open the overhead. The best way to get into a home is for my wannabes to unlock it for us. Little brothers can tell when the only people at home are old folks or women. Wannabes who are ten or twelve are perfect for the job because they aren't suspicious. And when they tell us where their grandparents hide their jewelry and stuff we go straight to the hiding places and don't need to coerce anybody by beatings or threats. And for all their effort they get money, beer, cigarettes, and their share of goodies and joyrides. I give them plenty to spend during the Tet Festivals.

Cars, stereos, gold, jewelry, diamonds, you name it and we have buyers. That's my specialty. I turn all that stuff to cash. We trade *trung* for *ga* [guns]. Everybody's got guns; no matter where you go and no matter what gang, everybody's got guns. Even homegirls and wannabes—they got handguns.

I always tell them to be careful. The Fs [FBI] may even have their photo. The cops have a huge file of hundreds of kids. If they're ever arrested I tell them to give a false name. The worst thing that could happen is that they get sent up to the Ranch for a few months. Their chances of getting caught for, say, breaking and entering around here are not good because I often send them out of town for home invasion stuff. That way nobody can identify them. And if they do an operation around here, I tell them to wear a ski mask or to pull a woman's stocking over their faces.

For *ghe* [girls] you have to plan. Sometimes they do not come easily and you have to work for them. But in this country children have their own bedrooms, you know? Since most parents work, I tell the wannabes just go to her house during the day. The place will be all yours. I know a rooster who hid his lover in his bedroom for days and his parents didn't know it!

"Put your books down, Canh, and party with us."
—A Vietnamese high school sophomore

Chapter 4
Drug Use

When Hong An moved with her baby brother, Jerry, and her mother, Hong Ngoc, from Dallas, Texas, to California, she was twelve—a petite and pretty Vietnamese girl. The little family settled down in southern California, where Hong An attended elementary school and her mother found a job with a local electronics company.

Mother and daughter lived a quiet life. During her free time on the weekends, Hong Ngoc loved to attend poetry readings. Hong An, who was a straight-A student, did her homework and played with little Jerry.

Hong Ngoc wrote poetry and began to read it aloud at literary appreciation meetings. When she found some acclaim as a writer and reader, Hong Ngoc began to fill her calendar with performance appointments. On weekends and holidays she was rarely home.

Hong An graduated from the elementary school and entered the seventh grade. She missed seeing her mother. Hong Ngoc was around less and less, only one or two weekdays and an occasional Saturday morning. But Hong Ngoc was loved and admired by a lot of people. She felt happy. The horror of Vietnam and the Thai refugee camp seemed far behind her.

One day, during a recess at school, a Vietnamese boy named Tong stopped by Hong An's junior high. He parked his car by the fence, slipped a cassette into his tape player, lit a cigarette, and sat back to observe the young girls who wandered about the schoolyard. They all seemed so beautiful, but one was more beautiful than the rest. With her pale skin and long black hair, Hong An was exquisite. He waved to her. Hong An, a little puzzled, waved back. Who was this boy?

Tong swung by the school again and again. One time he offered Hong An a bottle of Coca-Cola and a box of chocolates. Hong An liked the attention Tong gave her. Lately she had been feeling a little neglected. Remembering the times when her mother read poetry just for her, she felt sad. That never happened anymore. Her mother always seemed too busy.

Then Tong offered her marijuana. Hong An did not know what the stuff was—it looked like some of the spices her mother kept on a shelf over their kitchen stove. But if Tong, an eighteen-year-old who smiled sweetly and gave her Coca-Cola and chocolate, offered it, then surely it was okay.

She smoked it. At first it made her cough and she hated the sickeningly sweet smell. But Tong laughed and assured her that next time it would be better, next time she'd love it.

Next time she did. She smoked marijuana, sipped some wine cooler, and tried cocaine. The white stuff gave her the most incredible rush of wonderful feelings she had ever had. Cocaine made Hong An feel good, very good. It almost made her forget about her mother.

Within a very few weeks Hong An could not wait for Tong to show up at the schoolyard and give her cocaine. Marijuana was nothing compared to cocaine. The trouble was, when the effects of the white powder wore off, she felt inexpressibly sad and depressed, sadder even than she did when she came home and her mother was not there. A house without a mother was sad, but life without cocaine was unbearable.

One afternoon Hong An's mother came home from work to find that her daughter was not there. Jerry was alone. She waited all night, pacing from window to window, but Hong An never came. In the morning she called the school. "No," the attendance counselor said. "Our records show that your daughter was not in school yesterday, either." Hong Ngoc sat at her kitchen table and wept. She admitted that Hong An had run away.

Hong Ngoc did not feel like reading poetry anymore.

Hong An went to live with Tong at a safe house. When they could not sleep there they slept in motels or crawled into cars parked along dilapidated, treeless streets. Hong An snorted thousands of dollars' worth of cocaine. She had sex with Tong whenever he wanted. In exchange he supplied her with cocaine, using money he got from selling the stuff through his gang, the Bloody Panthers. He supplied her with crack, too, and she thought crack was ever so much better than cocaine, except when its effects wore off and she felt far worse than she did when she came down from cocaine.

Then Tong was caught and jailed. He was an adult, so he was sent away for a long time. Hong An begged Tong's friend Minh, a member of the Flying Dragon gang, to get her crack. Minh was more than willing, although he made Hong An understand that now she belonged to him. Minh had a tattoo on his chest, a great flying dragon with burning eyes.

Hong An's mother had burning eyes, too, eyes that burned with tears of sadness, of anger, of guilt. She could not sleep at night. She grew weak from an ulcer.

One afternoon the police called. Hong An was arrested and transported to the Juvenile Detention Center. Hong Ngoc rushed there to see her. But Hong Ngoc's joy evaporated when she saw her, for Hong An did not look anything like her former self. Her hair was filthy, her skin was blotchy, her clothes were dirty and unkempt, and her eyes, bloodshot and puffy, were those of a hunted animal. She looked ill, terribly pale and ill.

Hong An was under arrest for selling drugs. A probation officer explained that Hong An must seek treatment at the rehabilitation center. At the rehabilitation center, the counselors talked to Hong An and Hong Ngoc for a long time. Hong An promised her mother that she would follow all the dos and don'ts the counselor prescribed.

She would have to stay at the center until they helped her to be well again. Hong Ngoc thought that things would now be easy.

One weekend Hong An was permitted to return home for a visit. She played in the living room with little Jerry, and the house seemed filled once again with the poetry of family. Hong Ngoc busied herself preparing beef noodle soup for Hong An, elated to be her mother again.

The doorbell rang. From her kitchen window, Hong Ngoc saw a fancy black sports car parked in her drive with a Vietnamese boy behind the wheel. She felt afraid. Hong Ngoc put down a dish and stood on tiptoe to watch. Hong An answered the door and shouted into the kitchen, "Mom, I'll be right back."

Little Jerry ran out behind Hong An. "Get inside," Hong An hissed at him, pushing him savagely toward the house, "and don't tell Mom." Hong An climbed into the back seat and the black sports car sped away. Little Jerry watched it disappear around the corner. Wondering why his sister was so mean to him, the little boy repeated, "Don't tell Mom, don't tell Mom," as he toddled back into the house.

But Mom saw it all from the kitchen window. Hong Ngoc went searching for her daughter. She haunted desolate streets in desolate neighborhoods, neighborhoods where hollow-eyed people looked at her vacantly. She peered into pool halls that reeked of beer and urine, and into cafés where people smoked disconsolately and drank weak coffee.

Hong Ngoc searched for months. She quit going to the electronics plant. Unable to make payments on her house or car, she lost them both. But Hong Ngoc did not care. The poetry had gone out of her. Her daughter was gone.

She and Jerry moved in with relatives, where she lived as if among the dead. Hong Ngoc dreamed of Hong An: Hong An in a pink nightgown, the same color pink she wore when she was a little girl and they were in Vietnam. In her dream, Hong Ngoc rushed to embrace her and Hong An clung to her, mumbling, "Mother, Mother, I will stay with you forever." Hong Ngoc's tears mingled with those of her daughter and she stroked her long hair.

One morning Hong Ngoc opened a letter addressed to Hong

An. It was from a hospital, from "Oncology." Hong Ngoc did not know what "oncology" meant. She called me. I told her it meant cancer.

Cancer? Hong An? This was surely a mistake, Hong Ngoc thought. But her heart thumped as she phoned the hospital— perhaps they could tell her where Hong An was. Hospital officials told her to come down, that she could make an appointment to see Hong An's doctor.

The doctor told her that Hong An was indeed very ill, with uterine cancer. The doctor explained that she needed to see Hong An regularly in order to help her. Hong Ngoc replied that she did not know where Hong An was, since she had run away.

Hong An was still on the run, and having violated her probation, she was afraid to go back to school. School officials might notify the police and then she would be arrested. But Hong An was tired, very tired. She longed to be taken care of, to be held and stroked by her mother.

Then one day the doorbell rang. Hong Ngoc awoke from her dream to the insistent ringing. Her blood ran cold. Doorbells and the ringing of telephones chilled her because they summoned to her mind policemen and emergency room technicians. A doorbell rang and she would imagine the unimaginable, that Hong An was dead. She slipped into her bathrobe and went downstairs. She stood for a moment in the entryway and stared at the doorknob. She felt clammy, lightheaded. She held her breath and opened the door.

Hong An stood there. She looked utterly bewildered and ill.

For the next three months Hong Ngoc took her daughter to the hospital for treatment. Hong An seemed to be stronger and her fine color returned. "I am happy," Hong Ngoc told relatives. "Hong An is such a sweet girl and I have her back. It is like the old days."

Summer vacation began. One day Hong An came into the kitchen where her mother was preparing supper and told her she had found a job at the Café Hai Van in San Francisco. Hong Ngoc was distressed but tried not to show it. "That's fifty miles away, daughter. I shall miss you all day long."

Hong An began to work, and at first all seemed well. But one morning Hong An spilled $530 in cash onto the kitchen table and said, "This is my salary." Hong Ngoc was astonished. She never imagined that Hong An would make that much as a waitress, and said so.

"Mother, I am not a waitress. I sell *bia om*."

Hong Ngoc's face flushed. She knew exactly what selling *bia om* was, and she knew full well what it might lead to. "Daughter, this job of yours is degrading. I have read in our Vietnamese newspapers what this business of *bia om* is. It is something that was better left behind in Vietnam. You entertain men by doing everything but sell your body to them—all to get them to buy as much beer as possible. Do you fondle them? Sit on their laps? Kiss them? An, this is not something our family can honor. It is not an acceptable livelihood. Listen to me, An, please listen. Think not only of yourself but of your family. Summer school begins in two weeks. I will take you to sign up for a course in something that will interest you. You will use your Vietnamese name. The school will never know that you have violated your probation."

Hong An was not listening. She was removing her clothing from her bureau drawers, folding it neatly, and sorting it on her bed. Her suitcase was on the floor with some of her belongings already packed. "Mother, I must move closer to my workplace."

Hong Ngoc felt panicky but she composed herself. "Daughter, this money is dirty. You are worth more than this; you can do better than this. You are a good girl. This is beneath you. A *bia om* girl today is a prostitute tomorrow. I have seen these girls with their cigarette burn marks at the Ranches and at the Juvenile Hall, An. They are in and out, in and out, and they sleep with many boys for cocaine; bad boys who steal and carry terrible weapons and drink whiskey and deliver stolen goods for lots of money. *Bia om* money will not bring you happiness. You are clean. You do not wear these marks."

"Mother, Lien is downstaris. She is waiting for me."

"Daughter, you will go nowhere with Lien. You told me yourself that she is a member of the Green Dragon gang and that she uses drugs, that you smoked crack with her." She left the room softly and shut the door. "Stay here, Hong An."

Trembling, she telephoned me at the Ranch. I called the police.

Soon a patrol car with two officers parked in front of Hong Ngoc's building. Hong Ngoc was watching for them from her apartment window. She met them on the stairs and at the same moment she saw Lien fleeing down the street. "Please," she implored the officers. "Please don't handcuff her."

But they did. They handcuffed Hong Ngoc's daughter. Hong An looked at her, bewilderment and anger mingling on her face as she climbed into the back of the patrol car for another trip to Juvenile Hall.

Hong Ngoc returned to her apartment and sat down at the kitchen table. She put her head in her hands and wept—wept because she was sad and because she was relieved. For a time, anyway, Hong An would be safe. Counselors would help her; the counselors were wonderful. But her daughter's face rose accusingly before her.

"Cau ghe" is Vietnamese slang that literally means "to go crab fishing." For men like Thai Trang it means to look around for schoolgirls. Sue Huong and Lisa, his victims, became addicted to drugs because he lured them into experimenting with them. Sue Huong and Lisa had no knowledge of drugs. Their parents had no knowledge of drugs, and so they would not have known that it was important to discuss the dangers of drugs with them. There are many Vietnamese adolescents like Hong An, Sue Huong, and Lisa, and unfortunately there are many young men like Tong and Thai Trang.

Drug addiction often begins with simple curiosity. "What is grass?" a child wonders. "What is cocaine, or the 'white stuff'?" "Does cocaine have a taste?" "What does it feel like to 'boong'?" All too frequently there is an older child or a young adult around who is eager to answer these questions. Often a child feels enormous social pressure to experiment with a drug. Sue Huong's story about her relationship with Thai Trang is an illustration.

Sue Huong

I was in America only four months when I met Thai Trang. I came with my family from central Vietnam. When he first asked me to go joyriding with him I wasn't sure. I remember he asked me to dance, but I told him I didn't dance skillfully enough yet to go to a club. I learned a few steps at Christmas but I really didn't have the chance to practice. Also, I told him I didn't want to get home late. My parents would chide me. He promised to get me home in time.

We talked about my home. I told him I missed the steaming bowls of spicy *Hue* beef noodle soup that my family and I enjoyed in Vietnam. Thai said, "How about a bowl of *bun bo Hue*?" He took me to a restaurant, a Vietnamese restaurant. But before we left I made him promise me again that he would have me home by seven. I did not wish to disappoint my mother and father. I remember feeling a little scared, but I was excited. Thai Trang was very handsome.

After the dinner of *Hue* beef soup I began to feel more friendly toward him. In the car, Thai pulled cigarettes—or what I thought were cigarettes—from the pocket of his jacket and offered one to me. He told me it would help me to relax. I told him I don't smoke. He told me, "Just inhale a couple times; it'll refresh your taste. And it'll make you feel good. Real good."

I did not know what to say to Thai Trang. I was scared to look at him. He said, "How about sharing mine while I'm driving, okay? No big deal, okay?" So I did. I inhaled Thai Trang's cigarette. He bought me noodle soup. I did not want to be rude.

Thai Trang

I noticed Sue Huong at the Falcon Middle School and picked her up for the first time at the end of the school day. I asked her to go to the Lodi Nightclub with me but she refused. She didn't seem enthusiastic about any of my ideas and was very quiet. But I knew she'd be easy. She was incredibly naive. Besides, I never give up. I always get my way with girls and I know that some like just to smoke and others prefer crack. I am prepared for any eventuality.

I could not take my eyes off Sue Huong who is beautiful. She has full lips and shoulder-length hair and her body is slim and vibrant. When she told me she liked spicy beef soup I took her to the Trang Nha restaurant on Santar Road. After the soup Sue seemed happy. In my car I offered her a beer which she drank at once. She looked out the window excitedly and asked me many questions about the city. I drove up and down the back streets and around in circles so that she had absolutely no idea where she was.

When I could see that the beer and my Kools [young Vietnamese males often stuff Kool cigarettes with marijuana] were taking their effect and Sue was getting quieter I pulled my Prelude onto the shoulder of Central Expressway and kissed her. She didn't resist. I exited the expressway and circled back to East Stenry to the *nha bui* [safe house]. There are rooms there where the brothers bring their *ghe* [girls] for a good time. I parked in an alley near the safe house and helped Sue out of the car.

I brought her into the bedroom that Su [Thai's Big Brother, the "lieutenant" of the Flying Eagles gang] lets me use whenever I like. Sue was scared. They all wear that wounded-animal look at first but they always give in. I've seen it dozens of times.

Huong was good. She told me that she'd never been with a guy before and that she'd been curious about sex for a long time. Well, I satisfied her curiosity. She told me that she had once seen Hong Kong sex movies in a clandestine movie room operated by the VC deputy chief of her hamlet. Villagers paid 1,000 dong for a matinee.

I've done all right for a kid who got off a refugee boat two years ago. I drive a Prelude. I wear a gold necklace with the Flying Eagle pendant on my neck. I wear clean shirts and a black leather jacket. I always have plenty of *trung* in the glove compartment. I always say that I am prepared for any eventuality.

Lisa

Thai Trang knows how to party and he always has plenty for me to boong [crack to smoke]. And there's always roast pork and roast duck and lots of Heineken in the mo [motel room]. I met Thai at the Me-Ly Nightclub. Thai was good looking. When he asked me to a party the next night, I couldn't say no. At the party Thai snorted cocaine. I had never seen the stuff before and I asked him what he was doing. He told me he was snorting *tep* and asked me did I want to try it. Just a nailful. He helped me to try it and it made me feel lofty. He asked me if I wanted to try some more. I did the stuff eight times that night.

I boong two or three large eggballs a week and I live with Thai at the safe house all the time. I haven't set foot in my parents' house for two months. Which is fine with me, since my father beat me and my mother humiliated me.

Some Indochinese youth join "party gangs," and through them many are introduced to drugs and become steady users. Tu Hoang, known as the Red Bear, is fairly representative. The first Vietnamese American member of the Hispanic Norteno gang, he bears tattoos on his upper right shoulder and on his wrist that both read, "X Red Bear 4." Tu Hoang arrived in the United States thirteen years ago. The family settled in Stockton, California, where they lived for three years, then moved to San Jose. Tu Hoang's Eurasian father, Thong Hoang, was a heavy drinker. He was also involved sexually with a number of homegirls. One day Tu Hoang's mother came home early and was stunned to find her husband in their bed with a young girl. They divorced immediately.

Tu Hoang was devastated. He confided to me that his father's sexual escapades and his parents' divorce made him anxious and sad. He escaped through drugs and partying:

It all started with a party gang which I joined. I did not find happiness in the family. I wasn't yet familiar with street gang activities. I joined the party gang just for fun doing crazy things to deal with emptiness in the home. [In the party gang we did such things as] dancing, sniffing cocaine, smoking crack, drinking, making trips with acid—sometimes with nail polish soaked in hard paper placed under my tongue—and enjoying sexual encounters.

To be a member of a "party gang" or "party crew" you have to pay dues, monthly dues. The organizers are Mexican Americans. They circulate flyers periodically, usually twice a month, among high school boys and girls. In the flyers they announce the date and the location of the upcoming party. If you are interested in attending that party, [you] call for the cost. It is not disclosed in the flyers. The costs include admission fees—usually ten dollars—[plus] the cost of the "Horny Pills," known among the homeboys as XTC . . . or "Spanish fly" that costs around twenty-five dollars per pill, and the costs for the drinks. One of the most popular drinks is Sysco wine cooler . . . because it produces, if [drunk] by the bottle, the same effects on the female partner as "horny pills" or "Spanish fly." It only takes a little longer to turn your partner on. The neat thing about it is that you don't have to maneuver or wait until your girl steps away from your table to drop the pill into her drink.

I asked Tu how the party gangs were able to get these illegal substances:

We know where to buy them. That's one of the advantages of being [a] member of a "party gang" or "party crew." You've got to be "introduced." It's just like buying drugs or guns.

Do Vietnamese join "party crews"?:

Of course, but not many. Some Vietnamese girls are interested in having sexual experiences with boys of other races, like blacks, Hispanics, whites. They are dynamite!

Tu Hoang was involved in a drive-by shooting incident south of San Jose. Riding in one of eight truckloads of Varrio Norteno Locos and Outside Posse homeboys, he and the others had been at a drinking party. Five persons suffered gunshot wounds and he was arrested. Tu Hoang found himself at a Ranch where he has, unfortunately, become the leader of an inside gang.

San is a fourteen-year-old Vietnamese boy who recently moved from San Jose with his mother and three brothers back to San Francisco. San's mother, Ha Thi Ngu, noticed that his disposition had changed dramatically. He talked back to her all the time and disobeyed her, speaking to her in a contemptuous tone. He had never acted this way before; he had always shown her respect.

One day San came home wearing an expensive gold necklace. She was instantly suspicious—the necklace would have cost a lot of money, and how would he have gotten it? When she confronted him, San stomped out of their apartment and slammed the door. That was the moment that San's mother first suspected that he was involved with drugs. She had set clear rules against drug and alcohol use, but San appeared to be ignoring them. "I felt afraid," she told me. A few days later one of San's younger brothers saw him step out of an expensive-looking car in front of their apartment. He reported this to his mother. Ha Thi Ngu warned San that if she ever caught him with drugs she would turn him over to the authorities.

Shortly thereafter, San walked into the house with a plastic bag sticking out of his shirt pocket. When his mother yanked it out and opened it, she discovered some white crystalline powder and several plastic vials. She knew immediately that the stuff was cocaine. She grabbed the bag, dragged San into her car, and drove him and the cocaine to the police station. Later she told me her story:

> Until now San has been a good son. He was doing well at school and even worked at the grocery as a stockboy to help me out at home. But the moment he got in with this older crowd he got out of control, sassing me and no longer doing his schoolwork. I want to save my boy's life and I told him that I turned him in because I love him. And I don't want him influencing his younger brothers.

Generally the Vietnamese community is naive about drug use. Vietnamese newcomers to this country, those whose children are most vulnerable to drug abuse, know absolutely nothing about drugs. To combat this ignorance, Asian Community Mental Health Services prepared a pamphlet that is distributed widely throughout the Vietnamese community. The pamphlet provides insights into the extent of the cultural gap that yawns between Vietnamese and American cultures, and the ways that gap can push Vietnamese children into drug use:

> Your child is growing up into a world of uncertain values and cultural conflicts. This makes the world a confusing place for everybody, but particularly for your child who is learning what it means to be Vietnamese in an American context. This transition may be particularly difficult for your family because you are both adjusting to a new society. Please remember that adolescents are no longer

children, but neither are they adults: they have to learn to make decisions for themselves. You can help your child become a strong person by instilling pride in your Vietnamese heritage. Becoming American does not mean having to give up being Vietnamese.[1]

In fact, many parents feel they *do* have to "give up being Vietnamese" in order to survive in America. "Vietnamese families often are reluctant to talk about their feelings; learn to talk to your children about them," the pamphlet counsels. This is easier said than done. Unlike most American parents, Vietnamese people do not permit their children to express themselves when they are angry, frustrated, or feeling defiant—the child is expected to restrain himself, to exercise self-control. To fail to do so is to show disrespect, and respect for one's elders (one's father in particular) is at the heart of Vietnamese child-rearing practices.[2]

The pamphlet gives further advice that can be hard for a Vietnamese household to follow. "Learn to disapprove of the action without attacking the person," the pamphlet advises. This sounds reasonable, but Vietnamese parents will shame their children and even withdraw their love in order to teach them to exercise self-control and to show respect. This posture is so ingrained in some Vietnamese, so much a part of the tissue of their existence, that it is reflected even in the nuances of the Vietnamese language. I will tell the story of Vu Huy to illustrate.[3]

Vu Huy lives with his father, who received a high school education in Saigon and works in an electronics company, and his stepmother, who is currently a beautician. Vu Huy began to cut school and go out, and his father found out about it. One day his father stood in the doorway and forbade Vu Huy to go out. Vu Huy swore at his father, and when he tried to shove him aside in the doorway, his father fell down and Vu Huy fell on top of him. As they struggled, Vu Huy's gun suddenly stuck out from his jacket pocket.

"A *gun!*" the father gasped. Vu Huy lunged for his weapon. "Gun! Gun! Gun!" the father shouted like a madman. Vu Huy sat there holding the gun, not knowing what to do. Vu Huy's brother, Ba Huy, appeared from his bedroom, wondering what all the ruckus was about. "Gun!" the father cried again. "Your brother has a gun! Call the police! Dial 911!" With his father and his brother still on the floor before him, Ba Huy stood there completely bewildered. *"Call the police!"* his father shouted at him again. Ba Huy dutifully called the police.

The father told the police that his son intended to kill him. The police arrested Vu Huy and the judge sent him to the Ranch for six months on a weapons charge. Vu Huy's stepmother later told me that after the police left the apartment, Vu Huy's father sat at the kitchen table with his head in his hands until evening. He did not get up or move from the table, and he refused to eat.

I learned that Vu Huy was in the Asians Kicking Asses gang. Nobody in his family knew. I also learned that Vu Huy was bitterly resentful of his stepmother. "She favors her natural child," Vu Huy reported. One afternoon Vu Huy came with his father and step-mother to my office. She talked to Vu Huy using the term *"may."*

In the former South Vietnam most families addressed their chil-dren as *"may."* The word does more than imply condescension: it suggests that the speaker despises the addressee. It is generally used to address people who are not respected. It is used casually but im-plies distance, and it clearly *establishes* distance between child and parent. Being referred to as *"may"* has the effect of pushing the child away—a child simply cannot feel close to a parent who addresses him as *"may."* A parent's use of the word creates an atmosphere within which the child feels inferior, perhaps even unloved. *"May"* is a hu-miliating term, and it is powerful. Nevertheless, the word is used by the vast majority of South Vietnamese parents.

Interestingly, *"may"* was not a part of the North Vietnamese vo-cabulary. I am not sure why this is so, but it is probably a function of the fact that North and South Vietnam had very different cultural histories, histories that shaped vocabularies that are distinctive even to this day. In the North, parents called their children by their names or by the word *"con."* In contrast to *"may," "con"* is an endearment that implies a belonging by blood, and it conveys the special closeness that only parent and child can feel. It is a word that binds and im-plies mutual respect. Many South Vietnamese continue to call their children "*may*," but this is a tragic mistake, because in so doing parents are disassociating themselves from their children and weakening the parent-child bond.

I asked Vu Huy to leave my office and gently explained to his stepmother the effect of the word "*may*" on him. (The father told me he always used the term "*con*.") I suggested that she work very hard on not using it. She agreed to try.

Well-meaning people want to help Vietnamese parents help their children to avoid drug use and gangs. But glib advice that Vietnamese parents "show their children that they love them" and that they "learn to talk about their feelings" ignores the weight of a cultural tradition in which parents are the unquestioned authority to which children meekly submit. The "typical" Vietnamese American views the parent-child relationship very differently from other Americans.[4]

"Don't make your children feel that they have to succeed to please you," the drug abuse pamphlet warns. But for the Vietnamese, a child's success reflects the family, and family pride is sacred. A woman once came to me and said that because her son had been sent to the California Youth Authority, she was moving to Dallas. She would live with a friend until she was able to establish herself. "I cannot face my sisters with Nguyen in jail."[5]

The drug abuse pamphlet advises, "Don't expect your children to study all the time." But the Vietnamese value learning in a way that perhaps other Americans cannot understand. As I explained earlier, in Vietnam the learned man is a man of status, much more so than the man of wealth. Studying is the path not only to success but to living artfully and well, with grace. One might as well advise, "Don't expect your children to breathe all the time."[6]

Vietnamese children are "fishing on both sides"—they want to please their parents and yet they long to fit in with their peers. The story of a boy named Canh illustrates this dilemma well.

Canh was a child who left Vietnam unaccompanied, but as luck would have it, he met a granduncle in a refugee camp in the Philippines. They went to live in a small apartment in San Jose, while Canh's mother and father stayed behind in the southernmost part of Vietnam. He ended up at the Ranch as a result of attempted auto theft. "I don't want my uncle to see me," he told me tearfully. "We must be like the sun and the moon." One afternoon when the two of them came in for counseling neither of them would speak at all.

"I get constant lectures at home," the boy complained later. "He tells me I must *study, study, study,* but I don't have time to study." Canh was failing everything in school and was a chronic runaway.

"Why don't you have time to study?" I asked.

"Because of my work."

"Your work?"

"I work at the grocery, I work at the convenience store, and I work at the liquor store."

"How can you be doing all of that when you have to be in school?"

"I cannot be in school because I must earn ten thousand dollars to send to my parents. They need the money because they need to buy a rice mill. I go to school for my first two classes, but then I leave it to work at all these jobs. They pay at most only five dollars and fifty cents an hour, and so you can see that I will be working a long, long time before I can send my parents the money they need for their rice mill. They send me letters—'Where is the money, where is the money?'—but they don't understand that even in this country, ten thousand dollars is a lot of money. That is why I join the gangs. I need money and I need money quick. My parents need money." Canh put his head in his hands and wept. (He is only seventeen.)

He went on: "My parents, they think I'll be sponsored by some rich American and get an education. 'Do not neglect your studies,' my father writes to me, but I have no time to study. And when I do I'm so frustrated and depressed that I cannot. And my friends, they are always tempting me to have fun. 'Put your books down, Canh, and party with us.' I put my books down and drink and smoke marijuana and take pills, but it all makes me feel so tired for work and for study, and my uncle, he pressures me constantly. 'Canh, you must study! You must quit your work at these stores and study!' But he doesn't understand." Canh was too exhausted to go on.

Canh asked me to talk to his uncle and to write to his Vietnamese parents. I did both, explaining the situation to his parents. The father immediately wrote to me and thanked me. "Tell my son not to worry about the rice mill and just to study," he said.

Canh was adamant. "I'd rather live in a foster home than live with my uncle," he said. The county respected his wishes and put him in a foster home. Away from the constant lecturing of his uncle, Canh is doing well. He has dropped out of his gang and is studying hard in school. He no longer smokes marijuana or takes pills.

"I do this to please my father," he says. "My uncle, he never loved me. He just wanted to be able to say to his friends that 'Canh, he is a scholar.' "

"I try very hard but nobody wants me. I get my G.E.D., I go here and there and beg. I say, 'You hire me, please, I work hard for you,' but nobody wants me. So fuck the world. I got to get by someway somehow."
— Vietnamese inmate of the C.Y.A.

Chapter 5
Counseling the Alienated

I try to meet troubled juveniles on whatever ground they give me. The moment a child expresses interest in something—it can be virtually *anything*—I build on that. To illustrate my methods, I share in this chapter the stories of encounters I have had with Indochinese and Amerasian wards. Most of these encounters took place at the Ranches, but some were at other facilities—drug rehabilitation centers, Juvenile Hall, courtrooms, the homes of parents, and so forth.

Tien Duy arrived in the United States at the age of four. His father was an ARVN officer who died in a communist prison camp. The boy's grandmother has cared for him for as long as Tien can remember, and they have lived in the United States for thirteen years. According to Tien, his mother lived in the area, but he has had nothing to do with her—he has never told me why. His mother has several sisters who live nearby as well. Either his mother or an aunt will give his grandmother a ride to the Ranch to visit him, but they themselves never visit him. His mother sends him things—fruit and Chinese instant noodle soup.

Tien was first sent to the Ranch and assigned to me for counseling because he was in possession of an illegal weapon (a semi-automatic) and a nine-inch knife at the time of his arrest for riding in a stolen vehicle. When the police approached the vehicle, Tien fired two shots at the squad car. When asked why he had the gun, Tien said that some gangsters were after him so he had to protect himself. Tien was a heavy user of drugs and alcohol. He said he smoked marijuana regularly, had tried crack, and used PCP frequently. He drank heavily as well (ten beers and shots at one sitting, as he told it). It was clear that drug abuse was affecting his short-term memory, and during his first few weeks at the Ranch he showed little self-control. His first night there he attacked another ward for no apparent reason. Tien said he "didn't like the way he looked at me." His upper front teeth are missing—"blown out," according to another report I got on him. The bullet that entered his mouth came out his cheek, where he bears a nasty scar. His eyes, though, are young. His eyes are not the eyes of an old man. Not yet.

Tien responded surprisingly well to counseling, particularly when our talks together dealt with drugs. He devoured any reading material that I gave him about people whose lives were wrecked by drugs, about people who were able to free themselves from drugs, and about the drugs themselves. He did not know the dangers of heroin and said he had never tried it simply because "the others didn't," but he admitted that he was "curious." We discussed the nature of addiction and its effects (I pointed out to him that he was already manifesting short-term memory loss) and he said, "I will have to be careful. I will keep in mind about addiction and having to support [my habit by criminal activities]."

"Tien, do you know that mothers have tried to sell their babies in order to buy crack?"

"You've told me a lot of things, Mr. Dee [many of my wards call me Mr. Dee or Uncle Dee], but this I don't believe. That can't be so."

"It's the truth, Tien."

"Such a mother deserves to die."

"No one deserves to die, Tien."

"Maybe not. But maybe so. You told me that mothers die for their children. This I believe because my mother nearly died for me. [This was the only time I heard him speak of his mother, and he never explained what he meant.] But a mother selling her baby? That's unnatural."

"Of course it is. It's the drug at work. Drugs make people do unspeakable things. Tien, promise me that you won't smoke crack."

"I promise."

Tien struck me as exceptionally bright. He had picked up English readily, but he had also dropped out of school. I encouraged him to get his G.E.D. (General Equivalency Degree), and he began to work hard on doing so.

Not long after his release Tien telephoned to tell me that he had gotten a job. It was not much of a job—he was pumping gas. But a few months later Tien was back at the Ranch. According to official documents and reports in the news, Tien was involved in an extortion attempt at a Vietnamese restaurant, but according to Tien, he was merely standing outside while his friends were throwing bottles and breaking glass and shoving customers around. He swore to me he was clean. I asked him about his job. He said the service station had let him go, because it had less business and could not afford to keep him on.

During our counseling sessions he seemed hungry for any guidance I could offer him. "Tell me about the fighters," he asked me in a childlike way, and I told him again. Tien asked me to repeat particular stories almost every time he was in my office, the way a toddler begs for favorite nursery songs.

"General Tran Hung Dao was a great fighting man of the thirteenth century in Vietnam," I began. "He defeated the Chinese army by planting stakes in the Bach Dang River between Hanoi and Haiphong. At high tide the Chinese soldiers came in their boats and were grounded on the stakes. Most of their boats sank."

"Now tell me of Le Loi and Nguyen Hue."

"Nguyen Hue drove the Chinese out of northern Vietnam in the eighteenth century. Leading his army on foot on the eve of the new year, Nguyen Hue and his soldiers jogged all the way to Hanoi from Binh Dinh—a distance of about eight hundred miles. The troops cooked their food as they traveled, using bamboo platforms that they held as they ran. Le Loi is known as the liberator in Vietnam because he put up a resistance in the Lam Son mountains for ten years and eventually, because he was so persistent, drove the Chinese out."

On Tien's release day he told me that his grandmother would allow him to live with her for one month, but after that he would be on his own. Tien said he was determined to find and keep another job and to stay out of trouble. He was optimistic about his future. He would not cut school.

For months Tien looked for a job. "I tried everywhere," he said wearily one afternoon. He had walked most of the way and hitch-hiked part of the way to see me. "And I'll do anything, even wash dishes, but everyone says, 'hard times, hard times, come back when times not so hard,' and I do but then they say the same thing, 'hard times, hard times, come back when times not so hard.' My grand-mother has let me stay because I haven't been mad-dogging [pro-voking fights with gang members] and haven't been in any trouble, but she wants money. She says I pay or I get out. She says I'm a grown man now."

"Remember Le Loi and Nguyen Hue," I said to him gently. "You mustn't give up; you must keep looking, and you must keep study-ing. Are you studying, Tien?"

"I am."

" 'Hoc,' or studying, is terribly important. Someday you'll see that your experiences in trying to land a job will work for your good. Do you remember the story of Le Ly?"

"Le Ly was the lady who had to sell her body to survive during the war. I remember her."

"Yes, she even had to prostitute herself. She told her story to a writer and he told her story in a book. Now that book is a movie that was produced by a famous filmmaker. Le Ly was illiterate, Tien. She didn't have a G.E.D. and she couldn't even think about going to col-lege like you're doing, and yet she succeeded. Why did she succeed, Tien?"[1]

"Because she didn't give up."

"Her situation seemed hopeless, didn't it? And do you feel hope-less now?"

There was a pause as Tien considered. "I do."

"Le Ly achieved, Tien. And you will, too. Be persistent."

"I'll be like Nguyen Hue, Mr. Dee. I'll jog from place to place and cook my food as I travel. I won't give up."

"There's another thing you must consider." I point to a sign taped to the side of my desk:

Friends now
equals
Job connections
later

"You've antagonized other wards here. What good does that do you? You shouldn't make an enemy of anyone and you should seek friends among all people, not just Vietnamese. And if you find that you can't be friendly, or that someone has taken a dislike to you for no apparent reason, then you must try not to make him an enemy. 'Never burn any bridge because someday you may have to cross it.' Tien, you must have the trust of other people. Trustworthiness is a gold mine."

"You mean I can make money from trustworthiness?"

"Yes, you can. Let me tell you about my parents' store. They called it '*Nghia Tin*,' which means 'Loyalty and Trust.' My parents were evacuated from Da Nang into the countryside on the eve of the French landing in 1947. Everywhere people were afraid. What was going to happen? What would tomorrow bring? Despite their fear and anxiety, my mother and father made the best of their situation. The Chinese loaned them money and *trusted* my parents with merchandise in a war-torn country. My parents made good on that trust. Returning to Da Nang, they opened their store, made an honest profit, and paid their debt to the Chinese. You're never loaned money twice, Tien; remember that. As long as you enjoy the trust of other people, like my parents, you'll be given opportunities. '*Tin*' is the fifth and greatest of the five ethical rules of Confucius. People have to trust you. If you run away and join a gang you'll lose the trust of people who might have provided you with opportunities. And for people to trust you, you have to build bridges. You have to work at it. The relationships you have with people are very, very important, Tien."

"I have a relationship with you."

"You do, and our relationship is a good one, isn't it? I'm beginning to trust you, Tien. I trust you to listen to me."

"I'm listening."

"Do you know that one of this country's astronauts is a Vietnamese? And that another Vietnamese was recently made a captain in the United States Air Force?" I passed him the newspaper clipping and he grabbed it from me, reading it hungrily.

"No. I didn't know about him. Will he get to fly jets?"

"No doubt he is flying them now."

"Wow." Tien sat back in his chair and sighed.

"That's not all. There were two Vietnamese brothers who were carried here as little children in 1975 by their mother, who was fleeing the communists. They studied hard and kept their noses clean and applied to the United States Air Force Academy in Boulder, Colorado. They just graduated. Do you know who presented them with their degrees?"

"Ho Chi Minh," Tien replied, giggling.

"You're a wit," I said to him smiling, and I thought to myself, this boy is sharp, this boy has humor. He knows things. But he grew instantly serious.

"Tell me," he said. "Tell me about the boys. Who gave them their degrees?"

"The president of the United States. George Bush."

Tien whistled. "This Air Force Academy. Is this some place where I might go?"

"Tien, in this life anything is possible, but you must begin to make the right choices now, this very moment. None of these people got anywhere by themselves. Every single one of them—my parents, the Vietnamese air force captain, the Vietnamese astronaut, the two Vietnamese brothers—earned the trust of people every day and built their lives on their relationships. A Vietnamese high school student won first place in a haiku competition out of sixteen thousand contestants and he was flown to Texas to be presented with a monetary award. But he knew about haikus because he studied hard. He shunned foolish choices. He earned the trust and confidence of his teachers and proved to them that he was capable and worthy. In other words, he built a lot of bridges that he then walked over. The moment you leave your seat and get up and leave my office and go back to your dorm, you'll have choices, too. A number of Vietnamese have graduated from the police academy in San Jose and the new chief of police is a Mexican American. They all built bridges. All of them are charged with protecting the community and many people will look up to them. They'll wield authority. *Build*, Tien. Choose wisely. Seize your opportunities." I handed him a looseleaf binder and told him to open it to the first page. "What does it say?"

" 'The Past is Forgiven. The Present is Improved. The Future is Perfect.' "

"What does that mean?"

"That maybe I too could go to the Air Force Academy and meet the president of the United States?"

"Not if you continue to do the foolish things you're doing now. Tien, you're wearing the clothing of a gangster. Why is that?"

Tien's hand flew involuntarily to his oversize leather jacket and then into the pocket of his baggy pants.

"Tien, do you carry a weapon? Do you own a gun?"

Tien looked at me evenly. "I own a gun. I do because everybody else does. Every Vietnamese I know either carries a gun or owns one and keeps it someplace. Even the middle school kids. You're a fool if you don't have a gun. You tell me not to, but you don't live out there." Tien gestured with his arm out the window.

"Do you carry it?"

"It's buried in my grandmother's yard."

"Tien, think. Do your friends know you have a gun?"

"Some do."

"If your friend who doesn't have a gun knows that you have a gun, he'll think of some way to use your gun. Someday he'll ask you if he can borrow it. Most likely you'll say yes. That will make you accessory to any crime he commits. You're not safe. If someone dies because of your gun you'll be sent to the YA."

"I fear the YA. I fear the black demons in the YA."

"That's stupid, Tien. The blacks are not demons and neither are the whites. The demon is inside *you*. Do you fear death, Tien?"

The boy shrugged and looked at me. How many times I have seen this look! The look that says, "I fear the YA more than I fear death." Tien has seen friends murdered. He has seen blood and gore. He lives in an environment of killing and blood and does not seem to be affected by it. Nevertheless, reasoning about his future moves him. He has heard stories about the YA and these chill him. But he will be loyal to his gang brothers to his death and that loyalty seems to mitigate whatever horror he might feel about death. Tien came into the Ranch the first time wearing a camouflage fatigue jacket. On the back of the jacket were the words *"chet vinh hon song nhuc"* (death before dishonor).

Tien ended up at the Ranch a third time, this time for selling PCP to an undercover agent.

"Tien, you broke your promise."

"I did not." He looked at me indignantly. "I promised you I wouldn't smoke crack. I was selling PCP. I didn't make any promises about PCP. I'm running out of time," he added angrily. "I waste time here because I can't do anything."

"Time? Listen carefully to what I have to say about time, Tien. One day as I was taking a young ward to the children's shelter, he said, 'Mr. Dee, you're driving too slow and I'm tired.' 'Let me drive on the sidewalk to get around all the traffic,' I said. 'Oh, no, I'd get killed,' he replied. Then I said, 'Let me drive on the top of all the other cars and we'll get there faster,' and the boy said, 'No, no!' In other words, I was trying to suggest all the reasons why we couldn't go fast and to let him know that we had no choice. In other words, that things take time. Can you move the hand of my wristwatch, Tien?"

"Of course."

"But you can't move the sun down, can you?"

"No, I can't."

"So you see that time follows its own course. You said you can't do anything. When you wait for your sweetheart do you feel like you wait too long?"

Tien laughed. "Forever!"

"And when you have fun, you see time going fast? You do. Thus, time, fast or slow, is in your mind. Here at the Ranch the time may go slowly—one hour seems like six, right? It's your mind. You have two kinds of time: real time and subjective time. You are here and you must cope with that fact—with the reality of that time—and that's why you think about escape. Do you think about escape, Tien?"

"All the time." He smiled.

"Follow the Ranch schedule and you won't feel impatience. Forget about the time and do what you should and you'll be like the butterfly. You're confined at the Ranch like the butterfly in its cocoon, but when you're released, you can be beautiful. Consider the time that you went to Juvenile Hall: don't you feel that it happened just yesterday? The time behind seems fast; the time ahead seems slow. So it's useless to be patient or impatient, to count every hour. Don't think about it. When you look behind you at the past, one hour is the same as ten hours. So try to be comfortable. Try to profit from your time here. Once, a man's barn burned down. In great distress he went out to assess the damage, but his friend pointed out, 'Look, now you can see the sea!' The point is, the friend plucked something positive from a bad situation. A few months from now you might feel that you'd like to stay longer in order to get the full benefits from the Ranch. Work at a new view of yourself. You can see the sea from here, Tien."

"I need money. You're saying I can make a new self, but I never have enough money to buy things. I'd like to buy a car. My friends who do bad things—they always have money." He looked wistful. "Lots of money."

"Then you need to study so that someday you'll be in a position to buy a car—any kind of car you want. Think of your time here as a means to get that car because the Ranch gives you many opportunities to learn. There are many benefits here, Tien. Every part of this place is a school and you can learn here if you take advantage of it.

There is a school in the kitchen if you study the chef; there is a school in the rec hall if you study the players; there is a school in every room if you watch the grounds people doing their carpentry, painting, and electrical work. Look at them and learn. Ask yourself, 'Is this something I might like doing?' Watch and then you'll be able to do, too. Then when you get out and ask for a job you can say, 'I can cook' or 'I can do carpentry.' They won't turn you away. They'll want to pay you for your skill. They'll give you money and you can save your money for your car. A long time ago in this country there was a black man who was a slave. He was a skilled carpenter and he was very, very good at what he did. Noboby could build things with his hands the way this man could. Well, the people in the local church—the rich white slaveowners—told this man that they wanted him to build pews for them. The slave said, 'I'll build pews for you only if you'll agree to let me sit in one of them every Sunday.' The slaveowners got together and discussed this and decided that they really wanted the pews and that they wanted this man to build them, so they assented to his demand. And do you know that every Sunday until his death the black slave sat in his pew in that all-white church? What does that tell you about skills, Tien?"

Tien pondered all of this for a long time.

"I also want to tell you about Nguyen Chi Thien. Thien was a poet."

"I don't care to hear about poets. I want to hear about fighting men."

"Thien knew all about fighting men. Thien was confined twenty-seven years in a communist jail in Vietnam. There was no paper, no pencil, no books in that hole. It was a lot worse than the Ranch! In winter it was cold as ice and in summer like a steam bath. Thien survived only because he used his time. He composed poems and memorized them all, day by day. Another man, Vo Dai Ton, a former ARVN colonel, a soldier just like your father, was captured by the communists in Laos and wrote ten thousand poems. He used his time fruitfully. He used it fully. Neither of these men used his time to think of escape because it was useless. They'd have been recaptured immediately. They couldn't run or hide. They would've been like water buffaloes among the cows—they'd have stood out. You would too, if you tried to escape."

"I don't want to be a poet."

"But you want to own a car. You want to get a job. And in order to do both, you need to learn. So your job is to keep your mind open. Like a good soldier, be on the alert to your surroundings at all times. Ask yourself, 'What can I learn from this particular man, or this particular situation?' Play your role fully. You are at the Ranch for a short time, so follow instructions, do your work, spend your time well, and you'll get out on the prescribed day—and you'll be that much better prepared for school and to hunt for a job. If you change your attitude you may even get out earlier. Tien, what's that you have on your wrist and fingers? You didn't bear those marks the first time you were here."

Tien slipped his hand into his pocket.

"Don't hide it. It's a tattoo. It's the tattoo of the Born To Kill gang, isn't it?"

Tien nodded his head.

"Is that why you were born, Tien? To kill?"

Tien shook his head.

"And the burns on your other wrist. Show them to me, Tien."

Tien sighed. He pulled his tattooed hand from his pocket and lay the other one across my desk. I pushed back the sleeve and touched the five ugly burns with my finger.

"Tell me what these mean, Tien."

Tien looked at the floor. He looked at the floor a long time.

"If you won't tell me what they mean I will tell you." Tien was silent.

I did not remove my finger from the five cigarette burns arranged in a dice pattern on Tien's wrist. "These five-dot burns signify that you are willing to participate in criminal activities. Are you, Tien? Are you willing to participate in criminal activities?"

Tien did not look up at me. Nor did he remove his wrist from my desk. "Tien, I'll tell you what these five dots mean. They stand for 'Tien' [money], 'Tinh' [sex], 'Thuoc' [drugs], 'Toi' [crime], and 'Tu' [jail]."

"They do not. They stand for—"

"Don't lie to me, Tien. You are about to tell me that they stand for *Tuoi Tre Thieu Tinh Thuong*—Youth Needs Love. I know better, Tien. And you know that I know."

The boy removed his wrist from my desk.

Months later Tien was back in the Juvenile Hall. This time the charge was auto theft. Once again Tien came and sat in my office. I warned him that the next time he was likely to be sent up to YA. His eyes widened. "I don't want to go *there!*" he said quietly. It amazed me that in spite of his missing teeth and the scar on his cheek Tien looked almost cherubic.

"So this time you stole a car."

"They put me up to it."

" 'They'? Who's 'they'? You participated. You bear the responsibility."

"I bear the responsibility for this, too," Tien said, amused. He held up my pen. "I lifted it," he said to me giggling, "right from under your nose." He returned the pen to its holder.

"You're very good at what you do, Tien. You have a real skill. But it isn't going to get you anywhere but in trouble. You have an inborn, natural ability but of late you've been using your skill for ill. You can steal a car or break open a safe, but this will cost you an opportunity to go to school and to work. There are any number of ways in which you could use this talent for good. You could work for security in a giant corporation, design sophisticated equipment, even work for the CIA—any of these are positive things that you could do with your skill. Do you know that in 1947, during the war against the French in Vietnam, the Viet Minh used a twelve-year-old boy to sniff out the French soldiers? This boy had the most incredible nose. From a great distance he could smell the odors of the French—their sweat and their cooking odors—when nobody else could. You should mimic that boy. You have a skill. You need to find people who can use it. But you don't know 'The Way' yet. Maybe someday you will learn. I hope so."

" 'The Way'? What is 'The Way'?"

"Let me recite you a poem," I replied, and I recited to him "The Way of Life," by the Chinese sage Laotzu:

A man is born gentle and weak.
At his death he is hard and stiff.
Green plants are tender and filled with sap.
At their death they are withered and dry.
Therefore, the stiff and unbending is the disciple of death.
The gentle and yielding is the disciple of life.
Thus, an army without flexibility never wins a battle.
A tree that is unbending is easily broken.
The hard and strong will fall.
The soft and weak will overcome.

"In every circumstance you need to evaluate what you should do," I went on. "Imagine that you see a pretty flower growing on top of a cliff and want to pick it. That is '*tinh*,' or desire. You want something—you have an emotion, a feeling. There is a reason for your wanting, a reason for your desire. In the case of the flower, you want to bring it inside and put it on your table."

"I want to give it to my sweetheart," Tien interrupted.

"Okay. You want to give it to your sweetheart," I went on. "Your reason, your motivation, is '*ly*.' But then you must consider timeliness, or '*thoi*.' In the case of the flower the time is now because it's in bloom. Now is the moment to pick it. Then, lastly, you need a way, or '*the*,' a means to get the flower. You climb up the hill to pick it, or you get a ladder if it's growing high on a wall, or you use shears if it's thick and stalky. Then you might need a basket in which to put it. That too is part of the way. Do you understand so far?"

"I understand."

"Now. Consider yourself and the car you stole. You wanted the car. Did you have the right to take it?"

He did not answer.

"Was it the right time? You need not answer, Tien; I know that you know the answers to my questions. Obviously it was not the right time. You waited until nightfall when you couldn't be seen. Then you helped yourself to that car—the owner didn't invite you to take

it. You didn't have 'The Way,' either. You didn't have the car key or
his permission to get into the car. 'The Way' was illegal. And you got
caught."

"This time I will kick back [retire from criminal activities], Uncle
Dee."

"Tien, your eyes tell me you're still young. You can still bend.
But you may not always be able to do so. If you continue to do what
you are doing your eyes will become the eyes of an old man. You'll
become stiff and inflexible. Tien, listen to me. When you were arrested this time you behaved like a madman. You attacked the arresting officer, the undercover agent. And the night you were brought
in you had to be restrained."

"That boy taunted me. Rafael, he called me a gook, a Viet Cong
gook."

"So? You don't need to be angry. When someone says something
that makes you angry, just consider it a dog barking at the moon.
That boy angered you, but you played into his hands. If after a few
times he can't set you up, he'll go away. 'A kite rises against the wind,'
Tien. If your character is strong, when you're provoked you'll rise
above the provocation. Think of yourself as being like a piece of
iron."

"Iron. I like that. I like to think of myself as being strong as a
bullet."

"You're not as strong as a bullet, Tien! Touch your cheek. Which
was stronger? Your cheek or the bullet?"

Tien's cheek flamed. Where the bullet passed through, Tien's
skin looked raw and angry. He touched it.

"Think of yourself as being like a piece of iron," I repeated.
"The more you're in the fire, the better steel you become. Do you
understand?"

"I think so."

"Tell me what you think you understand."

"If they provoke me I must ignore them. When I ignore them I
become strong like steel."

"Exactly. You must be like the bamboo soaked in water. Soak
bamboo in water and it becomes incredibly strong; it lasts a long

time. The frogs will croak and they won't bother the bamboo. It lies there in the water. It's indifferent to any noise in the pond. Do you understand?"

"I think so."

"Then explain what you think you understand."

"That Rafael, he's a frog. But if I'm like the bamboo soaked in water I'm strong and his croaking won't bother me. I won't even hear it."

"Exactly. The next time Rafael croaks, what will you do?"

"Nothing. I won't even hear it."

"You'll walk away. Tien, tell me. Are you still with BTK [Born To Kill gang]?"

"I am."

"Then everything I'm telling you is for nothing. If you go back to the gang when you get out of here, everything you've learned will be so much straw blowing in the wind. You'll go nowhere with BTK except maybe to the YA or to your grave."

"I'm going nowhere now."

"But that isn't so, Tien. You're doing better at school. I see that you made an 'A' in your physical education class here."

"That's because of the Japanese teacher. I try to please the Japanese teacher.

"That's good, Tien, that's very, very good! Why do you try to please the Japanese teacher?"

"Because he's strong. He's as light on his feet as a lynx. I look at him and think, he's as strong as the strongest fighting man. I'd like to be like him."

"Is the Japanese teacher a fighting man?"

"He acts like one."

"Does he? And how does a fighting man act?"

Tien pondered.

"How does a fighting man act?" I repeated.

"He fights!"

"Have you ever seen your Japanese teacher fight?"

"No, but—"

"Then he's not a fighting man. Now think carefully, Tien. What is there about your Japanese teacher that makes you think he is a fighting man?"

"He moves like a commando. He thinks on his feet. He's quick with his tongue."

"In other words, he commands his body and it obeys, right? He's at home in his body, isn't he? You see in this man a kind of perfect self-discipline?"

"I watched a big tomcat leap to the top of a high wall at the edge of my grandmother's yard. It was so careless, you know? It did it without any effort at all. It sprang to the top of that wall; it *willed* itself to the top of that wall. Then it sat there and licked itself. It looked at me, blinked, and looked away. It could've cared less that I was impressed. I've thought about that cat a lot, Uncle Dee. It was—" Tien groped for words—"acrobatic. That's my gym teacher. He wears a white linen suit when he's not teaching gym and he looks—" Tien looked at me and shrugged.

"Elegant. You suggested he moves like a cat. So he's graceful. Precise. There is not a movement that's wasted in your Japanese physical education teacher."

"No," Tien smiled. "He looks *smooth*. Like he could leap over a garden wall without rumpling his white linen suit. He moves like a machine. Like the curl in an ocean wave."

"You're a poet, Tien."

He laughed.

"Before this Japanese teacher you stood in your physical education class and refused to do anything. You crossed your arms and said, 'This is stupid.' You even told me that you thought it was all stupid. Do you recall?"

"But like I said, now I'd like to be like him."

"That's fine, Tien, very fine. It's very good that you want to be like him, because Mr. A's thoughts strike like a snake. They're quick as the leap of a cat to a high wall. What did he say that impressed you?"

"He told me I had no honor, no self-pride."

"Surely you've heard that before."

"But he did these amazing leaps. Right in front of me; I've never seen a man move like that, except maybe in Kung Fu movies. And while he was doing this he had a look on his face that a lesser man wears when he's resting. When he was done he told a story about the Japanese people. It was a story of a youth who was so poor that he couldn't afford a sword. Well, this boy made a bamboo sword to carry around but his friends ridiculed him. 'That's only a toy sword!' they taunted, and that made the boy furious. So he killed himself with it. *That* is honor and self-pride. I liked that story very much, Uncle Dee."

"Does your Japanese teacher use drugs?"

"Never."

"But you use drugs and you said you'd like to be like him. What does that suggest to you, Tien?"

"That I should stop using drugs."

"Would your Japanese teacher carry a weapon?"

"He says that the best weapon is a powerful mind and that the man who is the emperor of his mind and body can rule a nation."

"Do you think he's right?"

"Anything that Mr. A. says is right."

"Do you remember 'Zero Defect,' Tien?"

"You told me about it the first time. Yes, I remember. It's there, on your wall." He pointed to the words ZERO DEFECT in big block letters on the wall behind me. "You told me that Japanese manufacturers have a policy of zero defect. It means that whatever they make they make of excellent quality, free of any imperfections or errors."

"You got an IR [Incident Report] last night, Tien. You used inappropriate language to one of the staff members and now you're going to suffer the consequences—you'll be here longer. That was an error, a defect in your behavior. Tien, you've got to be wiser. You've got to discipline your body and your mind to be peaceful."

Tien tapped his forehead. " '*Hien hoa*.' I remember what you said about that, too. '*Hien hoa*' means to be wise and harmonious or peaceful and harmonious. And I remember that you also said that 'Trouble comes out from the mouth; illness comes in through the mouth.' Mr. A. told me I should act like a heavy-duty shock absorber and not like a brick wall."

"You need to practice willpower, Tien, or what the Vietnamese call '*Nhin*.' '*Nhin*' means restraint. You need to be cool. If, like your Japanese teacher, you exercise your body, it will be that much easier for you to exercise your mind and to restrain yourself. Let me tell you about Mark Wellman. He was a paraplegic and at age thirty-seven he climbed to the top of Half Dome at Yosemite National Park." I pointed to the photograph taped to my window. "It took him thirteen days, and during that time Wellman had to face ice storms, fatigue, and loose rock. Today he is famous—a paraplegic climber. What did that take, Tien?"

"Willpower."

"Willpower and physical strength. What will it take for you to keep your mouth shut when you feel like cursing a staff member, Tien?"

"An ice storm, Uncle Dee." The boy laughed at his joke. "Mr. A. told me that John Major was a high school dropout and a common laborer but that he went on to rule Britain."

"He is the prime minister. Tien, have you ever heard of Colin Powell?"

"Yes. He's an American general and he's black."

"General Colin Powell is chairman of the Joint Chiefs of Staff, Tien. He is among the highest ranking soldiers in the land. Do you know who his boss is?"

"Who?"

"The president of the United States. Colin Powell was born in a ghetto, Tien. He was born in poverty. He went to a frightening school in a run-down, frightening place called the Bronx, in New York, and do you know that one time not long ago he went back to his alma mater—"

"What's an alma mater?"

"The school from which a person graduates. He went back to his high school and spoke to the students there, most of whom are as underprivileged as he once was, and told them, 'You can make it. If I can make it, you can too,' and they cheered him. You can make it, Tien."

"I wouldn't mind being a general."

"Then whenever there is trouble, play deaf, play blind, play dumb. The greatest victory you can ever have will be the victory you win over yourself. He who angers you conquers you. You're not the sort of young man who likes being conquered, so why do you allow it? And you don't have to be an older person to be a hero. You can act the part now. Did I ever tell you about the Trung sisters and how they fought the Chinese?"

Tien leaned forward and rested his chin in his hands on my desk. He loved hearing stories about brave military deeds, and his behavior was always childlike as he listened.

"Between 39 and 40 A.D. the Vietnamese people kicked the Chinese out, and do you know who led the people? Two women. Two young women warriors. The Chinese were chasing them and the only way the women could avoid falling into their hands was to hurl themselves into the river. Although the Chinese reoccupied the country for a thousand years after that, the Trung sisters became heroines. All Vietnamese schoolchildren know about the Trung sisters. They were vigilant and fierce. You need to be vigilant and fierce, Tien. And you're not being so now."

"But I am! I'm practicing to be like Mr. A!"

"You're not. You're a member of the Born To Kill gang and you're going to get killed. That's not vigilance. It's stupidity. You've fallen into a trap, Tien, and a young man who says he wishes to be like Mr. A., who's a man of great prowess and wit, must be wise to traps. You're being used, Tien. Exploited by your gang leader. Military leaders don't exploit their soldiers. They deploy them wisely to benefit the nation. When he is in the field General Colin Powell places his men in battle formation. Why does he do so, Tien?"

"To win!"

"And why does he want to win?"

"To save his country."

"Of course. But listen hard, Tien. He uses his men strategically. That means he tries to obtain a victory on the battlefield, but he does *not* do so in total disregard of his men. He uses them to win but he doesn't use them carelessly or recklessly. He would never, never abandon his men on the field of battle. He loves his men. Fiercely.

He does everything that's in his power to protect as many of them as he can and he grieves for every one who's killed or wounded. Now Tien, I want you to think hard. Think about your Big Brother. What's his name?"

"Cuong Ly."

"Does he love you?"

"He gives me things. He gave me a Rolex watch and a leather jacket."

"So? It's very easy to give away things that cost one nothing. Tien, the night you were caught, where was Cuong Ly?"

Tien shrugged.

"That's right, you don't know because by his own prearranged plan Cuong Ly was not anywhere near the field of battle. You went into the fight alone. He sent you out to deal with the 'enemy'—do you understand what I mean by 'enemy'?"

"I understand. The enemy wasn't really my enemy. The 'enemy' was the person whose car I stole."

"Cuong Ly sent you out *alone* while he, Cuong Ly, was looking out only for himself. Am I correct?"

Sighing, Tien said, "Cuong Ly dropped us off and told us where to go with the car once we stole it. He told us where to meet him later that night."

"Cuong Ly is as wily as a fox, Tien. And tell me, when you were caught, the arresting officers asked you about Cuong Ly, didn't they?"

"They did."

"That's because they know all about Cuong Ly but they're never able to catch him at anything because boys like you take all the blame upon yourselves. There are never any consequences for Cuong Ly. There are always consequences for Tien. The police asked you if he was involved, didn't they? Of course they did. And what did you say?"

"I said I acted on my own."

"So you get sent to the Ranch and Cuong Ly is out there at this very moment in a coffee shop someplace enjoying himself. Do you think he's thinking about you right now, Tien? Do you think he worries for you? Frets over the fact that it's because of him and his ideas that you've been in the Ranch three times now? And if you're sent up to the YA, will he weep for you, Tien? Will he lose sleep over the fact that there are tigers in the YA who are ready to tear you to pieces simply because you are Vietnamese? What was Cuong Ly going to do with the stolen vehicle?"

"Use it to transport the white stuff up the coast."

"Cuong Ly makes an awful lot of money selling the white stuff, doesn't he?"

"I suppose so."

"You know so, Tien. And how much money do you see?"

"Enough for 'do' [drugs]."

" 'Do' puts you right back where you started from, Tien. The drugs are a trap just like the money and the girls are a trap. Cuong Ly gets you addicted to crack so that you become his slave, a built-in consumer. He wants you to use drugs regularly. Did you know that Cuong Ly was a drug dealer in Vietnam, too? He sold all kinds of drugs just to survive there and now he's doing the same thing here. Cuong Ly also tempts you with material things, but he's only using you for the big money he gains. Don't be a fool, Tien. It's because of him that you lost your teeth and it's because of him that you bear the scar of a bullet wound on your face. He abandoned you. He left you and the other boy to hide in a drainage ditch where the police dogs found you. He sped away. Cuong Ly always speeds away. He's smart. You're not. Who do you admire most, Tien: Cuong Ly or Mr. A?"

Tien sat back in his chair and looked out my window at the brown hills. I watched his face closely as he struggled with my question.

"Cuong Ly gave me the key to his house."

"But you pay him for that key. You give him some money every month for food and your room. He doesn't really 'give' you anything."

Tien shook his head as if to clear his mind of a jumble of thoughts.

"Think about money, Tien. When you want to use a drug it costs money. Cuong Ly knows that. At first he gave you money, no questions asked, but now he makes you earn it, every nickel, and you earn it by doing all of the things that he won't risk himself. Then he rewards you with things that you think you want."

"But I *do* want them," Tien objected. "I don't just *think* I want them."

"Tien, what do you want more: do you want the things with which Cuong Ly rewards you or do you want to be like Mr. A.? Do you understand that you can't have both?"

"I understand."

"Mr. A. carries himself like a man of honor. Cuong Ly does not. Keep that in mind, Tien. Think about all that we've talked about today and ask yourself, 'Will I become a man like Mr. A. or a man like Cuong Ly?' I want an answer, Tien."

"I need to think about it, Uncle Dee. You've asked me a very big question."

"Indeed I have. Remember, I want an answer. And Tien, before you go I want you to promise me that this week when somebody barks at you, you'll ignore it. I want you to remember that 'avoiding the elephant's path is no humiliation.' "

Tien stood up to go. "Tien, I'm going to give you something and I want you to carry it with you. It will help you to remember some of the things we've talked about together." I handed him the little business card. Inscribed over a pale green line drawing of a kite rising against a whirling wind were the words

Hoc   Doc
Tap   Nhin
Tin

"What do these words mean, Tien?"

"*Hoc* means studying, *doc* means reading, *tap* means physical exercise, and *nhin* means be cool."

"Repeat them."

"*Hoc, doc, tap, nhin.*"

"While you're considering my big question, think of these words, Tien. And remember about trustworthiness. Remember *tin*."

"*Tin* is my ticket to the Air Force Academy."

"Study, read, assume control of your body like your Japanese phys-ed teacher and be cool."

"Cool as a fighter pilot."

"Prove yourself trustworthy and the United States Air Force will entrust you with its jets, Tien."

In our next session Tien told me that he had given a great deal of thought to my question and that he wished to be like Mr. A. When I asked him why, he said it was "because Mr. A. is like a warrior." I told Tien that he must be like a warrior, too, and that the word "warrior" refers not only to a person who engages in warfare but to a person who is struggling with some inner conflict as well. "Does the warrior care for his body? Does he care for his mind?" I asked Tien. To each of these questions he responded, "Of course!" When I asked him why the warrior cared for his mind and his body, he said that it was the only way he could fight well on the battlefield. "You're on a battlefield as well, Tien," I said to him, "and the only way you can fight it is to get out of your gang, to stay away from drugs, and to turn in your gun. And then you must hone your mind by studying hard at school."

Tien did all these things. He walked out of the Ranch more than eighteen months ago and has not been back since. He is doing excellent work at school. Recently I spoke to his grandmother, who reported that Tien will soon be applying for college. "My grandson wants to teach physical education," she said. She showed me a letter he left for her on the kitchen table as he left for school:

Dear Grandmother,

The way I [felt] about you is regretful because no one is better than you. Before I never listen to what you say because I think I didn't need you. But [now] I have a feeling of regret and anger at why I didn't listen to you. Now we are starting to be a family again. . . .

Chau,
Tien

In front of his mother and father Hy Tran put a gun to his brother's head and demanded two hundred dollars "in cash and right now." The boy's father was able to talk him into putting the weapon down, but because of this incident the judge sent Hy Tran to the Ranch on assault charges.

Hy Tran's parents were on welfare. Having come from a tiny hamlet southwest of Saigon, they had no skills. They had been a farm family living in a village that looked like any small village in the provinces; it could have been the setting for the village that American soldiers set fire to in the film *Platoon*. They grew rice and corn and manioc, used water buffalo to work the paddies, and kept pigs and chickens.

The father, Ha Tran, had fought as a soldier for the Republic and had risen through the ranks to become an officer. He had fought in a lot of different places in Vietnam, had sat on the bench behind door gunners in the big American choppers, and had seen the damage to the imperial buildings in Hue after the heavy fighting in the Citadel. But he was as ignorant as anyone could be about what life would be like in the United States. He had come for "freedom" and to educate his children.

Sent to the United States under the Humanitarian Operation program, he related to me what the communist bureaucrats had told them. " 'In the United States the government will give you two keys. One key will be for your new car and one will be for your new house. The government will pay you retroactively from 1975 to the present, so you need not worry about a job for a long, long time because it will pay you well.' " Ha Tran told how he had repeatedly bribed bureaucratic officials to put his file on top so he could be among those who would get to the United States early. When they informed him that he was finally scheduled to depart, Ha Tran said an official told him that

> after we landed at Bangkok airport we would be "greeted with full military honors" and then we would be "driven to a first-class international hotel." But at the airport Thai officials boarded us on buses and gave us straw futons on which to sleep. We were sent to the camps and told to sleep on the floor. I protested. "What about our military honors? What about the luxury hotel?" The official who

processed me asked me where I got such crazy ideas and I told him. He laughed and said it was "all lies." But I looked forward to the future. I still expected a car and a house. In the U.S. my friends laughed. We got eighteen months of general assistance and then we were on our own.

When Hy Tran came to sit in my office for the first time he said little. I passed him an article about a young Vietnamese boy who was killed in a drive-by shooting and he said he couldn't read a word of English. Then I gave him a similar piece written in Vietnamese; he said he couldn't read a word of Vietnamese either. I noticed, however, that he was avidly scanning the material posted on my walls.

Hy Tran was very short, a tiny boy of thirteen who looked like he was ten or eleven. He was a chronic runaway. The second time he came to see me he came of his own accord and proceeded to chatter away about his sex life with girls who were several years older than he. It was clear he had a sexual life, although I doubted his talk about these older women. He also announced, "I am against everything. Do you hear me? E-v-e-r-y-t-h-i-n-g," he spelled out.

When he came to me a third time he sat down and immediately blurted out, "My parents treat my older brother better than they treat me. When I asked my father for money he gave my brother two hundred dollars and me ten dollars."

"Is this the reason you ran away?" I asked.

"Yes. I think about this matter all the time."

"What are you going to do?"

"I'm going to kill them."

The boy said this in such a cold-blooded, calculating way that I took it seriously. He was bitter, very bitter, and frustrated. I drew a series of six concentric circles and wrote "Hy Tran" in the center ring. "Hy, tell me who is closest to you."

"My friends."

"Who are your friends?"

"My friends are my homies in the Asians Kicking Asses."

"Has this always been so?"

"Before this money thing my brother was closest to me. And my parents."

I wrote "Asians Kicking Asses" in the first ring, immediately out-side of Hy's name, and asked, "Where do I put your parents in these rings? These are relationship circles and indicate the people who are most important to you."

"Nowhere. They have no relationship to me." He said this with great resentment.

"How shall we fill in the rest of these rings? Besides the Asians Kicking Asses who is important in your life?"

"My girlfriends."

"Okay, so you have gang brothers and girlfriends. That tells me you're a most unfortunate boy."

He sat quietly while I spoke to him this way. I drew another set of relationship circles and wrote "Hy Tran" in the center ring. In the second circle I wrote "parents," in the third "siblings," in the fourth "relatives," in the fifth "friends," in the sixth "acquaintances."

"There is a natural order to things, Hy Tran. Just as the sun rises and sets and the seasons wheel around, there is a natural way in which children relate to the people around them and there is an unnatural way. One way makes for great happiness. The other—the unnatural way—makes for misery. You're miserable, Hy, in spite of your friends in the Asians Kicking Asses. Am I right?"

He looked at me, the anger in his face turning into sadness, and nodded.

"Your way is unnatural and it can only make you unhappy."

"My father's way is unnatural, too. He makes me miserable. All he does is scream and yell and curse me, and sometimes he hits me. And he's so moody! One day he's up and the next day he's down. Sometimes he spends the whole day walking from window to window and staring at the street as if he were locked in a cage. He's jumpy. He makes all of us jumpy, especially my mother."

"Let me tell you about your father, Hy. You think he doesn't understand you, but you don't understand him, either."

"He's impossible for me to understand. He's—" he groped for words. "He's angry, all the time angry, and when he's not angry with me he's angry with my mother who does nothing."

"What do you mean, she does nothing?"

"She does nothing to deserve his anger and yet he swears and yells and curses at her, too."

"That makes you angry?"

"It makes me want to get my gun and kill him."

"It sounds to me like you love your mother. Does she belong in your relationship circles?"

He shrugged. "She went along with the money thing. She didn't say anything when my father gave my brother the two hundred dollars and me only ten dollars."

"We'll have to talk about that too, Hy. Let me help you to understand what's going on with your father, first. Your father was a powerful man in Vietnam. In that country men have great authority. Nobody questions you if you're a man—certainly not your wife and never your children. This was the way he thought and was brought up. Everybody thought that way in Vietnam. It's hard for you to imagine it. Are you smart?"

"I'm smart. Yes, I'm very smart." Hy squared his shoulders and sat a little taller in the chair. I noticed that his feet didn't even touch the floor.

"Then you can imagine the things I'm telling you. Only a smart boy can imagine the things I am about to tell; only a smart boy can actually picture them in his mind."

"Well, I can imagine them. Just keep on talking."

"Not only did your father have authority because he was a man, he was a soldier also."

"My father was a *soldier?*" Hy Tran was astounded. Obviously the boy's father had never told him.

"He was a freedom fighter. Your father fought the communists in Vietnam."

"Did he carry a gun?"

"Don't all soldiers carry weapons? Your father used his rifle in an effort to free his country of people who were doing harm to it and to protect the people he cared about. He fought for your mother. For your relatives who are still in Vietnam. For his own mother and father—your grandparents whom you've never met.

Your father was an officer and a good one. Ask him about his wounds."

"My father was wounded?"

"Ask him! He fought many battles. Let me tell you more about your father. The war ended and the communists won, in spite of the sacrifices of your father and countless others like him. Your father left the country, a country for which he bled and for which many of his friends and comrades had died. But leaving cost him. In Vietnam he was proud because he had the respect of his family and his village; in this country he doesn't have the respect of anyone and so he's no longer proud. Even you don't respect him and you're his son. This is a terrible, terrible thing, Hy, to be a father and to see no respect in your son's eyes. More important—try very hard to understand what I'm about to tell you, Hy—in this country he doesn't respect himself. You're angry and sad, Hy, but your father is even more so. He's angry because he's still young and he has energy and he's willing to work as hard as he fought when he was a soldier, but he has no good work to do. And why does he have no good work to do? Because he wasn't trained. He wasn't educated. Your father is no doubt a smart man but what he did in Vietnam he did using his wits. People can't survive here using only their wits. They need tools and skills and your father doesn't have the tools and skills to do the kind of work that people do here. So your mother works. She works in a restaurant in the evenings and as a beautician during the day and your father has to bear this. She puts food on the table and that shames him—it shames him that he, a man, can't work to support his family while his wife, your mother, does. And yet she makes only a pittance, so little that they continue to collect assistance from the state. This is humiliating. And this is why he broods, this is why he lashes out at you and at her. He wants to be looked up to and needed. You don't need him. Nobody needs him. It isn't anger he feels. It's shame."

Hy Tran put his face in his hands and rocked himself.

"Hy, listen to me, I have to tell you more." He looked up at me momentarily and then put his face in his hands again.

"I'm listening," he said as he rocked himself.

"Your father can walk away from your mother and your mother can walk away from your father. People divorce; husbands and wives don't stay together for always in this country. But your mother and your father can never walk away from you. *Giot mau dao, hon ao nuoc la*: 'A drop of blood means more than a pond of water.' *Mau chay, ruot mem*: 'When blood spills, the body hurts.' Your father would fight for you, Hy. He would no doubt die for you because you're his flesh and blood. But he sees your contempt and it wounds him."

"So why did he hurt me? Why did he love my brother more?"

"We don't know that he loved your brother more. What we *do* know is that your mother and father belong right here"—I tapped the first concentric ring with the eraser of my pencil where I'd written "parents." "They love you. You don't think they do but they do. Sometimes it's very hard for a father to show his love. Let me tell you a story about my own father. Years ago when I lived in Vietnam I had to go away for a long time; I had to leave the country. I was eager to return, and longed to see my father again. I thought a lot about the day I left: as we said good-bye in the airport in Saigon, many in my family embraced me, but not my father. That hurt me. How many times I thought about that, that my father didn't embrace me! When I returned, it was the very same thing. All my relatives welcomed my return and everyone embraced me—except for my father. Well, that night I looked out the window and saw a huge firecracker—what Americans call a Roman candle—burning in our front yard. It was the biggest firecracker I'd ever seen. Well, my father put it there to welcome me home. That was his way of showing me he loved me. Remember this story, Hy. You have to be alert. Your father has his own ways of showing that he loves you. Does your father drink?"

"Not much."

"Then you're a most fortunate son, Hy. Many men who've been through what your father has been through drink and gamble. Many soldiers who were just like him languished in refugee camps where they weren't permitted to do anything. So they drank and smoked marijuana."

"My father doesn't smoke. But I want to know right now why he gave my brother two hundred dollars and me only ten dollars. I want to know why he loves him more than me. Call him. Call him right now." He was clearly agitated.

"I'll call him soon and you and I will talk again."

It turned out that Hy Tran's parents had given the older boy two hundred dollars so that he could oversee the repair of the brakes on the family car—they knew almost no English and entrusted this to him. The cost of the brake repair was $140, and of what remained they gave Hy ten dollars. Neither parent had any idea that it was this that had disturbed Hy. The older boy had apparently led Hy to believe that he had been given the money and had been teasing him. As soon as Hy Tran knew the truth his resentment dissipated like smoke.

But other problems remained. Hy Tran was a member of the Asians Kicking Asses and he was failing in school. The parents came in to see me and I counseled them and Hy Tran together.

The parents had virtually no understanding of the way American schools operated. As far as they were concerned, you sent your children to school and the teacher took care of everything, including their conduct. They never dreamed that Hy was cutting classes (in part because the school had been lax in reporting his attendance to them). I spent a lot of time explaining to them that they had to supervise Hy closely, that to a large extent the quality of their children's education was up to them. "We didn't know," the father said simply, but beneath his reserve I sensed a profound resignation.

"Life here is a war in which I cannot shoot," he said matter-of-factly.

"But you can help your son," I replied, and I directed my attention to Hy while the parents listened. On a piece of paper I drew the following Chinese character and held it up for everyone to consider:

"This is a Chinese character, Hy. It is the symbol for 'person.' One of the 'legs' stands for wisdom. The other stands for knowledge. Put a head on it, Hy."

Hy drew a small circle on the character so that it looked like this:

"What does it look like now, Hy?"

"It looks like a man."

"Now it's a complete person. The complete person knows how to do and how to live. Right now you're in school, where you're being taught skills"—Hy sneaked a sidelong glance at his father—"so that someday you'll be able to land a good job. But most schools don't train you how to live. Making a living is one thing; living is another. In order to be successful you need to be able to do both. Making a living is a science; living well is an art. If you have just one, you're deformed. One-legged."

I covered the knowledge "leg" with my hand. "What happens if the person has no knowledge?"

"He can't walk."

"And no wisdom?"

"Same thing. He can't live."

"That's good, that's very good, Hy." His mother smiled at him. "In order to walk, in order to function and to achieve a successful, happy life, you need two legs—one of wisdom and one of knowledge. Now, consider these fruit trees:"

"Describe the first one."

"It's dead."

"It's dead because it was not cared for.

"Describe the second."

"It looks kind of scrawny."

"Maybe it didn't get enough water, perhaps not enough sunshine. And the third?" I asked.

"There's lots of fruit."

"I'll tell you what these trees stand for, Hy. They stand for you. You have to care for yourself if you don't want to dry up and die. First, you have to straighten your relationships out. You have to know that your mother and father come first and that you come first with them. Second, you need to give your tree plenty of sunshine, that is, you have to do your job in school. No more cutting classes, Hy, or your tree will bear tasteless, underdeveloped fruits. If you lack skills you won't get a good job and you'll pay for that your whole life. Third, you must study hard and develop your skills. Merely going to class won't be enough; you can't just go through the motions. You have to give your tree a boost with fertilizer. Do well in math and science, English and social studies, and your tree will bloom with beautiful white flowers, and then big shiny fruits will grow in great numbers. And you've got to get out of the Asians Kicking Asses, Hy. [His parents were shocked when, a few days prior to our meeting, I informed them by telephone that Hy was a member of a street gang.] No tree will grow in the street, Hy. That's a scientific fact."

Today Hy Tran is back home and has lost his bitterness. He goes out with his brother and not with the gang. His mother says he is respectful of his father.

"I want to learn how to live," a boy of thirteen said to me simply. "Show me which direction I should go," said another. A third said, "When I get out of here [the Ranch] all I want is to get into sports, maybe baseball or boxing. I want to be a kid. That's all I want." And a fourth remarked, "It's a lot more dangerous to be a teenager these days. You can't even fight without worrying whether the other guy has a gun."[2]

These are young offenders who hunger for adult understanding, for someone who will sit and listen without judging. And this is what I do. Day in and day out I sit and listen and teach them. Although each and every one of the wards to whom I devote attention is a unique individual, the problems of Vietnamese young people have a troublesome sameness about them. The following are extracts from letters written to me by my wards:

Duoc

My problem is I cant consintrate in school. I no understand my work, doing not enough homework, and fool around. I know I fool around. At school I dont ask for help and always cut school, doing bad thing with friends like smoking fighting destroying property. At home I dont listen to family, dont communicat with family, and its boreing at home. I dont like lecure [lectures] from brother or sister. With my frinds I do crime and go out alot and fight and party. I own guns and illeagal weapons. . . . I dont have self control and is always getting in trouble. I dont have much disapline.

Ho

I got bored at home, so I ran away and got arrested.

Tuan

My old friends . . . would get me into troubles.

Khanh

I am go the wrong way and dont go to school.

Nhan

The only problem I have at home is that my mom always make me stay home and dont let me outside so I have to sneak out.

Nam

I never went to school and was never home.

Son

I cut school because I want to *have fun*.

Anthony

I am angry. I am always getting into trouble. I don't know how to control my temper and my anger.

They come into my office and sit shyly, shifting in their chairs and tugging on their fingers. They are criminals—they have stolen cars, burglarized, and invaded homes in the middle of the night, terrorizing even toddlers at gunpoint. Some are addicts. But they are all such young boys! They are short of everything.

Sometimes the girlfriends of the wards are a positive influence. For example, Kim Oanh was an eleventh-grader in San Leandro. Her boyfriend, Tan Ho, dropped out of school and ran away from home. She sent word through gang members, begging him to come home. She waited but heard nothing. Her last effort was to try to reach him through poetry—to touch his heart:

> Day by day, I miss you.
> Night by night, I see you, too.
> Are you near, or far?
> Over here, I keep waiting, waiting, waiting.
> Away, away, you keep running.
> Where are you going, going, going?
> Please, please kick back!

Kim Oanh's efforts were successful. Tan Ho wrote back to her:

Mot Mau Nhu Xua: As Ever
> As long as the earth keeps revolving,
> And the heart keeps beating,
> Even as the colors of flowers fade
> We will someday meet again.

Later, he sent her this poem:

Le Song
> Night by night I miss my dear;
> Day by day, my eyes are watered with tears.
> In the sleepless night,
> Under the silver moonlight
> Looking up at the dark blue sky
> Nowhere can I see the shadow of my darling
> To help assuage my suffering.

The Supreme Being does not allow
Her to meet me.

Where in the world are you now, honey?
Only one person can bring meaning to my life
And to my countenance a happy smile:

Her!

Tan Ho was committed to the Ranch three times for auto theft. His parents were on welfare and worked for cash under the table whenever they could, so Tan Ho was left alone and unsupervised virtually all the time. A handsome, lean-faced, light-skinned boy, he was attractive to girls, and during our first counseling session he informed me that he had two sweethearts, one in San Leandro and the other in Hawaii. (I promptly told him it was unethical for him to be stringing two girlfriends along. Ultimately he ended the relationship with the girl in Hawaii.)

Kim Oanh wrote to Tan Ho:

Try your best at school in there. Don't worry too much about me. I can handle myself. I'm decided to wait for you. A year is not a short time but not a long time, either. . . . I don't fool around. Don't worry. I'll be happy to see you become a good and successful man.

Linh Le, an eleventh-grader in Fresno, wrote to her boyfriend, Khuong Luu, who was serving his term at a facility in San Mateo County:

Khuong, I want you to know that you may be the first and the last man I chose as my boyfriend, perhaps for life, too. I am always thinking about you and have a weird feeling about you. Lots of guys up here like me, and they don't live too far. But I don't like them. Instead, I only like you, even [though] there is a long distance between you and me. I can just feel that there will be a chance someday that we will be together.

On every weekend that he was permitted "outside," Khuong went to Fresno to see Linh. Apparently she took his interest seriously, because after Khuong returned to the Ranch, she followed up their time together with a letter:

> Let me tell you the truth. I never take my love of you lightly. I take it really seriously. Once I got what I wanted, I'll stick to it, but if what I wanted didn't come, I'll never give up that easy. I'll try very hard to go through whatever I could to get whatever I really wanted. . . . No love is more fervent than my love of you now. . . . A fervent love is a lasting love.

Ngoc Tram, a freshman at the University of California, urged her boyfriend, Phu Trinh, who was in a drug and alcohol treatment program at a county rehabilitation facility in northern California, to "kick back" and not grieve his parents:

> Now, you are no longer a young adolescent. So, see that you are not going to cause any more problems for our parents. Yes, as I think of you, I think of you frensiedly. I'm truly in love. Please accept this love and cherish it. Don't lose it, because I never give a second chance.

In another letter Ngoc Tram said she could not sleep:

> I am thinking about someone on vacation at the Ranch. And I bet you never would believe someone is in love with you seriously and passionately.

Taking advantage of his feeling for her, Ngoc Tram continued to give Phu Trinh advice:

> You know that I don't like it when you get drunk. My advice is that you drink a little less each time until you can stop drinking.

Nhu Nguyen, an eleventh-grader in Fremont, wrote to her boyfriend, Nghi Tran, who was doing time at a Contra Costa County Ranch:

> Nghi, I love you truly. I can't think of losing you, but right now I keep thinking we are always so close, but we manage to stay together. . . . Please promise you will never leave me. . . . You are very sick. I

think you should stop using drugs, it's very bad for you. It hurts
your lungs and I am just worry about you.

Tenth-grader Loc Dinh wrote to her boyfriend, who was serving
time at a Santa Clara County Ranch, and admonished him:

Try not to drink or smoke too much 'cuz it's bad for your health.
Also try not to get into trouble. If you want to be a good person,
you still can. You can change if you really want to. Nothing is stop-
ping you except you. Whatever you do, always remember: is it worth
it? If you do good deeds, then you will meet a good person. Don't
ever think just because you made a mistake that's the end of it. It's
ok if you shoot for the stars and miss. It's better than shoot for a
pile of shit and hit!! Always remember this saying. If you don't follow your dreams, how do you know what would've happened? You
only get one life, so make the best of it. Don't ruin it, especially with
drugs. That's not the answer. If you really want to find a true love,
who respects, cares and loves you, then you have to be good yourself. Do things that are right. Who cares what your other friends
are doing? Sorry for teaching you.

Loc Dinh tried very hard to turn her boyfriend around. She wrote
him every week. Whenever he was home on Outside Time she
sought him out, but he eluded her. Frustrated that he chose to spend
time with former gang friends, she wrote to a *Hoa Hao*, a Buddhist
teacher:

I know that you have a great wisdom within you. For me, I'm very
useless. I can't do anything that could satisfy people around me.
Sometimes I feel extremely depress[ed].

Once I have a person that I trust and we talk about everything.
Somehow I have no secret [to] keep from him. On the contrary, he
keeps many secrets from me. He doesn't want me to know and I
don't ask him (unfortunately). I know almost all of his secrets from
his sisters and my brother. They all don't want to tell me, but I pick
up during their conversation.

Master, there is one thing that I don't understand. As a child,
I always think that if you're nice to a person, there are no reason

for [him] to do something bad to you. I never try to do anything harm[ful] to any person, or seriously lie to them, or talk behind their back. But everyone I know always commit one of the above. The one that make me feel very betray[ed] is the one that I share most of my secret. He creates a big hole in my heart which could never be refilled.

I remember another boy, Kinh Tran. Kinh Tran was a member of the East Side Terminators (EST) gang and was at the Ranch for auto theft and possession of a stolen weapon. One day I found him crying on the lawn. I took him inside and asked him what the problem was.

"I miss my girlfriend," he said simply. "And if I can't see her I'm going to run away again."

I was able to arrange for Kinh's girlfriend to visit him every Sunday with his mother and sister. It helped his morale and he told me he would not run away anymore. His girlfriend also wrote to him twice a week, and she encouraged him to help his mother in the family's fish business and to consider going to college. Kinh's father came only once. They were an upper-middle-class family that came to the United States in the second wave, and the father was more inclined to socialize with his former ARVN buddies than to visit his son. But the boy's girlfriend was apparently meeting his emotional needs: they are now married, and Kinh Tran is preparing to enter the police academy.

Sometimes when my own efforts fail, girlfriends have turned my wards around. Sixteen-year-old Hugh Ha had run away from home and joined the Cambodians with Attitude gang. During our counseling sessions he never looked up from the floor, and when his mother asked him a question he would not answer her. Hugh was not a provocative kid, and he adopted a very passive posture. He went through the motions at the Ranch and was released on his due date, but I had little hope for him. He had been in for his involvement in a gang fight and I fully expected to see him again.

But then Hugh met a Chinese girl and, in his mother's words, "he was crazy about her." Every night she went to his house and they did homework together. On the weekends they went out. He told his mother, "I'm worried about my past. If she finds out, or her family finds out, she'll leave me." But the girl never found out and they became engaged. Hugh Ha's mother was very happy, but she told me that the girl's family was extremely conservative and wanted their daughter to marry a Chinese man, not a Vietnamese. Ultimately they went along with it, and today Hugh Ha and his wife are in college.

Some of the girlfriends of the wards are clearly not positive influences—they are as bewildered by life and as isolated from society as the boys. One ward wrote to his mother in Vietnam, describing his new life in California. He drew a disheartening picture of life in the Vietnamese community as he was experiencing it:

> Vietnamese people are all over. They gradually took over the houses and businesses in my area. Americans also moved. A lot of Vietnamese boys my age are in prison. Theft, murder, smuggling, everything. A great number of them run away (*di bui doi*). Girls of 15 or 16 are running away after the boys. It is very hard to find a good [Vietnamese] girl over here.

Often the correspondence between boys and girls reveals that they have become sexually active at very young ages, as young as twelve. As I mentioned in chapter 1, traditional Vietnamese are extremely conservative with respect to sexual morality. In the United States a depressing number of Vietnamese children appear to have no sexual standards and feel little responsibility to the children that come along as a result of their liaisons. The following rambling letters, written by a girl to her boyfriend at a Ranch, reveal someone who is obviously wrestling with a host of sexual and social demons. Note that the girl's slide began the moment that a boy gave her "stuff." She has subsequently become a chronic runaway.

Letter 1

> I don't know about us kicking together cause I don't know what I'll think of myself. I mean you went with Trang. That's your type. If we go out, we aint going to have a good communication going on.

Do you understand? Maybe not. But, whatever. My sis is trying to set me and some [guy] together. She wants me to find Love. Fuck that Eh. . . . It aint worth breaking mine or someone else's heart. I remember the nights we kicked it together. It was fresh huh. I really don't know about really know about this shit. Each time I think about it it gives me a headache. I don't know. Draw me something. I can't still believe that you had a kid. Damn. Aren't you sad? Okay sorry cuzz. Baby, I won't remind you. I was doing so good in school. Straight motherly A's. Then went out with this dick. I only did cause he gave me stuff. I don't know why. Ah well. I miss my gang life. Really. I want to go kick it with everyone. Give myself a name. I don't know why. But I like to walk somewhere and . . . someone knows me. like when I was in Santa Ana. Ask anyone down there during the time though. New fuck[s] are everywhere, so I don't know about now. Probably there was still people that didn't know me though. They're the loser. So, are you lonely? I went jogging in the rain today. Damn it felt good. There's this one dude that wanted me to go live with him. . . . And another mother that wants me to go to New York. Dumb fucks. Ah well. I'm innocent. Want a future. Then I own houses in those places. I'm afraid of living with guys. Cause then, what happens if one night that some dick makes me horny and I fuck him. That's why when those guys go to my sis house, I sleep alone. Keeping my pussy clean. . . . No matter what, I'm going to use CONDOMS. If you can't read it, it says condoms— scared yet Baby—should be. If we do fuck. You aint going to feel jack. But knowing you, you'll probably suck my tits. I know I'm sick.

The Ranch informs all wards that every letter that is sent out or that comes in will be screened. Staff members look for anything that is inappropriate or harmful, and I constantly remind my Vietnamese boys that all their correspondence will be read. This is part of Ranch efforts to prevent the wards from doing harm to themselves and to others. Some of the correspondence is obscene. When a letter comes from a girl to one of my wards that is inappropriate, I call the ward in and inform him that a girl wrote him an unacceptable letter. Sometimes I read parts of it to him and explain why it is inappropriate. Often this provides opportunities for instruction, even with a letter as shockingly sexual as the following:

Letter 2

> Eh, I just got paper. This is the second letter. Eh, I bet you I can get your dick up for at least 3 seconds. Ready, no, it be in this letter though. So, how's ya doing? How's it in there. I miss my sister. [name], can you imagine me and you naked together. Both of us in your bed. The big bed. I'm on top of you, grabbing your dick with my hands and sticking that wet shit up my pussy. Me moaning while sucking your nipple. You holding my hips while I ride you. What did I say. I told you I could get you wet. Yep yep. I told you so. . . . Eh Baby, do you want to get horny again. I thought so. Anyway, how's it in there so far. You know what, I don't want to get you wet cause you might rape some yellow nigger. . . .

I called in the boy to whom this letter was addressed and we talked about sex (a subject on which he felt he was a preeminent authority). Most of these children have a moral sense and they are aware of the Vietnamese tradition with respect to sexual morality. Most have sex only with Indochinese girls, although we are seeing more boys who have sexual relationships with young Hispanic girls. Many have come right out and said they know that indiscriminate sex is wrong and exploitative.

None fears AIDS. All have an attitude that it cannot happen to them and are convinced that the girls with whom they have sex are "clean." The AIDS virus has not made significant inroads in the Vietnamese community in the United States (there have been a few isolated cases), but there is evidence that it is spreading in Vietnam as a result of the influx of foreigners who are seeking to invest and trade there. It is only a matter of time before it strikes Vietnamese children in the United States.

When the wards leave the Ranch, they go back to girlfriends who are often equally lost and perplexed, overwhelmed by seemingly insurmountable problems and pressures. Boys and girls continue to seek happiness in sexual pleasure with any number of partners and work hard at "having fun." But many face problems so bewildering that they suffer far more than the usual adolescent "angst." For them, the fun goes out of life at a tender age.

Holly Huynh arrived in the United States in 1984 with her parents and two brothers. Her father had been a rank-and-file soldier. Within months after the family's arrival, her older brother, Dao, joined the East Side Terminators. Later Holly did, too. Dao spent time at the Ranch for hitting a rival gang member over the head with a baseball bat during a fight.

Holly and two friends confronted a Cambodian girl who, according to Holly, had insulted her. With a .357 Magnum in her hand, Holly threatened the girl verbally. As a result she was sent to a detention facility for girls. At this facility, Holly repeatedly got into fights with other wards. I asked her why. "Because this place bores me," she answered. "I have to figure out something to get into action." She ran away from home the very night she was released and was gone for weeks.

Dao got sufficiently straightened out to return to school, and when I convinced his father to quit smoking, Dao also quit. But meanwhile the younger brother had run away and was killed in San Francisco during a brawl with a Chinese gang. Distraught, the father came to see me. Holly had run away again, he told me, and this time she was pregnant. "My life is nothing without my children," he wept, and it grieved me to watch him. He had loved his son enough to quit smoking, but he was the most physically abusive father I ever counseled, and he seemed unable to control himself. "Look at this," Holly said to me one day, "look at what that man did to me." She pulled her sweater from her shoulder to reveal a laceration that had required stitches. "From a beer bottle," she said matter-of-factly. Before she ran away the first time Holly wrote the following letter to one of my wards:

> It has been raining for two days already. Usually I enjoy the rain, but today, the rain made me feel so lonely and cold. I would sit on my bed and look out my open window at the rain. Its really cold but somehow I don't seem to care anymore. I feel so sad right now.

Everything is pouring hard on me. There is so much to do and so little time to do it in. I look out the window hoping maybe the rain can relax me and comfort my worries and depression but it is as helpless as I am.

I cried alot today but I can't seem to know why. I'm so strange huh? I guess it really started a few weeks back when a friend told me that you flirted with her at fourth street. I wasn't really mad at that I was just pist-off that you left the party for that. Then to top it off, *someone* told me that you were messing with [another girl] the next day.

I started smoking when I was in 7th grade but I hated it so I quit but I guess I can't fight the craving anymore. The other day I got drunk with my friend and we [called] up the one guy that I knew because he was a very close friend of mine and he is the only guy that I trust. He is my friends boyfriend but I talk to him on the phone alot. That's why I called him. It was the only number that I remember then. So I called him up and told him all these secrets about [name] that I wasn't suppose to tell. Well I guess they're not secrets anymore huh? I knew what I was doing but I didn't know why. It was a terrible mistake because my close friend is mad at me. I shouldn't have drunk in the first place but it was the only thing that can make me feel better. Next to smoking though. The bad part is I'm hooked, but the good thing is I losted 2 pounds. I guess its because I haven't been eating lately either. I have been cutting classes too, but for no reason though. Me and my friend just kick back and smoke [marijuana]. Dumb thing huh?

Did you ever knew that I got in a fight with 4 mexican bitches in P.E. class. I don't know though. I guess I was crazy that day. She told me to give her the ball so I threw it and told her to fetch it. She dogged me so I asked her if she wanted to fight. She said right now so I punch her. I was on a roll until her friends came from behind, pulled my hair back and punch me in the stomach. Oh, only about a few thousand times. My friend knew that I was losing it so she jumped in and helped me. Fucken [name] was there to but the shit didn't even jump in. She held me back which even give those bitches better chances of hitting me. Well it all came out as a five day suspension for me and [my friend] and those girls didn't even have Saturday school. I cutted class ever since and failing most of my classes. Great life huh???

I went to "Call Me Dragon" two weeks ago with Thi and her stupid chinese boyfriend. God, it was so fun. I got to see them kiss, kiss and kiss and kiss. Exciting night huh? I was lonely that night. . . .

Another young girl wrote to her boyfriend in the Ranch that "it seems like we're living in two different worlds. You're in the dark, and I'm in the light." It is clear, though, that both inside the ranches and outside, many of these Vietnamese children feel "in the dark."

So do many of their parents.

I always involve (or try to involve) parents in my counseling efforts. All the counseling in the world has little or no effect unless parents are made to understand the pressures their children face and are willing to change some things in their own lives that are having a bad effect on the children. My experiences have made it clear that the vast majority of Vietnamese parents whose children end up at rehabilitation and detention facilities are unaware of the kinds of obstacles and pressures their kids face virtually every day. And because so many Vietnamese parents spend little time at home, they are partly to blame when their children get in trouble.

Tu Phong and his wife, Ba Le, arrived in the United States about six months ago, a little more than a year after they sent their four sons (who ranged in age from fifteen to twenty-five) ahead to live with Tu Phong's sister. By the time the couple arrived, the oldest boy had gotten an entry-level job as an assembler at an electronics plant and rented a house along with his nineteen-year-old brother. But the two younger boys had dropped out of school and joined the Big Time Killers. They were arrested for auto theft (the youngest was in possession of a sawed-off shotgun at the time of the arrest) and ended up in a rehabilitation facility. On the very day they were released they were involved in an extortion attempt at a Vietnamese restaurant (planned by Big Brother Binh, who was not arrested), and both were sent to the Ranch.

I asked the parents to visit me at the Ranch and saw immediately that the father was not going to cooperate. He avoided eye contact and laid all blame on his wife, which was absurd, since neither of them was in the country when their sons began their rapid downhill slide. I asked them both to participate in group counseling sessions with other parents and to come in so the two of them could work with their sons, but the father never came again. When the couple left, the mother thanked me. Tu Phong just walked out the door.

Ba Le persisted. Every Sunday afternoon her sister-in-law drove her to the Ranch, and waited patiently outside while Ba Le attended the sessions. As a result of the counseling sessions she came to understand the nature of the "gaps" her children faced—the language gap, the academic gap, the cultural gap, the generation gap. I stressed that she and her husband had to help their sons build bridges over those gaps. The generation gap was aggravated by the fact that neither parent could speak English, while the two younger sons had picked the language up with remarkable speed. "Speak *English!*" her youngest demanded the first time they sat together in my office, and his face flamed.

Ba Le was fierce in her determination to do what needed to be done, but her devotion was not enough: she needed Tu Phong's involvment as well. "I changed my hours at the beauty parlor in order to be home for my sons," she told me, "but when my boys come home and I tell them to study my husband doesn't support me. He hardly speaks to them, but the boys continue to look to him. They prefer to watch Kung Fu videos with him when they come home. I can't compete with Kung Fu."

When the youngest son was involved in another auto theft and was sent to the Ranch a third time the father left home. Ba Le has not seen him since and has decided to divorce him. "He had a furnace in his heart," she said to me. She went on:

> I tried to tell him what you said about physical punishment and terrible words—but when Song came in late, my husband threw a chair at him. Song spat at him and told him, "Go back to Vietnam, motherfucker. Go back where you belong." That was when my husband walked out. I had told him that we needed to sacrifice our

preferences for the good of our sons. I told him that he needed to make an effort to be with the boys as much as possible and that he must set aside his preferences for smoke and drink, but my husband, he is a very stubborn man. "No one tells me how to live under my own roof," he said, and he struck me several times in front of the boys.

Many parents do change their ways. The parents of a fourteen-year-old named De Tran owned an auto body shop and were doing quite well financially—they had a large, comfortable home and were respected in the Vietnamese community. Then one day they got a call from the police. De Tran was under arrest for carjacking.

The parents were stunned. "We saw no signs of this," the father told me. But they had seen no signs because they were almost never home. Often they even slept in a small apartment over their body shop. According to De Tran, sometimes he would not see his parents for days at a time. "They left me money to order out Chinese food and I'd cook some stuff for myself," he volunteered indifferently, "but I was lonesome. I started to go out with friends who were lonely like me. We looked out for each other." De Tran's friends were his gang brothers in Viet Crips.

Although De Tran's mother was rarely at home, she loved her roomy, well-furnished house and enjoyed driving her fancy car. But she also loved De Tran and understood that she was on the verge of losing him. She changed her ways immediately and made it a point always to be home for him. "De Tran was living two lives, one in front of us and one behind our backs," she said. She reported that De Tran's father takes time to do things with their son on Sundays and is teaching him body work at the shop. De Tran is responding. "I can always earn money later," she added. "Having lots of money means nothing if I lose my child." De Tran has not been in trouble since his release many months ago. During our final counseling session he said, "I want my family to treat me like a son that never got into trouble before."

Intensive counseling brings many of the wards to a place where they begin to comprehend, and regret, the heartbreak they have caused their parents. Some cry. "When I get out of here, I will go back to school and stay out of trouble," one ward told me tearfully. "I want to find a good job to help out my family. Especially I need to take care of my parents. Because of me, they take all the pain and patience waiting for me to get out of here. When I get out of here, I will go back to school and stay out of trouble because I really want to do something for my success myself and for my family."

I counseled a thirteen-year-old boy who had been in this country only nine months when he was involved in a home invasion that resulted in the death of the homeowner. During his detention he wrote me a rambling letter that was as full of contradictions as it was of good intentions:

> I want to change myself and want my both parents to get happy. When I get out . . . [I want to] go away with my brother to another place and start my life over with my brother. I really want to buy a house for my mom and dad, and take care of them, make them happy cause I owe them alot[.] I will be a good man when I grow up. And I'll take good care of myself. I am sure I won't repeat and will never make a mistake again. I will stay away from my old friends and I will become a good son to my parents. I will never go back the old way. I am able to know what is right, what is wrong. I know how to exercise self restraint. Knowing what is right, what is wrong helps me stay out of trouble. I just want to go home and be a good boy. I am a man now I'm not a little kid no more I have to take care for myself and my family. I know I don't like it much in lock-up in here but I'm very glad to be here. For me I dont really want anything. Just a peace life and a family myself and a little business. *I love my Parents.*

When this young man was about to be released he came to me to say good-bye. He said:

> I have changed into a good person. I feel very happy. I can do what I promise to do. After I finish my homework I will help my parents at their liquor store, not for the money but for the experience in case I ever want to start some kind of business. I am planning to

have a good future. You have taught me how to self-restrain myself. I'm very regret for doing my crime. That's why I did my best to get out.

Others do their best but may never get out.

Red Bear, the Amerasian who became a member of the Nortenos, a Hispanic gang, headed down a "one way street." In gangland, that means you can "jump in," but if you "jump out," it costs you your life. "Once you join the Nortenos," Red Bear told me, "you're either a life member or you're dead. Dead dead dead."

Despite this threat, Red Bear seems at peace with himself. He dreams of a new life and told me that his mother is willing to move away if that will help him. "But if I go to another area and there are Nortenos there they will kill me. So why run?"

But he looked wistful. "Perhaps you can take a look at my poetry?" Reaching into his pants pocket Tu Hoang (I always called him by his Vietnamese name rather than by his gang name) removed a well-worn piece of paper that had obviously been read many times. The paper was torn along the folds and I could barely read the words that were written in faded pencil:

A Gang Member in Jail Remembers His Loved Ones

Over here, I remember, every night
My peers over there: some in jail, some have died.
Remembering my old mother—I hold back my tears,
And my lover—I wait year after year.

Too Late

When I set foot in prison
Then I felt remorse.
When I loved that girl
I dared not confess.

Now I have repented,
Now I want to speak up.
It's already too late.
When I get out from jail,
When I meet her again,
I might not have a chance.

"I'll have no other choice than to join the homeboys."
—Phung kee-kee

Chapter 6
Last Chance Ranches

Recently I received a letter from a young inmate whom I spent many hours counseling:

Dear Uncle Dee,

I guess you must be surprised to receive this letter from me. Today, I feel so bored. So, I decided to write you a few lines. It's been over a year since I was sent here. I'll be released in about 18 months. To tell you the truth, it's very boring here. Recently I had a fight with a black inmate, and was thrown in a "hole" days and nights—24/24, you know [a 24-hour isolation cell], for several days. Only then, I remembered what you had taught us at the Ranch. Uncle Dee, all that you have taught us are true. But I only realized your invaluable lessons of wisdom through personal experience.

My concern is that when I get out of here, I will be over 18. And I don't know what to do. I am afraid, if I violate parole I will be sent back here. I am scared. Please, help me. I need your opinion and advice. After all, you are my godfather, right? Please write me as soon as you can.

So long,
Hoat Nguyen

Hoat Nguyen is a young man who, despite his criminal record, is full of resolve—he wants to make something of himself. In 1987 Hoat's parents sent him and his older brother to the United States from a hamlet some sixty-five miles south of Saigon. The parents dreamed that their sons would get good educations, find good jobs, make money, and send for them. But two days after they arrived, Hoat's older brother abandoned him. Having nowhere to go, Hoat joined the Viet-Ching gang and shortly thereafter was arrested for stealing stereos. He was sent to the Ranch. After his release he was arrested a second time for auto theft and sent to the Ranch again. When he was released he got involved in an armed robbery for which he was sentenced to serve three years and seven months at the California Youth Authority.

Hoat Nguyen is afraid. He is afraid because he does not know how to create a future for himself. When he is released, what kind of life awaits him? He is uneducated and unskilled, and he has no family to go home to, only the same friends with whom he got into trouble in the first place.

Hoat chose the wrong path and wants desperately to find the right one. But he does not "know what to do." Too often juveniles feel that they have no viable alternatives to criminal activity, so rates of recidivism (the tendency to relapse into criminal behavior) are high. Only 20 percent of the juveniles who walk through the doors of the C.Y.A. never come back. The vast majority do, like Phung kee-kee, the young Vietnamese author of this poem:

From the jail back to the street

I turned down a 2-year deal
To kick back [get on] with my life.
But the Court cheated me,
And gave me five!

Day and night I worried: no mail,
Ever since I landed in jail.
I feel lonely, as we live apart.
Still no words.

—My lover must have changed her heart.
Then, a peer wrote me: she has flown away.
In three years, if I have my day,
I will have no money, no place to lay a sheet.
I will wander at night in the dark streets
With my soul full of bitterness and sorrows.
But nobody knows . . .

So, I'll have no other choice
Than to join the homeboys.

Unless Hoat can find an alternative to the streets—unless he is provided with the opportunity to develop the skills he needs to do meaningful work and to associate with people who are not inclined to criminal activity—it is likely that, in spite of his resolve not to violate parole, he will "join the homeboys" and find himself back at the C.Y.A.[1]

"I am afraid," he says matter-of-factly, and with good reason. Approximately 80 percent of juvenile offenders who have served time in the C.Y.A. are returned to prison within two years of their release. All the rehabilitation in the world is unlikely to work unless Hoat can do something productive when he is released. There are many Indochinese youths like him and the odds are against all of them.

For most of the wards, the psychological effects of mistreatment are only intensified inside a facility. "I hate authority," one boy said. "My father, the guards, they're all the same." "Life was crazy at O.H. Close," a ward recalled, referring to one of many training schools that are part of California's corrections system. "They expected you to work on the problems that got you there, but your real problems are right there in front of you: the gangs, the sexual pressure, the violence."[2]

In a training school it does not take much to push emotionally disturbed youths over the edge. Some become suicidal simply because the detention centers are unbearably stressful. At the Youth Training School in Chino, suicidal youths are dealt with severely. Staff strip the child naked and make him sit in a tiny barred cell with no bunk, no toilet, and no sink. What are we to make of "treatment" like this? As one journalist observed:

> They still call the state agency that rules California's labyrinth of prisons the Department of *Corrections*. As if the purpose of prison were to return criminals to the straight and narrow path before handing them back to society. But burrow into the state's penal code and you'll find the real reason: "The purpose of imprisonment for crime is punishment."[3]

In contrast, the goal of staff at the Ranches and Conservation Camps is to reform juvenile criminals—children who have committed the crimes of arson, assault, robbery, rape, and even murder. The juvenile justice system is flooded with young people who are rapidly growing as violent as the adults who are locked up in state prisons, but there are alternatives for them. Ranches and Conservation Camps provide wards with an opportunity to do community service, to clean up parks and fight fires, and the wards appreciate it. "Here, they respect you," one boy said of Ben Lomond, a Conservation Camp. "The work is hard but they respect you. You don't learn responsibilities and how to handle life in the institutions. [The training school] was a bad, bad, bad place, and my attitude was mad and bad." In Santa Clara County, where I work, the Harold Holden Ranch and the adjacent William James Ranch represent the community's commitment to give these children one last chance.[4]

These "last chance ranches," as the juveniles refer to them, are extremely important, because California is notoriously tough on child offenders. The state locks children up at twice the nationwide rate; it has more juvenile offenders behind bars than any other state (three times the number currently being held in Texas and Illinois, and four times that in Pennsylvania); it detains the most violent children an average fourteen months longer than other states for the same crime; the number of detainees has increased by more than half in spite of a drop in the state's juvenile population; and since 1985 the number of wards has increased by 202 percent.[5]

However, the state does not seem to be gaining by locking more criminals away for longer periods—violent crime has increased dramatically. In 1992 in Santa Clara County for example, felony assault and child molestation were up 26 percent, rape was up 60 percent, arrests for arson tripled, and murder and attempted murder nearly doubled since 1991. In other words, despite the fact that the penal system is tougher than ever, California citizens are less safe than ever.[6]

The state's prison system is also failing the children. According to Jerome Miller, the founder of the National Center on Institutions and Alternatives in Washington, D.C., "a tremendous number of gang leaders are graduates of C.Y.A." A former director of juvenile corrections systems in Massachusetts, Illinois, and Pennsylvania, Miller argues that the system as it is now actually creates criminals: "It's a natural product of overuse of incarceration for kids. It gives leaders status and confirmation. It's like you're not anyone until you've done time." As one juvenile recalled, on the day he was committed to the C.Y.A. for a maximum of ten years, "at that moment of sentencing, I felt a strange sense of accomplishment that I was now making the 'Big Time.' "[7]

Social scientists, enlightened state officials, and many families of the wards are also convinced that the C.Y.A. turns youngsters into hard-core criminals. They believe that many of the wards "graduate" from California's detention facilities with experiences and attitudes that toughen them and dispose them to criminal activity. The testimony of the wards confirms this, as seen in the following story, narrated by a C.Y.A. inmate named Robert:

> I did my best to fit in with the other "wards." I soon became gang-related and started getting tattoos. . . . I went before the Parole Board to determine what institution I would go to and for how long. I was categorized a 6, with 1 being the worst and 7 being unsophisticated. I was then sent to the . . . Training School in Stockton for one year. I soon learned the new slang and how the Y.A. games work. I was determined to do my own thing, which only got me another 21 months . . . added to my original sentence.
>
> At 18 I became old enough for the infamous Preston School of Industry in Ione, Calif. I was slightly nervous on the ride to Preston,

but tension quickly turned to fear as I glimpsed my first sight of "The Castle" and the 70-foot guard towers. I was coming from "Disneyland" [the Karl Holton Training School] where security only used mace to break up the occasional fight. At Preston, all security guards are equipped with mace, billy clubs, Taser stun guns, and .37 riot gauges that shoot CN mace powder which can take out an area the size of a basketball court. There were two or three fights daily—along with the gang assaults and stabbings.

That was the scaredest I'd ever been in my life. There I was, barely 18, up there with inmates who were labeled the "worst of the worst." My first night in Preston was the beginning of my adult life. *I had to adapt to my new surroundings, so I did. I . . . spent the next year . . . becoming hard-core in order to fit in.*

[After being transferred to the new facility at "Chad"], I saw more violent incidents happen than I ever saw in my whole life. I'm talking endless eight-on-one group assaults, attacks with weapons, staff assaults. . . .

I was transferred to Ventura School to start my college education. Ventura is co-ed and the most sought-after institution among Youth Authority males. I was also the first person ever to go from the worst institution . . . [to] the very best institution. . . .

I arrived at Ventura School. . . . A few days later I was jumped by four . . . Hispanic wards because I [had] "SJ" tattooed on my arm. *That was the end of my positive thinking and goal setting.* [Emphases mine][8]

For the Vietnamese wards in the C.Y.A. the experience is virtually identical to that of Robert. In order to get through a day one has to "adapt to new surroundings" and one must become "hard-core" not just to "fit in" but to survive. As one adolescent put it:

When you get there, you go to your own race, and they run down what you have to do. . . . If someone disrespects you—bad-mouths you or your family or your city—you either fight or flee. Fighting gains you respect. If you run, you're a "lame" or a "lop" or a "leva." If you give in to pressure—and the older boys pressure you all the time—you're a pressure case, a "P.C." And if you're weak they could rape you.

One Vietnamese ward also reported the danger of being raped by other inmates:

> If you don't stand up for your self-respect, you risk being raped at night—all night, every night, not just by one inmate, but in some cases by two, or more. I'm referring to the homeboys up there. They could coerce you to do oral copulation or anal sex for hours til day breaks!

From one training center a Vietnamese boy named Diem wrote of his experiences:

> You can find all kind of people up here. The majority are Blacks. There are also Cambodians and Laotians. Asian guys stick together. Up here you got to join one gang or another, regardless. Either Crips or Bloods [or] X 3 for the Mexicans. *Instead of making you doing good, the jail forces you, against your will, to gang up.* [Emphasis mine][9]

Over and over Vietnamese inmates of the C.Y.A. have told me that one must fight or join a gang in order to establish a reputation and thereby avoid being raped or assaulted. A Vietnamese ward detained in the C.Y.A.'s Main Facility wrote to one of my wards at the Ranch:

> We are ready to jump into any fight. We don't take fright of nobody. That's the game here, at the C.Y.A. Do you know of any homeboy who has changed after he had walked out of here? Anyway, when you get out [of the Ranch] this time, just kick back or else you will end up in this hell. Tell Vo to watch his steps if he don't want to get locked up here. . . .
>
> You know . . . we are locked up for crimes and criminal violence. In this micro-world, in these cell worlds, violence erupts anytime, and for no real causes. . . . In here, we fight fight fight, all the time. We can't stand the Mexicans. If you don't hit them first, they hit you and dislodge a couple of your teeth. Therefore, in every fistfight, all the Vietnamese, Cambodians, Laotians and Hmongs jump in and

fight viciously. . . . I know that sooner or later you will end up in
this hell if you keep messing around.

These letters show clearly that conditions in the C.Y.A. compel juvenile inmates to behave violently, to "gang up" to make it through
a day.

The growth of gangs and the virulent racism that fuels them are
a fact of life at the C.Y.A., and both are aggravated by overcrowding.
Indeed, overcrowding is a primary reason that California's juvenile
justice system is not working. Approximately nine thousand juveniles
from age twelve to twenty-five are locked up in the California Youth
Authority. The state operates eleven vocational schools and six correctional or "reform" schools that are spread across the state from
El Centro, near the Mexican border, to the Washington Ridge Conservation Camp near the Oregon border. By 1996 these facilities will
hold ten thousand; they were designed to hold 6,700.[10]

The Chino Youth Training School, intended to house the most
incorrigible juveniles, was designed for 1,200 wards. Currently it
holds 2,100, giving it the dubious distinction of being the largest
facility for juvenile criminals in the country. As one journalist observed, the wards are "compacted like so much garbage."[11]

Overcrowding has turned the C.Y.A. into a veritable nightmare
of fights, hate crimes, and murders, in which juveniles gang up with
others of the same ethnic background. Robert recalls that it was com-
monplace for a ward to "just hit someone with a lock in a sock or
stab someone mercilessly 50-something times [so that they had to be]
flown out via Life-Flight Helicopter." At the overburdened training
schools fighting is even worse. Like adult prisons, they are gang-
lands, and the more wards, the more gang activity there will be. Staff
at Chino work around the clock to suppress gang activity, but even
at the Ranches gang fights are a constant threat. At the Holden
Ranch we eliminated the red belts of the uniform and the red and
blue of the cafeteria trays because red and blue are the colors of the
San Jose area's two rival gangs, the Bloods and the Crips.[12]

"We can control some of it, but the things we cannot control are
the hard looks and the flying hand signals," says John Cunningham,

former superintendent of the Holden Ranch. Staff simply cannot see everything. "It's a minimum-security facility and the standards were set in the 60s," Cunningham explains. "The population has changed dramatically, but we've still got the same staffing, one staff person for every twenty youths." A fourteen-year-old complained, "The staff can't watch us enough. People fight behind the handball court or behind the school. But the one thing you can't do here is snitch. You can have a bad time here, get spit on, pissed on or beat up. So nobody says anything."[13]

Despite these problems, the Ranches are facilities where counselors like me are helping wards to change their lives. They are California's final effort to reach its youngest criminals before they end up in state prisons. In bucolic settings, with swimming pools and no fences, the Ranches (and "Camps") have more in common with resorts than prisons. "I was expecting something with guard towers and barbed wire," said a seventeen-year-old boy who is serving one year at the James Ranch. At the Ranches, young persons have real opportunities. The are run like army camps, to provide discipline and structure often absent from these boys' lives. The Ranches also give the boys opportunities to study, work at meaningful tasks, and receive counseling. At the Holden facility a typical day runs like this:

6:30 A.M.:	Wake up, head count.
7:00 A.M.:	Breakfast, head count.
7:30 A.M.:	Boys return to dormitory to take care of personal needs; medication is dispensed if necessary.
8:00 A.M.:	English.
8:50 A.M.:	Social sciences, including history.
9:40 A.M.:	Math, one class regardless of academic level.
10:30 A.M.:	Remedial English for boys behind in reading skills.
11:20 A.M.:	Physical education or wood shop.
12:15 P.M.:	Classes file directly to cafeteria for lunch and another head count.
12:45 P.M.:	Boys back in dorm for personal needs; dispensing of medication if necessary.

1:15 P.M.:	Boys break up into afternoon schedules, which vary from day to day. Some might be assigned to ranch maintenance, which includes such chores as cleaning and weeding. Some boys go into individual or group counseling, typically for hour sessions on subjects including drugs and alcohol, sex abuse, and anger management.
3:30-4:30 P.M.:	General recreation, free time.
4:45 P.M.:	Boys file to dining hall for dinner, head count.
5:15 P.M.:	Boys return to dormitory for personal needs, including showers. Another head count.
6:30-8:30 P.M.:	Recreation, free time.
8:30 P.M.:	Boys return to the dorm; final medication dispensed, personal needs, get ready for bed.
9:30 P.M.:	Lights out, head count.
10:30 P.M.:	Last head count.[14]

"You can say the Ranch is like a hothouse," Holden superintendent John Cunningham told a reporter. "You can take a plant out of San Jose, nurture it and fertilize it with love and discipline for a few months, then we turn around and put that plant back into the same ground and expect it to bloom. Sometimes it does and sometimes it doesn't."[15]

For Luong Tre it did not.

Luong Tre was born of a black GI father and a Vietnamese street merchant in Ben Tre (Bamboo Dock), a city southwest of Saigon, and was named after his hometown. Since he was a black Amerasian and thin in stature, local people nicknamed him Tre Den—Black Bamboo. On the eve of the communist drive into Saigon, his father fled, leaving him and his mother behind. One year later his mother disappeared, leaving him with his grandmother. She sold him to a woman who used him as her fake son in order to get to the United States.

The "family" came to California where Tre Den's "parents" operated two small markets in Sunnyvale. After one year in a San Jose

middle school, Tre Den could not read English. His grades and behavior were poor. He dropped out, ran away, and joined the Black
Eagles. Living in a safe house and on the streets, he eventually decided the time was right for revenge. His homeboys had run out of
money. Tre Den led them to his "mother's" house.

Tre Den stood outside in the street to avoid being seen by her
and to act as a lookout. Four homeboys stormed into the dwelling
and forced her at gunpoint to surrender all her cash and valuables,
even the jewelry she wore on her wrists and fingers. Then they took
turns raping her. Tre Den's "mother" did not report the incident to
the police, although her rapists were familiar to her.

Tre Den found himself at the Harold Holden Ranch for Boys.
He "posed a threat to the community." Meanwhile, his "mother" left
town.

When he was released, Tre Den stole a car. He was sent back to
the Ranch, and then to a group home in Salinas. There he met a
white girl and fathered a child. But he missed the homeboys and his
life on the streets. Fleeing from his group home, he abandoned his
child and returned to the Bay Area to live with his gang brothers
once again. The Santa Anita Boyz hired him to make a big delivery
of cocaine to Northern California and the Bay Area, escorted by
members of the Wally Girlz so as not to look suspicious. He stole a
car to use for the delivery and made good money. On his way to
Los Angeles to pick up the stuff, Tre Den delivered a trunkload of
computer chips. He netted three thousand dollars.

Back in San Jose, with money bulging in his jacket pocket and
the Wally Girlz for company, Tre Den threw a party for them and
some old friends in the Motel Paradise in Sunnyvale. There was
plenty of beer, drugs, and sex. The commotion drew the attention
of neighbors, who called police. Most of the young roosters and Big
Brothers got away, but Tre Den did not. The girls were detained at
Juvenile Hall. Tre Den was sent to the C.Y.A. for two years.

Tre Den has just been released. I saw him briefly. His eyes never
stopped moving while I spoke to him, and he rocked on his feet, as
nervous as a caged animal. "What will you do now?" I asked him.

Tre Den, now nineteen, shrugged. "Where can I go?" And with that he turned and walked out.

At the Ranches, tremendous efforts are made to rehabilitate boys when they are still malleable—before they find themselves at a dead end, like Tre Den. Delinquent children can earn high school credit, develop good work and study habits, and escape the chaos of their homes and neighborhoods. A lot of the rehabilitation is done through counseling. (Counselors work sixteen-hour shifts so the boys benefit from staff consistency.) Social workers and sex abuse counselors spend a lot of time with the boys; in the evenings wards attend meetings of Alcoholics Anonymous, Narcotics Anonymous, or Bible study groups, and they participate in group counseling or in programs designed to help them build their self-esteem, resist gangs, and manage their anger. Vietnamese children talk to counselors and social workers from Asian Americans for Community Involvement, based in San Jose. Most of the wards in the Ranches belong to gangs, and half have committed violent crimes, but counselors report that the programs at the Ranches are turning some juvenile criminals into good kids within a matter of weeks. About 50 percent of them, anyway: slightly fewer than half will be rearrested not long after their release.[16]

Most realize that they are very well off at the Ranches. Said one ward, "I know I'm lucky to be here. The judge said I could have gone to the YA." The Vietnamese wards are acutely aware of the uniqueness of the Ranches, particularly those who have come from Vietnam and whose fathers told horror stories about their experiences in Vietnamese prisons. Chronic runaways refer to the Ranches as "playboys' inns," and compared to the C.Y.A. they are "paradises." Indeed, the Ranches are not that much different from the motels where delinquent youngsters gather to use drugs and indulge in sex.[17]

Their own testimonies reflect the fact that Vietnamese child offenders profit by the Ranch programs. The following are excerpts from letters Vietnamese wards have written to me about their Ranch experiences. They show that Ranch programs help them to discern the difference between right and wrong and to formulate goals:

- After my pre-release I go to school everyday. And help my dad. Now I take care my life, If my friends ask me go some where, he or she good person I go.
- I learned to respect people things and feelings. . . . I think this is a good program here at JAMES RANCH it does lots of people who have problems solve it.
- I have radically changed. After school, I will seek part time job to save money to buy a car. . . . I will not go out as frequently as before. . . .
- I now how to react to the environment and me and know when to disapline myself. Now I have been doing good.
- Counseling here has given me a second hand look on all the peer-pressure that is happening . . . and would be very glad to know more from all the Counsler from the Ranch.
- I got bored at home, so I ran away and then got arrested. . . . I committed a lot of thefts. I didn't listen to [my counselors]. Now I repent. I am sure I won't repeat will never make mistake again. . . . This is my last repentance to my sister.
- I will stay away from my old friends, and I will become a good son to my parents.
- Before I came here, my English was not fluent, but since I came here, thanks to the teachers, my English have steadily improved. . . . I will not make the same mistakes again. This is the truth.
- I learn [from reading the article Uncle Dee gave me about Helen Tran, the only Vietnamese dancer with a major ballet company in the United States]. I read it two time. She is a girl that change her life by ignoring all the things that happens in the past. She change her life by *working hard*. I know that her family suffer a great deal of pain by leaving Viet Nam. I myself love my own country. When I was little, I didn't know what my own country looks like. I think that I'm the luckiest kid out of the whole refugee. . . . I like the part that Helen has said that when she left Vietnam, it was like leaving half of her heart behind. About the gap language, its telling people to do well and learn *english* and believe in self-esteem. . . . I didn't hear anything about my little sister when she past away. I didn't have a single clue how she died. When I cry I think of her. . . . The last girl I was with was Judy. I was going to be a gangster because of some emotional feelings. EST [East

Side Troublemakers] was formed to keep my brothers out of danger. [I learned] to ignore all the traps from people. HOC DOC TAP NHIN [studying, reading, physical exercise, cool] I . . . remember *saying that everyday.* . . . I enjoy listening to Vietnam's story. I have always been a little child. Now *I'm seeking new life.* When I was a child, all I can remember is when I was on a boat in THAILAND. The *pirates* had taken away our stuff. . . .

• I'm not trying to be a Fake so that I can leave this program. I've learned alot since I've been here. I learned how to be . . . calm with myself. . . . And if there are trouble between my family and I I will talk instead of taking off from home.

These are not "buzz words" the children have learned to utter in knee-jerk fashion. In fact, all are working toward their goals. Not one of the authors of these letters has returned to the Ranch.

Before I came to Holden as a counselor, Asian American wards were perpetual runaways, fleeing from the Ranch at a rate higher than that of any other ethnic group. I was hired to solve the problem, and in the seven years I have been working here, only ten of four hundred have run away. Ninety percent of those whom I have counseled have not returned to the Ranch and are no longer gang members or criminals. However, in spite of the good work that we are doing at the Ranches, the state may shut them down. In June 1993 only eleventh-hour maneuvering prevented the closing of the James Ranch. The facility was saved in part because supervisors warned that closing it and other institutions would inundate the C.Y.A. with two thousand more wards.[18]

What is the state's solution to increasing crime and growing numbers of juvenile criminals? Even though Ranches are less costly to operate and have chalked up a far better track record, and even though evidence suggests that the prisons make bad kids worse and that locking up more and more of them is not making us any safer, California's response is to build more prisons.

But the cost of building new facilities and creating more space in existing facilities is staggering—estimates have run as high as half a billion dollars. In practical terms, that means that programs like the Ranches will have to be eliminated because the state appears determined to coop up juvenile criminals. A corrections consultant observed:

> If the resources that now go to construction and maintenance of lock-ups went instead to communities, 45-50 percent of the wards could be handled at the local level. The choice is almost upon us: education and health care on the one side, and prisons on the other.

As one journalist noted, the state of California

> spends more than $25,000 a year for each child it locks up—more than it costs for a year at the University of California, including tuition, books, housing and living expenses. It spends four times more to keep one juvenile in custody for a year [$25,000] than to keep a family of four on public assistance, including food stamps.

And another pointed out that "every dollar spent for one thing can't be spent for anything else [the Department of Corrections spends 1.3 billion dollars annually]. What else could that 1.3 billion dollars buy?" He notes the following:

- 280,000 students could go to school, based on California's average K–12 per-pupil spending. That's equal to about nine San Jose unified school districts and is nearly triple the number of people in state prison at any one time.
- 2.9 million people—about the entire population of Los Angeles—could go to a 21-day heroin-detoxification program.
- 4.9 million people could get a month's worth of "family maintenance," to help their families stay strong and straight.[19]

Note that these are preventive measures, and prevention is always less costly than a cure. If society invested properly in these kids before they got into trouble, it would pay off for all of us in the long run. We must provide meaningful educations for children, proper outlets for their mental and physical energies, and opportunities for meaningful work in the community, all priceless commodities that allow children their dignity.

"Even violent kids don't need to be controlled by brute force," says an expert in traditional juvenile corrections, also an expert in its alternatives. Abused kids "are more threatened by love. And in a strange way, the public is also threatened by love because it indicts us all—it says these are our failures."[20]

Some months after he became a ward at the Holden Ranch, a young Vietnamese boy wrote:

> Mother, now I belatedly realize
> That the law of vagrancy has blotted my life.

Remorse, however, can come too late:

> Keep in mind that flowers bloom only once,
> And will disappear among the clouds and fogs.
> Sailing into a sea of uncertainties.

Indeed, our children bloom only once. Unless we rescue the troubled ones, they will sail into a sea of uncertainties.

"We pay for our mistakes, don't we?"

—Xinh Xinh

Chapter 7
Xinh Xinh and Tom

Tom Nguyen is an Amerasian, born on the South China Sea not far from Cam Ranh Bay. His grandmother, Kim, told me that Tom's father worked on the flight line at the gigantic American air base there. "He was from Texas," she recalled, "and he was an honorable, Christian man. He married my daughter." Kim says she still has the papers to prove it—she fled the country with them sewn into a fold of her *ao dai*. Her son-in-law was killed in a freak helicopter accident on the base, and she lost her daughter to a mortar shell as the three of them were fleeing the communists in April 1975. The concussion of the exploding shell was so great that she sustained inner ear damage and has suffered severe dizzy spells ever since. Tom lives with her. He believes this 73-year-old woman is his mother.

One day Tom was sitting in a restaurant in Santa Clara when police walked in, handcuffed him, and took him to court to charge him with attempted extortion. On the way to Juvenile Hall he could not stop crying.

"I know nothing!" he insisted to the district attorney.

"You came in with another young man and demanded two thousand dollars of the restaurant owner," the attorney replied.

"I tell you I know nothing. My cousin just asked me to come along with him and to sit in the restaurant and wait for him."

Like countless other sob stories the attorney heard, Tom's was fishy. The judge sent him to the Ranch for five months. A short while after his release from the Ranch the police found out that Tom was telling the truth. His cousin Hoa, nabbed by police in the middle of another extortion attempt, confessed that he had plotted the scheme and that Tom did not know a thing about it. Hoa had walked into the kitchen and demanded that the owner turn over two thousand dollars for "protection." Jerking his thumb into the restaurant he ordered, "Give it to him, sitting there." The owner called the police, who arrested Tom. The cousin had set Tom up so he would not be caught holding the money himself.

According to his grandmother, Tom had always been meek and mild. The injustice turned him into a tiger. At the Ranch he got into fights nearly every week. Once, when his grandmother was a little late in picking him up for his outside time and reprimanded him for fighting, he flew into a rage and began to curse her in Vietnamese. "Go back and pluck chickens in Cam Ranh, you deaf old woman!" he shouted at her. Kim sank to the floor weeping, and this made Tom crazy with anger. "Get up!" he screamed. Staff people came running. "Get up, you fool!"

I helped her to her feet and sat her down in a conference room where she wept uncontrollably. I took Tom into my office.

"I miss cigarettes," he said simply.

"Because you miss cigarettes you treat your mother like a dog? Tom, you can't abuse her this way. She is old and working very hard to make a living for the two of you. Since you've been here her headaches have grown worse and it's a tremendous effort for her to come to see you. She has sent you a package every week that you've been here. Has she ever been anything but kind to you?"

The young man hung his head.

"Instead of cursing her you should tell her to rest and sleep until she feels better. Show her that you're a good son, a pious son. Just now you showed stupidity. You showed blindness to what she has been going through."

"What about what I've been going through! I've been here four months for something I didn't do!"

"Life is full of injustice, Tom. Remember the story about Nguyen Chi Thien? What did he do?"

"He wrote poetry."

"He wrote poetry that people were afraid of! Imagine being afraid of a poet—so afraid that you'd jail him for nearly thirty years and starve him and beat him. I showed you Thien's photograph, Tom. Was Thien's the face of a bitter man? No. But you're wearing the face of a bitter man. Show them you're better than they are, Tom. You say you're here unjustly. Show them that that's so. Be good. Be good and things will work out for you in the end. You've learned from this experience. You've profited by it. It has cost you some time, but so what? The world can throw you in a hole but it can't deprive you of your thoughts, of your imagination. You're always free if you remember that, Tom. You're not 'mere flesh and bones, to be locked up.' Bear this injustice like Thien."

Tom did not get out until two weeks after his release date because of his fighting, but he seemed to put the five months at the Ranch behind him. He studied hard his last year in high school to prepare for a career in social services. Then he met Xinh Xinh.

Xinh Xinh's parents both worked as support personnel for the American Army in Vietnam. When they came to the United States they opened a coffee shop in downtown San Jose. When she was a little girl Xinh Xinh helped her mother in the kitchen. When she became a teenager she waited on customers. That was her undoing.

One day a good-looking Amerasian fellow came into the coffee shop. He flirted with Xinh Xinh and for her it was love at first sight. She ran away with him. The Vietnamese wards at the Ranch told me that Xinh Xinh had an abortion each year until the Amerasian was sent to the C.Y.A. for armed robbery. She then returned to her parents' home and met Tom.

Xinh Xinh had learned to use drugs with her Amerasian lover. She smoked pot and crack. When she was down she took Dexedrine and Biphetamine, Preludin and Voranil, and when she felt agitated she took Nembutal and Methaqualone and Serax. Xinh Xinh was only fifteen years old, a raven-haired beauty, but physically she was a wreck.

One night she got Tom to smoke Kool cigarettes sprayed with Angel Dust, and then they took LSD together. Tom babbled incoherently. He took a glass, smashed it on the floor, and swallowed it piece by piece. He ended up in the emergency room and was in surgery for four hours while doctors removed the shards from his esophagus and stomach.

Not long after Tom's recovery he and Xinh Xinh and some members of the Flying Eagles gang were involved in a home invasion in which the sixteen-year-old son of the homeowner was shot in the shoulder. The boy survived, but nerves in his shoulder were permanently damaged. Xinh Xinh was sent to the Ranch and underwent treatment at the drug rehab center. Tom was sent to the Youth Authority for three years and nine months. I learned all of this from his grandmother. "Xinh Xinh put him up to it," she said. "She wanted money for designer clothes and a gold necklace. She said to Tom, 'If you love me you'll do it.' Well, he did it. And now he's paying for it."

At the request of Xinh Xinh's mother, I visited her at the rehabilitation center. As we sat together in the group therapy room Xinh Xinh asked, "Uncle Dee, do you think that I, too, can dance?"

Sensing that she was thinking of Helen Tran, the beautiful Vietnamese dancer about whom she'd read on my last visit, I replied, "You can do anything you set your mind to, Xinh Xinh."

"Then watch me, Uncle Dee."

Xinh Xinh stood up (she was quite ill; her skin was pasty and she looked jaundiced) and danced around the room in a very sensuous fashion. "Do you like this Uncle Dee?" she said, and I understood that this young girl was dancing to arouse.

"Xinh Xinh! Stop that immediately or I'll have you sent back to your room. Stop degrading yourself."

She looked at me sullenly.

"Listen to me, Xinh Xinh. You're smart. You're beautiful. And you can do anything. You've made mistakes. But you can put them behind you."

"My ass is behind me. And I have a nice ass."

"Xinh Xinh, when you speak like that I don't hear you. It's so much chaff blowing in the wind."

"You hear *me*, old man. Talk! Talk! Talk! I'm tired of your talk. Yesterday you told me about your daughter. I'm sick of your bragging."

"I told you about Tiana to show you what you can do and that you can do *better!* Do you think it was easy for my daughter to make a movie, Xinh Xinh?"

"I don't give a shit. I don't care if it was easy or not. What does your daughter have to do with me!"

"She was a lot like you. She ran away once, too."

Interest flitted over her face.

"Your daughter? I don't believe it. You're saying that so you can talk at me."

"My daughter ran away to be a star. To be an actress. She never got really good parts, so she asked herself, 'What can I do with my life?' She decided that if she couldn't be in other people's movies she'd make her own. Good ones. Movies that have important messages in them. And she has. She has worked on a movie for years, Xinh Xinh, and now people all over the country, even important people in Washington, D.C., have watched it. For years she thought of nothing else. She lost sleep working on that movie and sometimes she didn't even eat while she worked on it. Have you ever thought about anything that hard?"

Xinh Xinh looked out the window and considered.

"I've thought about being more beautiful."

"Oh?" I watched her walk over to the mirror by the window and gaze at herself intently. Then she looked over her shoulder at me.

"You can put your beauty to work for you, Xinh Xinh," I said to her quietly.

"How? How can I do that?" She said this contemptously, as if defying me to tell her. But she turned to face me when I answered.

"Maybe you can be a fashion model, Xinh Xinh. But if you're going to be a model you have to take care of yourself. I know of Vietnamese and Amerasian girls who model. But they look healthy.

You look sick. Nobody wants to photograph a girl who looks sick. You look sick because you use drugs. Stop using drugs and you'll bloom again. Then you can go to agencies. You carry yourself like a model. Now you have to act like one."

Xinh Xinh sighed and waved her hand as if to dismiss what I said. "It would be too hard. I wouldn't know how. I wouldn't know where to begin or what to do."

"You begin by deciding to begin. The rest evolves. Step by step by step. That's how it was for Helen Tran, remember? Nobody in her family had ever danced before, and nobody in her family—except for her uncle who wrote songs and poetry—was an artist. Thirty years of war had made that an impossibility. But Helen Tran wanted to dance. She didn't understand a word of English when she started school, but she knew that she wanted to dance."

"I want to do things too, Uncle Dee, but wanting isn't enough."

"Oh, no, Xinh Xinh, wanting is *everything*. *Tay lam ham nhai*—if you don't want you don't work, and if you don't work you don't have food. Now listen to me, Xinh Xinh. Helen Tran wanted to dance so badly that instead of doing what everybody thought she should do and going to college, she did something different. Do you re- member?"

Xinh Xinh shrugged her shoulders. "I don't know what she did and I don't care." She looked at me insolently.

"Yes you do, Xinh Xinh. You care very much. You taped her pic- ture and her story on the door of your locker. I saw it. You showed me."

"Okay, so she went to New York. She auditioned for a dance school."

"It wasn't just any dance school, Xinh Xinh. It was the Alvin Ailey American Dance Center School—one of the finest dance schools in the country, if not the world. Helen Tran took a chance, Xinh Xinh. And why did she take a chance? Because she wanted to dance. And she got in. She got into the school and she got a scholar- ship."

"But she had talent." Xinh Xinh sighed.

"A lot of people have talent. And there were probably a lot of girls with a lot more talent than Helen Tran. But she worked. It was hard for her, very hard, to learn to dance, but she worked hard, and then one day the company asked her to perform. How do you suppose she felt, Xinh Xinh?"

"Excited. Nervous. Happy. All those feelings, Uncle Dee." Suddenly Xinh Xinh stood up and twirled about the room, coming to a stop in front of me. "I like the part where she said she was a light."

"Which part was that?"

"When her family was fleeing from Saigon and they were at Tan Son Nhut Airport and Helen could see the lights of the cars and buses hurrying out to the airport—when all the people were trying to escape the communists. The lights twinkled at the airport and along all the streets leading to the airport and Helen watched them. She said that when they flew away she watched the lights grow smaller and smaller until they looked like dying stars." She sighed again. "And then, later, when she was dancing, she'd remember them, those tiny dying star lights, and how she felt as if she were one of them."

"But Helen Tran's light didn't go out, did it?"

Xinh Xinh looked at me, and there was a brightness in her eyes—whether it was from the drugs with which she had been abusing herself, or from keen interest in the story of Helen Tran, I could not tell. "Helen said she was one of the lights that flew away into the night. I love that, Uncle Dee. Sometimes I wish I were a light that could fly away into the night."[1]

"Oh? Why is that, Xinh Xinh?"

"Because everything is too hard."

"What is too hard?"

"It is too hard for me to get what I want. To be what I want."

"Of course it is, Xinh Xinh! You will need to work very, very hard to get what you want and to be what you want." I paused, studying her dreamy expression. "Do you know who won the 1989 Miss America contest, Xinh Xinh? A black girl. A beautiful black girl. Do you know how hard that must have been, Xinh Xinh? Do you know how much discrimination black people face in this country? She knew that, but she decided—she simply *decided*—that she would work her way to the top. She used her beauty. You can too, Xinh Xinh. Not everyone has beauty. You do. You can use it as you would any tool. But first you have to decide to. This rehab center is a good place for you to begin. You can decide to make yourself well here. Think to yourself, 'If I make myself well I'll make myself beautiful, and when I've made myself beautiful I'll have some professional photographs taken and I'll go to a modeling agency.' When Tom was at the Ranch he showed me a picture of you, Xinh Xinh. You looked beautiful in the picture. Memorable. You were wearing a short white blouse and blue jeans and you looked beautiful—you have the looks a modeling agency might pay top dollar for. You're a natural, Xinh Xinh. You looked relaxed. As if you'd been modeling for years. You're not afraid of the camera."

"I remember the picture," she said thoughtfully. "It impressed you? It impressed you!"

"It did, Xinh Xinh. But you don't look like that now. Have you looked at yourself lately, Xinh Xinh?"

She put her face in her hands and began to cry.

"Xinh Xinh, stop crying. Crying is a waste of energy. Stop crying and listen to me and I'll tell you more. Have I told you about Maya Lin?"

She looked up at me.

"Who's Maya Lin?"

"She's a Chinese American artist, Xinh Xinh."

"I'm an artist too. I'm an artist with makeup, Uncle Dee."

"Let me tell you about Maya and then you can tell me about your makeup. After the war in Vietnam was over for the American people, they counted their war dead. More than fifty-eight thousand American boys died there fighting the communists. Americans wished to do something to honor them and so they had a contest to see who could come up with the best design for a monument. A committee of important people gathered together to consider the entries. Many famous artists submitted their designs, but the committee was unanimous: it chose Maya Lin's design. When the people on the committee discovered that the winner was only a college girl, they were shocked! A girl only a few years older than you, Xinh Xinh."

"So? What's your point?"

"That anything's possible, Xinh Xinh. Anything is possible if you don't make things impossible. Violence and ganging up and breaking the law make things impossible. And drugs change all the possibilities. You can't model in a drug rehab center, can you? In some countries the color of your skin makes things impossible. In the United States some people will be against you because you're Vietnamese and others will be against you because you're a young woman. But if you want to do something very badly none of this will stop you. It didn't stop the black girl who became Miss America, it didn't stop my daughter Tiana, and it didn't stop Maya Lin. But you're building a wall that will block your own success, Xinh Xinh. Pill by pill, injection by injection, cigarette by cigarette—each one of those is a brick in a wall behind which nobody will ever see your face. Xinh Xinh, you were saying you're an artist with makeup. Do you have any makeup with you?"

She laughed. "Of course I do."

"I want you to make yourself up. Imagine that you're getting ready to go to a modeling agency. Make yourself up and we'll talk."

"Now?"

"Why not? Have you got anything else to do?"

I watched her as she left the visiting room and retreated down the hall to her room. She returned a few minutes later with a bag and moved to the mirror that was lit with reflected sunlight. I watched her rummage through her bag. Then she worked on her face, her hands flitting back and forth from her bag to her skin, eyes, lips, and brows. She was birdlike in her movements—quick and purposeful. "War paint, Uncle Dee," she said, holding up tubes of makeup in her small hand and smiling at me. When she was done she brushed her hair. Then she turned to face me.

"Now study yourself in the glass."

Xinh Xinh shook her head. "I feel silly."

"You're a professional model, Xinh Xinh. You can't permit yourself to feel silly. Look at yourself. What do you see? Is she beautiful?"

She considered herself.

"I've always thought of myself as being beautiful, Uncle Dee."

"That's good, Xinh Xinh! That's very good! If you think you're beautiful, then you are beautiful. You'll carry yourself that way. And the fact is you are very beautiful, Xinh Xinh. But you're throwing it away. You're wasting it. Every time you pop a pill or smoke a cigarette or inject yourself with methamphetamines, you're destroying yourself. Cell by cell by cell. Are you smart, Xinh Xinh?"

"I'm smart. Yes, I'm very smart."

"Imagine somebody who's smart and beautiful, Xinh Xinh. What should such a person do?"

"Be in the movies."

"Okay, the movies. When this smart and beautiful person tries out for a part in the movies, what does she have to do?"

"Look beautiful."

"What else?"

"Read her part."

"No. She has to memorize it. Xinh Xinh, one of the nurses told me that you got lost going to breakfast the other morning. You couldn't find the dining hall and then they found you crouched in front of your door, weeping. Why was that?"

She shrugged. "Maybe the Angel Dust. The PCP. There were strange faces in the hall, strange distorted faces, and they were coming after me, trying to swallow me. Then I saw myself melt. I melted like a wax doll into a grate in the floor. It was the only way I could escape the faces."

"You were hallucinating."

"That's what the nurses told me. They said it's in my head from the drugs. But it all seemed pretty real to me."

"Xinh Xinh, imagine you're onstage. A producer and a director are there listening to you and watching you. How do you feel?"

"Excited!" She flung out her arms. "Overjoyed, Uncle Dee!"

"Suddenly the faces of the producer and the director look distorted. You think they're chasing you. What do you do?"

"Run like hell," Xinh Xinh laughed.

"Do you get the part?"

"I guess not."

"What's my point, Xinh Xinh?"

"I get your point."

"Do you?"

She looked at herself in the mirror and nodded. "I do."

"Xinh Xinh, you're strong. You're a woman and you're strong. Did you know that women in your homeland have been fighting for years?"

"Bah. Women don't fight. They clean up the messes made by men."

"They fought, Xinh Xinh. They fought, using the same weapons the men did. What does this tell you?"

"That women can do anything men can do. But I know that."

"Good. I'm just reminding you. Xinh Xinh, think about your mother. Has she stuck by you?"

Xinh Xinh looked at herself in the mirror, blotted her lips on a tissue, and eyed me cooly. "She has stuck by me, Uncle Dee."

"Every Sunday your mother has come here for counseling. She has sat by you every Sunday for months now, holding your hand."

"My father quit me."

"But your mother didn't. She is strong, Xinh Xinh, and you're just like her."

"I don't want to be like her. I don't want to be a woman that a man leaves. Tom will not leave me."

"But you are not together. His new trouble has put him in the YA for a long time."

"My father quit me," she repeated.

"This may be too large for you, Xinh Xinh; perhaps you're too young to understand what I'm about to say. Your mother has accepted all of what has happened to you. Your father couldn't. It was too much for him. He and your mother quarreled and your father went away. She has been persistent. She has been strong. And she has been strong for you. As I have told you before, a husband may walk away from a wife or a wife may walk away from a husband, but mothers almost never walk away from their children. It's a great mystery, but it's a great truth. Your mother is not 'a woman that a man leaves' but a woman who is stronger than a man."

"My lover is strong."

"Tom is strong but foolish. He listened to you when he shouldn't have and look where it got him."

"He sent me a poem. Do you want to see it?" She reached into her makeup bag and retrieved a crumpled piece of paper. Unfolding it, she read it aloud:

Ranch meals are as good as restaurant meals.
Ranch dorms are as comfortable as motel rooms.
The cops' beatings are like my lover's massages
His curses sound like *vong co* songs.
Their punches are like my workouts.

Checking into the ranch is like a prince
    entering the royal palace.
Noon break in bed is like the king's nap.
A lock-up place is like a funland.
Ranch meals are like restaurant meals
(Everyday three hearty meals are served.
Soft drink is readily available) and
Ranch stay is like in a motel.
Doing crew work in the morning is like General Quang Cong
    demonstrating his martial art.
Rooting out the weeds in the afternoon
    is like a Prince picking flowers.

"I've heard this poem before, Xinh Xinh. Boys who are sent to the YA almost always regard the Ranch as having been a paradise."

"Tom has been raped there," she said softly. "Repeatedly."

"The YA is a dangerous place, Xinh Xinh, and Tom will be there for years."

"We write to each other. In the letter he sent with this"—she pointed to the poem—"he told me that the Vietnamese and the Cambodians fight the blacks and the Mexicans, and that if you don't fight they don't respect you and they go after you. Tom doesn't want to be bad, Uncle Dee. But he said the YA is making him bad."

"He was accessory to a shooting, Xinh Xinh."

"It was an accident. He didn't mean to."

"Maybe not. But an innocent person is injured because of him. Tom will be in the YA a long time."

"We pay for our mistakes, don't we," she said bitterly. Observing her reflection in the mirror, Xinh Xinh studied her face and shrugged. "But my mistakes don't show now, do they?" She lifted her chin.

Afterword

Ban Vuong was fifteen when he arrived at the Ranch to spend six months for burglary. When he appeared in court his manner was so coldly superior and cocky and his perjury so blatant, that the jurors approached the district attorney to ask how they were supposed to deal with his lies. In their estimation Ban was "another hopeless case."

When I reviewed a letter he wrote to a friend (it attracted the attention of Ranch staff), I wondered if perhaps they were right. "I'm going to have a girl killed," Ban Vuong wrote, "only I'm not going to do the shooting; I'm going to watch." In that same letter he spoke admiringly of a Big Brother who "deals chips . . . and just bought a Mercedes Benz 300SL brand new." He mentioned a "stolen Supra" in his possession, "but I don't know . . . anyone who wants to buy it." Then he rambled:

> I told your brother everything that you told me. I told him to send money . . . and he said he will do it. The $1000, beeper and gold leaves, your brother tried to get it out too but he couldn't. Two days

[after] I get out your brother asked me to go to Santa Ana with him, but I said no because I had to stay home. He went anyway with 4 other guys. They went and succeeded. They all got $2000 each but I think Cao gets more money. A week later I saw Dong he got released. Dang went and got a Maxima, he went down to L.A. and sold it for $2000 dollars give $500 to Pham the guy that help him sell the car. Do you know anyone or any connections that buys Cars or ICE [drug] because I need connections to do business with your brother and friends. Tell me if you know, give address, phone number or beeper number or any information. Cao send his guy to Santa Ana to get a gun and a cell [cellular phone]. He asked if I wanted to go with him, but I said no, I have to go to school and stayed home. My probation officer is watching my movements. Huynh just got out of YA. . . . I'm sorry I can't hook you up with any *ghe* [girls] because they are all 14 and 15 no older girls.

Beneath his signature, Ban wrote, "True friends look after friends."

Drugs, girls, negative peers, a total preoccupation with and involvement in illegal (and highly profitable!) activities, references to a Big Brother (Cao), easy cash—many of the elements of Vietnamese criminal activity are apparent here, especially the casual tone Ban used to discuss murder and the procurement of a gun. But today this boy—"another hopeless case"—is a sophomore at Berkeley.

When he came to my office for counseling, Ban told me that his parents never let him have any spending money and that he hated his room. In my first counseling session with Ban's parents, the boy's father asserted that he wanted his son to experience the poverty he had known in Vietnam because he felt it would be good for him. It would force him to appreciate money. Whenever Ban asked for a few dollars to see a movie or play video games, his father denied him, usually accompanying his negative answer with a lecture about Honda, the auto manufacturer of Japan who made his children walk to school every day so they would know the value of a car. Itching for the easy money he knew gang members had, Ban began to hang out with the "homies" at his school. He tuned his father out.

Having built up a big auto body business, Ban's parents were very well off. As I talked to Ban's father, I inquired about the boy's room. Mr. Vuong proudly said that his son's room was spare: "I don't allow him even a radio, much less a TV." Ban told me that he wanted a stereo more than anything in the world. He said that if he could listen to music, he would enjoy doing his homework. When I mentioned this to Ban's parents, his mother said that the boy had a comfortable bed and a desk with a good lamp, but that his room lacked decoration of any kind, and a stereo was out of the question. "My husband knew the jails of Vietnam," she explained, "and never enjoyed luxuries until we grew rich in America. He is fearful that Ban may be spoiled by luxury. Ban is too young for luxury and must concentrate on his studies."

Fortunately for Ban, his parents were not close-minded. I explained to them the relationship between Ban's attraction to gang life and his anger about his room and lack of spending money. We talked about the negative peer pressure confronting the boy at school, and the pressure to excel that he was feeling at home. They were completely ignorant about drugs and were stunned when I told them that their son talked about selling dangerous and illegal substances. I explained the dangers of addiction to them, and told them how Big Brothers get children addicted and then use them to sell drugs in order to make a lot of money. I reminded them that children like their son are shooting and killing one another with the guns Big Brothers give them.

Ban's father told me that before Ban was arrested, it had gotten to the point where he was disappearing from home for days at a time and was insolent to him, even cursing him. Now their son was in the Ranch a second time, on a weapons charge. "Your son has access to more firepower than the average police officer," I warned them. Mr. and Mrs. Vuong were terrified, and they struggled to absorb all that I was telling them. As a result of our discussions, Ban and his parents worked out a deal. They would give the boy a stereo and help him decorate his room, if he worked Saturday mornings at their auto body shop with his father and studied in the evenings. That arrangement marked the beginning of a new life for all of them.[1]

I try to save Vietnamese children one by one, and even the

"hopeless cases" like Ban are savable—most of them. But the Ranches and other similar institutions may not be able to respond effectively to Vietnamese criminal activity because it is growing so rapidly.

In 1994 the number of Vietnamese offenders detained at the Juvenile Hall of Santa Clara County averaged between twenty and thirty juveniles a day. In the first three months of 1995 that figure jumped, and the number of Vietnamese offenders averaged between thirty and forty on any given day. The population of Vietnamese juvenile offenders is increasing at the Ranches, as well. In 1994 Vietnamese inmates at the Ranches made up less than 10 percent of the population. As of March 1995 they were approaching 14 percent. The situation is likely to be aggravated by a new generation of children—the offspring of the most recent immigrants from Vietnam who are coming of age and may very well contribute to yet another "wave" of juvenile crime.

In March 1995, when three innocent Vietnamese men were gunned down execution-style in a coffee house in San Jose, many in the community expressed the fear that Vietnamese criminal activity is too big for anyone to handle. The three people murdered in the back room of the May Tim Café were not gang members—their deaths were a tragic case of mistaken identity. At the Ranch, wards are certain that one of the assassins was Wah Ching and the remaining gunmen were Asian Boyz. The triple homicide (the first in San Jose in more than a decade) is a clear indication that despite an array of preventive and punitive programs in place in the San Jose area, the problem of Vietnamese gangs and Vietnamese criminal activity is not getting any better.[2]

As a result of a fifteen-month official investigation, the U.S. Senate ranked Asian crime as a "problem of dramatic proportions." It also reported that efforts to deal with it have been woefully inadequate. This is not surprising. Law enforcement agencies have been fighting Asian crime for decades, but the difference between the current situation and that of twenty years ago is that today, criminals with Asian connections in Hong Kong, China, Taiwan, South Korea, and Vietnam have established themselves in metropolitan staging areas on every continent, conducting their marketing research and development as scrupulously as any Fortune 500 company.[3]

Early in the winter of 1994, sixteen members of a Vietnamese and Chinese-Vietnamese gang were arrested in Santa Clara County on charges of importing "China White" heroin from Asia and trading in stolen weapons, computer chips, and other extremely sophisticated technologies—they were, as we say in Vietnam, "eating the cake at both ends." Asian criminal groups such as this one specialize in drug and weapons trafficking, trading stolen computer technologies, money laundering, extortion, credit card counterfeiting, home invasion, and alien smuggling. Their tentacles are so far-reaching, their operations so complex, and their contacts so interdependent, that some authorities have said that Asian crime is a global octopus.[4]

As we confront its manifestations here, we cannot blame one another. For seven years I have listened to parents blast their neighborhoods and schools. School administrators and teachers rage at parents. Schools and parents accuse the police of "not doing enough." Churches and courts attack the media for their focus on violence, arguing that they promote a "violence culture." Neighborhoods denounce politicians for their failure to provide "opportunities for young people," and whine that society is "indifferent." But hurling blame at other people or institutions has not brought us any closer to solving the problem.

Many people in the community (including the Vietnamese community), in the schools, in law enforcement agencies, and in government are convinced that more counseling, prevention, and intervention programs are the answer and it has been my experience that these programs do help individual Vietnamese children. An expert observed that gangs are "incredibly complex organizations [that] demand equally complex solutions," and he advised that it is "high time to rethink the old, to jettison what does not work, expand what does, and experiment with new ideas." This is sound advice, but it requires of us a certain attitude. We must be willing to consider innovative solutions and to listen to creative ideas about how to implement them, no matter how unorthodox or revolutionary.[5]

For example, the idea that a municipal government might declare certain places in a city off-limits to gangs sounded impossible to residents of San Fernando, California. Critics warned that the strategy would deprive citizens of their constitutional rights and would never hold up in the courts. But open-minded people listened to the idea and pursued it. As a result of their efforts, in spite of attacks from various quarters, including the American Civil Liberties Union, the city successfully declared limited states-of-emergency in places where street gangs had taken over, such as in public parks. Gun-toting gang members were fined for each violation, prosecuted, and jailed for violating the terms of the emergency. Now law-abiding citizens are enjoying their public parks.[6]

Similarly, law enforcement officials in Tulsa, Oklahoma, came up with an unusual idea to combat a dramatic increase in auto theft — offenders and their parents would sign contracts with local authorities that committed youths to ride patrol with the police. Residents scoffed at the concept initially, but the Youth Intervention Program is working: adolescents are getting a good view of what "the other side" of crime is like and in the process are developing positive relationships with police officers. The success of these programs suggests that, given the proportions of the Vietnamese gang problem, any idea for dealing with it should be taken seriously.[7]

The Department of Justice reported that "specialized gang units are common in police departments of cities with established, as well as emerging, gang problems." But the response to a survey it recently conducted indicates that prosecutors in 368 offices across the country are not optimistic about the ability of the law enforcement community to combat the gang problem: "gang members who come to their attention are often far beyond the reach of social interventions designed to deter youths from involvement in gang lifestyles." In fact, gang prosecutors agreed that "early intervention and more effective services to strengthen families" are the best ways to prevent ganging up and the violence that accompanies it.[8]

It makes sense for communities across the country to experiment with gang prevention programs designed to reach children at an early age; it is good news that the federal government is investing in efforts that, like the popular D.A.R.E. (Drug Abuse Resistance

Education) program, are attempts to keep children from ganging up. For instance, the Bureau of Alcohol, Tobacco and Firearms is funding the G.R.E.A.T. (Gang Resistance Education and Training) program to help students "learn how to act in their own best interest when faced with peer pressure and say no to gangs." Programs like this appear to be enjoying some success, but they may prove to be inadequate because of the scale and complexity of the problem—and its growing international dimension.[9]

Asian (including Vietnamese) criminal activity is increasing dramatically in Great Britain, Canada, and Australia, and these nations have taken steps to cooperate with the United States to exchange resources and information in an effort to deal with it more effectively. But the headquarters of gang activity in the Far East have thus far proven impossible to penetrate, and authorities have made little significant progress.

Meanwhile, juvenile Vietnamese and Chinese-Vietnamese in this country are at the business end of the octopus's tentacles. They steal and deliver cars, money, and computer technologies, collect "protection money" on an increasingly grand scale, sell guns and other weapons imported from all over Asia to schoolchildren, and, under the watchful eyes of their Big Brothers, recruit new gang members every day. Only with time will we have a sense of what array of responses by individuals, communities, governments, and law enforcement agencies, both inside and outside the United States, have a chance of diminishing the size of the problem.

Notes

Note to Preface

1. Gene Beley, "Visit with Gang Expert Patrick Du Long," *Country News* 4, March–April 1993, 15–16.

Notes to Introduction

1. "Six from Oakland held in slaying at San Jose video store," *San Jose Mercury News,* July 8, 1991.
2. T. T. Nhu, "Commentary: Sacramento Siege," *San Jose Mercury News,* April 19, 1991.
3. "They saw their sons kill—and get killed," *San Jose Mercury News,* April 6, 1991.
4. Ibid.
5. De Tran, "Gunmen never missed Mass," *San Jose Mercury News,* April 7, 1991.
6. Thomas Farragher, "Injured hostage recalls 8-½ hours of fear," *San Jose Mercury News,* April 6, 1991.
7. Gary Webb, "Six dead in gunfire at mall," *San Jose Mercury News,* April 6, 1991. "Step-by-step walk into a Sacramento hostage nightmare," *Sacramento Bee,* June 4, 1991. Mitchell Benson and Gary Webb, "Gunmen's goals were blood, infamy," *San Jose Mercury News,* April 6, 1991.

8. "Six from Oakland held in slaying at San Jose video store." "Step-by-step walk into a Sacramento hostage nightmare."

9. U.S. Department of Justice, Federal Bureau of Investigation, *Vietnamese Criminal Activity in the United States: A National Perspective,* March 1993, 1 (hereafter cited as FBI, *Vietnamese Criminal Activity*).

10. "18 Vietnamese held in East San Jose, robbed," *San Jose Mercury News,* February 27, 1990.

11. "Gilroy's Susan Black—Mother of a Gang Leader—Teaches Danger Signs to Other Parents," *Country News* 4, March–April 1993, 15.

12. "*Canh sat bat giu 60 nghi can thuoc bang dang A Chau, Nam Cali,*" *Viet Nam Tu Do,* October 29, 1992.

13. FBI, *Vietnamese Criminal Activity,* 3.

14. T. T. Nhu, "Commentary."

Notes to Chapter 1

1. Linda Hitchcox, *Vietnamese Refugees in Southeast Asian Camps* (New York: St. Martin's, 1990), 25.

2. Ibid., 27, 28.

3. Ibid., 28–29.

4. *Tho,* Nguyen Chi Thien, "*Nhom phat huy tinh than.*" A group of Vietnamese who claim to have been in prison with Thien and I printed Thien's uncopyrighted poems for distribution in the Vietnamese community in the United States. As of this writing, Nguyen Chi Thien continues to be under close surveillance by security forces in Hanoi because of his anti-communist writings. For information about the poems write: Nguyen Chi Thien, P.O. Box 3087, San Jose, CA 95156.

5. Hitchcox, *Vietnamese Refugees in Southeast Asian Camps,* 59–60.

6. Ibid., 62–63.

7. Nguyen Chi Thien, "*Nhom phat huy tinh than.*"

8. Hitchcox, *Vietnamese Refugees in Southeast Asian Camps,* 225.

9. Ibid., 63–65, 76.

10. Ibid., 76–77.

11. Edna Booth, "Vietnamese Assimilation into American Culture," in "A Selection of Readings on Socio-Cultural Values and Problems of the Vietnamese in the United States" (hereafter cited as "A Selection of Readings"), Book II, 145–146. Paper presented for symposium, A Special Project for the Vietnamese Culture Day at San Jose City College, June 5, 1993.

12. William T. Liu, Maryanne Lamanna, and Alice Murata, *Transition to Nowhere: Vietnamese Refugees in America* (Nashville, Tenn.: Charter House, 1979), 170.

13. Chung Thien Cuu, "Young Vietnamese Confronting the New Life," in "A Se-

lection of Readings," Book II, 197. Liu, Lamanna, and Murata, *Transition to Nowhere*, 107.

14. Liu, Lamanna, and Murata, *Transition to Nowhere*, 170.

15. Andrew Lam, "American nightmare: a Vietnamese perspective," *San Jose Mercury News*, May 15, 1992.

16. Hitchcox, *Vietnamese Refugees in Southeast Asian Camps*, 136.

17. Ibid., 70.

18. Nguyen Thanh Liem and Alan B. Henkin, "Vietnamese Refugees in the United States: Adaptation and Transitional Status," in "A Selection of Readings," Book II, 77–78.

19. Ibid., 82, 86–87. See also chapter 2, "Who Are the Refugees?" in Liu, Lamanna, and Murata, *Transition to Nowhere*. Note that the Vietnamese who chose not to respond to the surveys of scholarly researchers on which these generalizations are based may have been former military and government officers reluctant to reveal their prior occupations.

20. Liem and Henkin, "Vietnamese Refugees in the United States," 88.

21. Ibid., 88–89.

22. Ibid., 89.

23. Ibid., 90, 94.

24. Ibid., 93–94.

25. FBI, *Vietnamese Criminal Activity*, 19.

26. Ibid., 3, 4, 9–11.

27. Ibid., 3.

28. Ibid.

29. Ibid., 4.

30. Calvin Toy, "A Short History of Asian Gangs in San Francisco," *Justice Quarterly* 9, December 1992, 664.

31. Ibid., 653, 656.

32. Ibid., 660–661.

33. Liem and Henkin, "Vietnamese Refugees in the United States," 71.

34. Liu, Lamanna, and Murata, *Transition to Nowhere*, 30. Liem and Henkin, "Vietnamese Refugees in the United States," 71–72.

35. FBI, *Vietnamese Criminal Activity*, 5.

36. Ibid., 4–5.

37. Ibid., 5.

38. Ibid., 7.

39. Edward Behr and Mark Steyn, *The Story of Miss Saigon* (New York: Arcade, 1991), 7.

40. Marilyn Lewis, "Amerasians pawns in scam to get to U.S.," *San Jose Mercury News*, February 21, 1993.

41. Vietnam Veterans of America Foundation, "Report on the Amerasian Issue," Washington, D.C., August 1989, 18, 21, 24–25 (hereafter cited as "Report on

the Amerasian Issue"). Vietnam Veterans of America Foundation, "Merger of the Indochina and Vietnam Projects," March 8, 1990.

42. "Report on the Amerasian Issue," 16–17, 19. Vietnam Veterans of America Foundation, "Merger of the Indochina and Vietnam Projects."

43. In July 1983, "250 single Amerasians [were] sleeping on the sidewalk in front of the Office of External Affairs in Ho Chi Minh City." See "Report on the Amerasian Issue," 11, and Lewis, "Amerasians pawns in scam to get to U.S."

44. "Resettlement plan riddled with fraud," *San Jose Mercury News*, February 22, 1993. Lewis, "Amerasians pawns in scam to get to U.S." "U.S. cracks down on phony Amerasians," *Phuc Vu*, March–April, 1993. "Abuse, disfigurement for a ticket to America," *San Jose Mercury News*, February 21, 1993.

45. Lewis, "Amerasians pawns in scam to get to U.S."

46. Ibid.

47. "U.S. cracks down on phony Amerasians."

48. Ibid.

49. Ibid.

50. "For a Few Caught in Repatriation Fraud, Life in Limbo," *Phuc Vu*, March–April 1993.

51. *Thoi Bao*, May 4, 1991. *Phu Nu Dien Dan* 90, July 1991.

52. "Report on the Amerasian Issue," vii.

53. Ibid., vii–viii.

54. *Phu Nu Dien Dan* 90, July 1991.

55. "Report on the Amerasian Issue," 31–32.

Notes to Chapter 2

1. Le Thanh Viet, "Education and Cultural Adjustment," Sacramento Community Forum, April 24, 1991.

2. FBI, *Vietnamese Criminal Activity*, 10.

3. Asian Community Mental Health Services, *Xi-Ke, Ma-Tuy, Xi-Ke, Ma-Tuy O Chung Quanh Ta . . . Hay Giup Con Em Tranh Xa No.*

4. T. T. Nhu, "Commentary."

5. "Six from Oakland held in slaying at San Jose video store," *San Jose Mercury News*, July 8, 1991.

6. *"Cao Pho Tu Con," Trieu Thanh* 618, November 2, 1991.

7. Dennis Rockstroh, "Vietnam-born teen on road to Harvard beats big odds," *San Jose Mercury News*, June 2, 1993.

8. "Lessons in graduation: Boy turns nightmare into Harvard dream," *San Jose Mercury News*, June 16, 1990.

9. T. T. Nhu, "Schools work for those who need them," *San Jose Mercury News*, June 21, 1992.

10. From official assessments of wards who have performance problems in school.

11. Patrick Du Phuoc Long, "The Whys of Vietnamese Gangs," in "A Selection of Readings," Book II, 132.

12. "Hostage: Relative Questions Tactics," *Sacramento Bee,* April 8, 1991.

13. Carol Izumikawa, "Hitting Home: Why Asian Gangs Often Target Their Own Communities," *City on a Hill Press,* March 10, 1994.

14. *Saigon Nho* 96, November 29, 1991.

15. Text from a film written, produced, and directed by Tiana Thi Thanh Nga, *From Hollywood to Hanoi* (New York, 1993).

16. Ibid.

17. Ibid.

18. Ibid.

19. Ibid.

20. Vi Khue, *"Phong Su Xa Hoi, Buon Tre My Lai," Phu Nu Dien Dan* 90, July 1991.

21. Nguyen Huu, *Vietnam Tu Do,* June 8, 1991.

22. Ibid.

23. "Why more dads are drifting away," *San Jose Mercury News,* June 14, 1992.

Notes to Chapter 3

1. Interestingly, at Camp Pendleton, Calif., where thousands of first-wave Vietnamese were processed before resettlement, researchers observed the "Vietnamese youths' strong sense of family solidarity." See Liu, Lamanna, and Murata, *Transition to Nowhere,* 123–124.

2. Hitchcox, *Vietnamese Refugees in Southeast Asian Camps,* 166.

3. Ibid.

4. Betty Barnacle, "5 masked bandits raid house, beat 3 S.J. family members," *San Jose Mercury News,* January 21, 1992. Betty Barnacle, "Four robbery suspects arrested," *San Jose Mercury News,* December 19, 1991. Betty Barnacle, "Robbers terrorize South S.J. Family," *San Jose Mercury News,* July 16, 1992. "Four teens sought in latest home invasion," *San Jose Mercury News.*

5. FBI, *Vietnamese Criminal Activity,* 10.

6. Carol Izumikawa, "Hitting Home."

The best way for the community to protect itself against criminals is to enlist the aid of law enforcement agencies, but some Vietnamese are reluctant to do so. In Vietnam a defendant was presumed guilty until proven innocent, there was no bail system, and the penal code was designed to protect the community and preserve public order, rather than individual rights and liberties. The American system is exactly the opposite, and some Vietnamese find it frightening, believing, for example, that a criminal out on bail is free to retaliate and harm a witness. As a result, some will refuse to testify against even the worst offenders. Unfortunately, Vietnamese criminals understand the system perfectly and know precisely how to use it to their advantage. The Justice Department reports that "one of the first things that a Vietnamese criminal out on bail will do is to drive by his victim so that the victim will erroneously assume that the criminal has 'paid off' the police and is now free to retaliate. He may also attempt to initiate conversation with the arresting officer, in full view of the victim, sometimes with his wallet or cash in hand." According to the FBI, the result is that the victim is convinced that the American judicial system is as hopelessly corrupt as Vietnam's and that he has just observed another payoff. He therefore refuses to testify, and he relates his observations to others within the community. The belief spreads that law enforcement in the United States is not to be trusted (FBI, *Vietnamese Criminal Activity*, 20, 21).

There are things that law enforcement personnel can do to elicit cooperation from the Vietnamese community. Because bail is understood by some Vietnamese to be a form of bribery, police should take the time to explain how bail works and that people who cooperate will not be subject to revenge as a result of it. Police should explain how the American criminal justice system differs from Vietnam's, and stress that when people cooperate with law enforcement personnel, they are helping themselves and their neighbors. When police make contact with the Vietnamese, it helps to approach the oldest male of the household first. This encourages cooperation from the rest of the household. If language is a problem, police should seek assistance from school-age children, who generally speak both English and Vietnamese, and tape record the interview. It is important that police be patient with the Vietnamese person being interviewed and with the interpreter—"Vietnamese will take twice as long to tell you what you need to know." Police should obtain the suspect's given Vietnamese name, not a nickname or chosen American name. These guidelines were developed by the San Jose Police Department and Douglas Daye, Cross Cultural Trainer.

7. *Saigon Nho,* May, 1991.

Notes to Chapter 4

1. Asian Community Mental Health Services, *Xi-Ke, Ma-Tuy, Xi-Ke, Ma-Tuy O Chung Quanh Ta . . . Hay Giup Con Em Tranh Xa No.*
2. Ibid.
3. Ibid.
4. Ibid.
5. Ibid.
6. Ibid.

Notes to Chapter 5

1. Le Ly Hayslip with Jay Wurts, *When Heaven and Earth Changed Places: A Vietnamese Woman's Journey from War to Peace* (New York: Doubleday, 1990).
2. Gina Boubion, "Last Chance Ranches," *San Jose Mercury News,* July 13, 1993.

Notes to Chapter 6

1. Michael A. Kroll, "Locking Up the Problem," *San Jose Mercury News, West Magazine*, February 19, 1989, 23.
2. Ibid., 14, 17.
3. Christopher H. Schmitt, "No Exit," *San Jose Mercury News, West Magazine*, June 7, 1992, 9.
4. Kroll, "Locking Up," 22.
5. Ibid., 14.
6. Gina Boubion, "Last Chance Ranches."
7. Kroll, "Locking Up," 12. Robert Lee McConnell, "Hardcore," *San Jose Mercury News, West Magazine*, June 27, 1993, 8.
8. McConnell, "Hardcore," 11, 12.
9. Kroll, "Locking Up," 12.
10. California Youth Authority Information Office, *California Youth Authority*. Pamphlet.
11. Kroll, "Locking Up," 12, 17.
12. McConnell, "Hardcore," 11.
13. Boubion, "Last Chance Ranches."
14. Ibid.
15. Ibid.
16. Ibid.
17. Ibid.
18. Ibid.
19. Kroll, "Locking Up," 23, 14. Schmitt, "No Exit," 10.
20. Kroll, "Locking Up," 25.

Note to Chapter 7

1. Larry Engelmann, "The Lovely Rebirth of Helen Tran," *American Way*, April 15, 1988.

Notes to Afterword

1. Claire Johnson, Barbara Webster, and Edward Connors, "Prosecuting Gangs: A National Assessment," *National Institute of Justice*, February 1995, 1.
2. "Three slain by mistake: Six young men arrested in shooting at Monterey Road Cafe," *San Jose Mercury News*, March 16, 1995.
3. "Efforts to halt Asian crime hit in new report," *San Jose Mercury News*, December 29, 1992.
4. "Long arm of Asian gangs reported," *San Jose Mercury News*, January 4, 1994.
5. Long, "The Whys of Vietnamese Gangs," 139.

6. Ibid., 137–138.

7. Ibid., 136.

8. Johnson, Webster, and Connors, "Prosecuting Gangs: A National Assessment," 5, 9. The authors note that "more than 80 percent of prosecutors responding [to the survey] from large cities acknowledged gangs in their jurisdiction [and] agreed that the presence of gangs has become more widespread, that the amount of gang-related violence has been increasing, and that violence and drugs have become paramount problems with regard to gang crime." See p. 9.

9. Bureau of Alcohol, Tobacco and Firearms, "G.R.E.A.T. The effective new program that follows D.A.R.E. into the classroom to keep kids out of gangs." (For free information write to ATF at P.O. Box 50418, Washington, D.C. 20091-0418. Telephone 1-800-726-7070 or 202-927-8329.)

Selected References

Books and Pamphlets

Asian Community Mental Health Services. *Xi-Ke, Ma-Tuy, Xi-Ke, Ma-Tuy O Chung Quanh Ta . . . Hay Giup Con Em Tranh Xa No*. Oakland, Calif.: Asian Community Mental Health Services, n.d.

Behr, Edward, and Mark Steyn. *The Story of Miss Saigon*. New York: Arcade, 1991.

Bureau of Alcohol, Tobacco and Firearms, "G.R.E.A.T. The effective new program that follows D.A.R.E. into the classroom to keep kids out of gangs." 1992.

Contra Costa County Probation Department, Contra Costa County District Attorney, and Pleasant Hill Police Department. *Youth and the Law: A Handbook for Parents and Their Children*. Pacheco, Calif.: BFI, n.d.

Hitchcox, Linda. *Vietnamese Refugees in Southeast Asian Camps*. New York: St. Martin's, 1990.

Liu, William T., Maryanne Lamanna, and Alice Murata. *Transition to Nowhere: Vietnamese Refugees in America*. Nashville, Tenn.: Charter House, 1979.

Tollefson, James. *Alien Winds: The Reeducation of America's Indochinese Refugees*. New York: Praeger, 1989.

Articles

Beley, Gene. "Special Report on Escalating Gang Violence." *Country News*, March–April 1993.

Boubion, Gina. "Last Chance Ranches." *San Jose Mercury News,* July 13, 1993.

"Canh sat bat giu 60 nghi can thuoc bang dang A Chau, Nam Cali." *Viet Nam Tu Do,* October 29, 1992.

"Cao Pho Tu Con." *Trieu Thanh* 618, November 2, 1991.

Engelmann, Larry. "The Lovely Rebirth of Helen Tran." *American Way,* April 15, 1988.

"For a Few Caught in Repatriation Fraud, Life in Limbo." *Phuc Vu,* March–April 1993.

Izumikawa, Carol. "Hitting Home: Why Asian Gangs Often Target Their Own Communities." *City on a Hill Press,* March 10, 1994.

Johnson, Claire, Barbara Webster, and Edward Connors. "Prosecuting Gangs: A National Assessment." *National Institute of Justice,* February 1995.

Khue, Vi. *"Phong Su Xa Hoi, Buon Tre My Lai."* *Phu Nu Dien Dan* 90, July 1991.

Kroll, Michael A. "Locking Up the Problem." *San Jose Mercury News, West Magazine,* February 19, 1989.

Lewis, Marilyn. "Amerasians pawns in scam to get to U.S." *San Jose Mercury News,* February 21, 1993.

McConnell, Robert Lee. "Hardcore." *San Jose Mercury News, West Magazine,* June 27, 1993.

Nhu, T. T. "Commentary: Sacramento Siege." *San Jose Mercury News,* April 19, 1991.

———. "Schools work for those who need them." *San Jose Mercury News,* June 21, 1992.

"Police Arrest Members of a Vietnamese Gang in Westminster, California." *Thang Mo Magazine,* July 1991.

Schmitt, Christopher H. "No Exit." *San Jose Mercury News, West Magazine,* June 7, 1992.

Thanh, Nguyen Liem, and Alan B. Henkin. "Vietnamese Refugees in the United States: Adaptation and Transitional Status." *The Journal of Ethnic Studies* 9, 1982.

Toy, Calvin. "A Short History of Asian Gangs in San Francisco." *Justice Quarterly* 9, December 1992.

"U.S. Cracks Down on Phony Amerasians." *Phuc Vu,* March–April, 1993.

"Vietnamese Gangs in the Eyes of an American Journalist." *Saigon Nho Weekly,* July 1991.

Unpublished Works

Booth, Edna. "Vietnamese Assimilation into American Culture." In "A Selection of Readings on Socio-Cultural Values and Problems of the Vietnamese in the United States," Book II. Paper presented for symposium, A Special Project for the Vietnamese Culture Day at San Jose City College, June 5, 1993.

Cuu, Chung Thien. "Young Vietnamese Confronting the New Life." In "A Selection of Readings on the Socio-Cultural Values and Problems of the Vietnamese in the United States," Book II. Paper presented for symposium, A Special Project for the Vietnamese Culture Day at San Jose City College, June 5, 1993.

Long, Patrick Du Phuoc. "The Whys of Vietnamese Gangs." In "A Selection of Readings on the Socio-Cultural Values and Problems of the Vietnamese in the United States," Book II. Paper presented for symposium, A Special Project for the Vietnamese Culture Day at San Jose City College, June 5, 1993.

————. "Vietnamese Students and Our Schools." Remarks made to Vietnamese-American Parent Teacher Association, Santa Clara County, Calif., June 13, 1993.

Thien, Nguyen Chi. *"Nhom phat huy tinh than." Tho.* San Jose, Calif.: n.d.

Viet, Le Thanh. "Education and Cultural Adjustment." In "A Selection of Readings on the Socio-Cultural Values and Problems of the Vietnamese in the United States," Book II. Paper presented for symposium, A Special Project for the Vietnamese Culture Day at San Jose City College, June 5, 1993.

Vietnam Veterans of America Foundation. "Report on the Amerasian Issue." Washington, D.C.: Vietnam Veterans of America Foundation, 1989.

Public Documents

U.S. Department of Justice. Federal Bureau of Investigation. *Vietnamese Criminal Activity in the United States: A National Perspective.* Washington, D.C.: GPO, 1993.

Film

Alexandra, Tiana [Tiana Thi Thanh Nga]. *From Hollywood to Hanoi.* Text from a film written, produced, and directed by Tiana Thi Thanh Nga. New York, 1993.

Acknowledgments

Thank you to the following persons who made this book possible:

John William Cunningham, former superintendent of Santa Clara County Juvenile Rehabilitation Facilities, for his invaluable advice and guidance; Deputy Chief Probation Officer Patricia L. Shannon, for her encouragement; Probation Counselor Joseph A. D. Trione, for his expertise in controlled-substance abuse; my daughter Elizabeth Du Long Galaznik, her husband, John Galaznik, and my grandson, Aaron, for their insightful advice when this book was in draft form; my other children—Tiana (Thanh Nga), Michael, and David, and Mariane Du Long Reedy and her family for their material help; Eddie K. Ruiz, for his knowledge of Hispanic gangs; Maria Ascher of Harvard University Press and Dr. Leigh Hafrey of Harvard for their advice; and for having made this work possible, To Ha and Bob Carlson. I am deeply indebted to Laura Ricard for her painstaking collaboration with me on this book and her personal commitment to my cause.

Finally, for her continuing devotion I wish to thank my wife, Anh Du Long. When I first told her of my wish to write a sequel to *Bui Doi Cali* she liked the idea immediately. "Do you remember the Vietnamese wife of years ago who encouraged her husband's studies with these words?" she asked, and recited this poem:

Di dau cho thiep di cung,
Doi no thiep chiu, lanh lung thiep cam.
[I shall be always with you,
O my man,
In happy days and needy days, too.
Whether it rains or shines,
I shall be yours, and you shall be mine.]

San Jose, California   Patrick Du Phuoc Long
February 1995

Index